THE DANGERFIELDS
MUNITIONS & MEMORIES

JEAN DEBNEY

BREWIN BOOKS

First published by
Brewin Books Ltd, 56 Alcester Road,
Studley, Warwickshire B80 7LG in 2011
www.brewinbooks.com

ISBN: 978-1-85858-464-5

A Cataloguing in Publication Record
for this title is available from the British Library.

Typeset in New Baskerville
Printed in Great Britain by
Hobbs the Printers Ltd.

THE DANGERFIELDS
MUNITIONS & MEMORIES

How simple a thing seems to me to know ourselves as we are, we must know our mothers' names.

Alice Walker

TABLE OF CONTENTS

With grateful thanks to:
Iris, Win, Daisy, Kathleen, Jenny, May, Evelyn, Eileen, Iris.
Without their wonderful memories none of this would have been possible.

*   *   *   *

This book is dedicated to the memory of Margaret and Joseph.
Thank you to: Sharon, Helie and Hessel, for all your support.

INTRODUCTION

For over two centuries, the nation's second city, Birmingham, has pulsed with industrial activity and as its heart beats, so its factories have created and distributed a wealth outward. The canals, the railways and the roads are like arteries and veins, passing the life blood of Birmingham's production, across the country and beyond. It has known incredible prosperity and wealth from the endeavours of the entrepreneurs who have been attracted to the remarkable capacity that Birmingham has to encompass the new. It has known deep recession, and when many other places have declined, failing to return to their previous position, Birmingham has always managed to emerge, charged with new energies, stronger than before. When faced with extreme adversity, as the whole global economy is today, Birmingham has the dynamism to diversify and meet those challenges head on, and evolve with new ideas and vitality. What is at the centre of this chameleon-like quality to adapt, is the people of Birmingham, the Brummies. They are a city of many people who came together, all with the desire to work, get on, and make something of themselves. Throughout the Industrial Revolution and beyond, people were attracted to a place where ingenuity and creativity, came together to create opportunity for those who through sheer hard work would aspire to better things.

This book is a collection of reflections from women who were living and working in the city during the most troubled and fearful time of the city's history, the Second World War. They are all ordinary women, who were called on, as all were at that time, to play a key role in the national production of arms, munitions and aircraft, that were so vital to the Total War Economy. They all have very personal and individual perspectives of that dreadful era, and reflect the many differences of the people who made the city, most importantly, they are the last. The last that hold the living history, that unless it is recorded now, and taken account of, will be forgotten forever.

This is why I have undertaken this work, to collect and convey those memories, for I am a Birmingham girl, who has a passion for my city. A passion, I know, not shared by many who do not know Birmingham's proud heritage, who see only a city which still bears physical scars of post-war reconstruction, always in state of flux and change. My parents were of the same generation as the women that are remembered here, and shared many of the common experiences of this city at war. I used to ask my father and mother, as a child, to write their stories down, to save their memories, even then I understood how profoundly challenging these things had been for them like so many others. However time and life causes things to take different priorities and unfortunately, my parents are long gone, and their memories have died with them. All I could do now, is give a second-hand story, a reflection of their reflections, filled with inaccuracies and error, and without the sentiment and feeling of their souls and time.

A history of anything is a subjective remembrance repeated by another at a later time. That history can become corrupted by misunderstanding, by false reflection and complexity, by removal through time from the actual events and people. Celtic tradition is of oral history, it is of the handing of stories down through word of mouth, often mother to daughter, in order to keep the stories alive, but once that chain is broken the history is lost, and the continuity of that historical experience is gone. The 'voice' is the key to everything, and we have to save that 'voice' for all to appreciate, which is why it is critical to record the spoken voice for accuracy. When the 'voice' is recounted to the reader in the transposed narrative, it is essential to stay as faithful to the actual spoken word as possible, displaying grammatical inaccuracy, common through local dialect. All the narrative remains in the raw state, unless it has been negotiated between myself and the women to edit their narrative for grammatical correctness.

It is important to realise that this 'voice' has almost been lost in the shadow of the Great War, for the women placed at the centre of this story, are the generation who have been instrumental in giving respectful remembrance to all those who fell in that previous conflict. These two wars were so close within history, that it has provided us with a false sense of there being more time at a later date to devote to memories of the Second World War. For these women have all achieved great ages, their late eighties and early nineties, and they were the youngest of their generation that gave of themselves to these endeavours. The vast majority have long since died and we are left with very few from whom to collect reminiscences, creating a research imperative to do so now.

Birmingham and World War Two are inextricably linked; both from a political and economical position. Politically, because of Neville Chamberlain being the Prime Minister at that time, who was beset with an impossible task, how to best manage a national inadequacy of resources for war. This set against the international view that war was unavoidable, when the horrors of the previous conflagration were so fresh in living memory. Economically, because the city had always been the 'workshop of the world', and had historically been the key manufacturer of arms and munitions. There was an expectation that, if only as a defence deterrent, the city would be expected to contribute a considerable effort to re-arming the nation.

When the call did come, in the late 1930's, Birmingham had amassed all the vital skills and technologies necessary, through the infant car industry, which was already the centre of car manufacturing for the UK. Within Birmingham itself, there was Herbert Austin and the early Rover factory, Lord Nuffield (William Morris) offered his services at Castle Bromwich, and down the road in Coventry, there were Rootes, Daimler and Standard Motors. From this the Shadow Factory scheme was born, that was going to prove so critical to the war effort. Erstwhile munitions factories, that had changed their production to bicycles and the like, found their services for armaments once more being requested. The BSA in Small Heath, ICI Metals Witton (formerly Kynoch), like so many other countless firms around Birmingham.

The ladies within this book, who had already been undertaking factory work and making; cigarette cases, compacts, and zip fasteners, found themselves turning detonator caps and shell cases, and reaming rifles. In so doing, Birmingham became the most sensitive, strategic target of the war, its many trials and tribulations which followed, had to be kept not just from Hitler's gaze, but from the UK population's knowledge.

In this book I shall explore this emergence of the second capital as the industrial heart, and its historical importance to war production, and how it rose to the challenge once more. This book is not a history of the Second World War, or of Birmingham per se, it is merely a snapshot view of where Birmingham was placed within that war through its heritage and remarkable achievements. Primarily, it is about how the city's most valuable resource at that time, the women of Birmingham, rose to the immense challenge on a daily basis, through often incredible hardship. The one and a half million women who worked in munitions, and the three hundred thousand who worked in Birmingham alone, have never received any public recognition for their sterling efforts, and this is in some part a small response to that by creating awareness amongst the population as a whole.

By using their personal stories, interwoven into contextual primary research, I hope to give a picture of what life was like for them through these extremely dark days; the blitz, rationing, the blackout, losing friends making new ones, the camaraderie, personal suffering and joy. The day-today existence in a forever altered world for these very young girls, who are now the last of so many that have gone.

I am a researcher first and foremost, and realise the importance of staying as close to primary sources of evidence, or the 'horse's mouth' so to speak. Rather than an over-reliance of second and third hand accounting through textbook sources (however valid), I feel it is vital to go back as close to the time as possible, As such, I have made extensive searches into the National Archive at Kew. There, I have been able to access, Cabinet and Ministerial papers of that time, looking in some detail at the decade pre-war, through to the declaration of war, the collapse of the Chamberlain Government, and the Wartime Cabinet overseen by Winston Churchill. I have sought, wherever possible, specific references to the city and various events, people and places, that put Birmingham in the centre of the wartime strategic map. This access to close research, added to the texturally-rich narrative supplied by the ladies, has enabled me to progress from anecdotal evidence and to emerge with a convincing account based on sound fact.

A history is a subjective view, and changes with the effects of political accounts and time. Views can be contradictory and contestable, especially if only given by a single voice. Which is why the use of multiple narrative is so important to create a convincing history, this through its negotiated position between author and narrator, enables a shared understanding to be formed, and with several narratives, a consensual history emerges, thus creating greater validity to that history.

Even these narratives are changed within the minds of their creators, for as I have already touched on, hindsight and the passage of time alter things. Memories become cloudier, or more easy to explain due to reflection of other things that were happening at that time, changing the narrative by effect. This then places even greater emphasis on the need for multiple narrative in order to reach a shared-collective understanding of those times and happenings. The narrative creates the person who is contained within it, it becomes the discourse of that person (of that time). As Mills (2004) comments (after Foucault) discourse produces 'something else (an utterance, a concept, and effect)'. The relatives and friends of the women now view them as grand old ladies, with the various attributes that are required within that personal subjectivity to be that, they are not regarded as they once were, or as they 'have been' but viewed as changed.

Our own personal story, creates our personal subjectivity, within any period of our lives, we live our own discourse, in some of their cases 'girly girl' to their families at that time, then 'macho girl' to their male colleagues that they worked with, now to their families and friends 'wise older woman' (Debney, 2006). Further, Butler (1999) stresses that we do not just create ourselves in this way discursively, but we also perform what we see ourselves as to others, knowingly.

They are also always different. As women, they have to cope with 'otherness', it is something that most women do not even notice as it is part of the fabric of society to always be perceived as different from men 'the other'. Most of the time these differences and otherness, are masked by being in different roles, different places, different employment. Otherness does become most apparent when women enter any field that is traditionally seen as a gendered employment area for men. Engineering is still to this day, retaining that ignominious position of being something that men generally do, and women generally do not. In the Second World War, although these women were desperately needed they were always going to be seen as the other, and never fully accepted. This happened for two reasons, firstly, as a response by their male colleagues who initially resisted their entry in to the male domain and were only pacified when women were designated with the unskilled title (and paid less) and as a consequence, set apart and seen as different. The Government had no desire to see women become accepted into these roles, because of the destabilising effect that this could cause to society as a whole, through constant propaganda campaigns they reinforced the message, that women would be returning to their pre-war roles as a caring wife and mother. In fact, Birmingham probably has another boast that it was one of the only places where women were traditionally in the majority of the factory working population especially in the allied metal trades, but always in a lesser role to men, which possibly only acted to reinforce the 'other' stereotype.

Women in Birmingham factories were in the position to be both 'outsiders' and 'insiders', a dual mismatch which probably was not found anywhere else at that time. Outsiders because they would never be truly accepted by their male colleagues as part of the semi-skilled and skilled workforce, and insiders because they were part of a majority of women (a greater population than the men) who did work in factories and had done for several generations. To them the women who had never worked in factories were the outsiders, and it follows that it made the ones who had done so, 'insiders'. The incoming women had to learn the ropes, come into the new environment which was alien to them. The most startling of these transformations, were those women who not only had never worked in factories, but had to be brought in from much further afield, through the

Essential Work Order, to fill the gaps in production. For many of these women, their 'outsiderness' was most apparent, through a lack of experience in industry, coming from a culturally different part of the country to Birmingham, having a different dialect, coming from different classes. They could display multiple differences, distinguishing them as higher on the scale of being set apart, and outside their women colleagues on the production line.

I have considered myself previously very much an insider. I am a woman, I am a Birmingham woman, a Birmingham woman with parents who were from that generation, and I have a background in engineering. However, that's where my own position switches from insider to outsider. I am removed by age significantly, and by that fact from experience. I come from a semi-professional background, which means my experience in factories, has been just that, 'experience', I have never had to work in a large industrial factory and live on the weekly wage. My engineering expertise is on a professional level, rather than a craft or technical level. So it follows that what I had perceived my status to be is very far removed from what it actually is. One's position as an outsider or an insider, affects your acceptance within that culture, and affects your perceptions and understandings of that culture. I can never truly claim to know absolutely what it felt like to work under those appalling circumstances from 1939 to 1945, but have more empathy than most women of my generation through my personal experience and understanding.

All I give here is a 'truth', my view of that truth and how I perceive it to be. My aim has been throughout the writing of this book to try and convey this truth as I understand it to be, to the best that I can to you the reader. To try and evoke the same passion and sense of drama that it has captured in me. Truth is akin to history, and because history is constantly changing and shape-shifting, so, the truth can only ever be true at a given time. I hope that in revealing this truth, this story brings some recognition to the few that are left for their amazing undertakings, at a time when our country needed it the most. I will end with a quote from probably the most enigmatic of wartime leaders, Sir Winston Churchill, a man capable of the most profound thought that was carefully crafted into dry wit:

"Man will occasionally, stumble over the truth, but most of the time he will pick himself up and continue on."

Chapter 1

THE CITY OF A
THOUSAND TRADES

The industrial city of Birmingham, was not an accident of geography, it was a coming together of material wealth, circumstances and entrepreneurial vision. As I was proudly informed by my geography teacher whilst at school, it emerged out of the vast availability of natural resources, particularly minerals so important for the manufacture in metal trades. In fact the famous painting by J. M. W. Turner "Rail Steam Speed" 1844, evokes the red skies of industry which were ever present at that time, and the power of the new technologies. So it was, J. R. R. Tolkien looked towards the city centre from Sarehole Mill at the turn of the last century, and he was able to conjure up strange imaginings of a harsh world beyond hobbit country. Birmingham was indeed the workshop of the world.

When Abraham Darby smelted the iron ore at Coalbrookdale, from which Thomas Telford created his iron bridge, a whole new world was opened up to engineers and inventors of that time. One such engineer, was James Watt, one of Birmingham's most esteemed fathers, and inventor of the steam engine. Together with his partner Matthew Boulton, the Boulton and Watt company had produced their first two steam engines by 1776 and by 1800 a further 400 had been produced, the industrial revolution was born. These groundbreaking advances in machine capability, evolved the manufacturing potential of Birmingham and combined with the influx of cheap Irish Labour, the 'navvies', the city began to develop in all directions.

The logistics of a city on a plateau, is to get materials in and then the goods out. James Brindley began the planning and excavation of the extensive canal networks that crisscross the inner city and beyond. This network was set very firmly at the heart of England and enabled materials and food to flood in for the ever burgeoning population, and the finished goods and products to be sent out across the country for retail. By 1820, the Irish population numbered 5,000, and was rising steadily. They came for the construction of canals, factories, houses and then the railway by

1830, with the impressive Curzon Street station, becoming the gateway to Birmingham.

The city was alive and buzzing, it was a hive of activity, which began to attract those with ideas and dynamism from other parts of the country, drawn to the city's potential to produce. The most renowned of these settled entrepreneurs was Joseph Chamberlain, at first a driven businessman exploiting that potential to the optimum, then a politician and philanthropist, envisioning an architecturally impressive civic centre, with the Town Hall dominating. The population in 1851, was recorded (given as the inner wards) as standing at 232,841, by 1891 that had nearly doubled to 478,113, and by 1911 it had nearly doubled again to 840,202.

This second wave of business development brought others too, the key figures of the manufacturing industry reflected in this book. Within the gun making quarter of Birmingham, fourteen of the master smiths, took the decision to form a trade association, in order to protect their interests as gun makers in times of peace when the order books were quiet. On June 7th 1861, The Birmingham Small Arms Trade association decided to form a public company The Birmingham Small Arms Co. limited. Meanwhile, on the Witton side of Birmingham, a Scotsman called George Kynoch, was in the process of building up from humble beginnings, Kynoch and Co. which would become a very impressive munitions producer within twenty years. After that time, it would then operate under the chairmanship of Joseph Chamberlain's younger brother, Arthur, for the following twenty five years.

Another young man emerged from the shadows of Birmingham, by the name of Joseph Lucas. Born in 1834 and an apprenticed Electro-Plater, he became a journeyman touting his wares around the streets of Birmingham, selling buckets, bowls and lamps. By 1873 he was listed as a producer of tin-plate, and lamp and oil dealer, from simple beginnings the company Joseph Lucas Ltd, would rise to be one of the foremost producers of gas turbine engines. It would soon go on to produce all the associated mechanical and electrical parts for anything, particularly motor vehicles.

The arrival of an Irish born, Australian immigrant by the name of Fredrick York Wolseley in 1889, was going to launch Birmingham into the next stage of its manufacturing fame. Wolseley had revolutionised the sheep shearing industry in Australia, through the development of mechanical aids for shearing. He moved his manufacturing company to Birmingham, and began to export his machines back to Australia. Wolseley went back to Australia the following year, only to return with his English born manager to supervise his operations in Broad Street, his name was Herbert Austin. With Wolseley's sheep shearing enterprise faltering within a few years, Herbert Austin gained permission from the board to venture into building the 'horseless carriage'. By 1899 the first Wolseley motor car was on sale to the general public, for a sum of £120. Unfortunately, Fredrick Wolseley himself had run out of steam and he sold both businesses to Vickers Son and Maxim, though Wolseley Cars were to re-emerge later. A young Austin had big ideas and went off to pastures new.

Herbert Austin envisaged expansion, and found a site on the outskirts of Birmingham, at Longbridge. There he founded the Austin Car company, he started with 270 personnel and made 120 cars in 1906. By 1914, his annual production was nearly ten times that, at a thousand per year and he was employing two thousand people.

That same year another famous brand was beginning to emerge in the city with the building of a new factory in Tyseley. A young gentleman called John Starley had been a bicycle manufacturer in the 1880s in Coventry, one particular machine was called the Rover. In 1896, motorisation of these vehicles began in earnest under the title of the Rover Cycle Company. Unfortunately, John Starley barely saw the new century in, and died in 1901. The new management decided to join in the new developments that were being pioneered in Birmingham and began to develop their first motor cars, but lack of direction (and an intervening war) led to intermittent difficulties, and production of their first small cars from the Birmingham factory did not commence until 1920. However, by then, they were in direct competition with a highly competitive Austin Motor Car Co. and the 'Austin 7'.

Another young man by the name of William Morris had started to produce his first motor cars in 1913, down the road in Cowley, although he cast envious eyes on expansion towards Birmingham and his path would cross significantly with the others. By 1925, 'the English Henry Ford' was turning out 56,000 cars per year and had secured his dominance over Austin and Rootes Group (based in Coventry and Wolverhampton). There was also Daimler and Wolseley in the background. These companies formed the core of the British car industry and all the necessary skills, equipment and knowledge that the government would need to call on.

During this period, first the BSA and then after the Great War, Kynoch's had diversified. The BSA had found a market in making bicycles, as those who had pioneered this industry had moved into motor cars. The BSA motorised their bicycles and eventually produced motorcycles. With the first world war,

Birmingham was called on to supply reserves. Obviously, munitions and armaments brought the BSA and Kynoch's back into full production of unbelievable proportions, but so too were many of the motor car factories, which had the plant, machinery and skilled men, to train women dilutees. The rest of the industry would be involved in the manufacture of every conceivable item, from mess tins to uniforms.

The depression was not a good time for any of the companies. Kynoch's moved into producing other goods such as zip fasteners and by 1929 the name of Kynoch Ltd had been subsumed into ICI Metals Ltd. Rover suffered huge losses, but the appointment of Spencer Wilkes as general manager, helped to bring the company round. Only Austin and Morris did particularly well, William Morris acquired Wolseley during the twenties, and began the manufacture of cars under the Wolseley banner in Birmingham, with the launch of the Morris Minor, to compete with Austin.

Both Morris and Austin emulated the aforementioned Joseph Chamberlain, and were noted for great charitable donations and other philanthropic endeavours. As a consequence, William Morris was created Viscount by 1938, taking the name Lord Nuffield. Austin was created a baron in 1936, becoming Lord Austin. Both men had risen from very humble origins, worked hard and become engineers of great insight, exploiting the wealth and character of the melting pot of Birmingham. Like many others in the city, they had left their agricultural background, to seek work and opportunity in a rapidly expanding city.

The government, particularly Neville Chamberlain who was at that time Chancellor of the Exchequer, had embarked on a plan to emerge from depression through sheer hard work and enterprise. Chamberlain, coming from Birmingham, had much personal experience of development and growth being generated through enterprise and understood its inherent value. They developed factory schemes in what were called 'special areas', what we now call areas of deprivation. Wales, Scotland, Liverpool, all came under these auspices, these places were then put into production as government-owned enterprises. This helped to restore the national morale and cure the malaise. Pride came back to deprived areas and work meant income, for those that had been impoverished by the Great Depression. This was an international problem, and a particular problem for Germany, which considered itself to have been harshly treated after the previous war, by others in the Treaty of Versailles. The rise of the National Socialists under Chancellor Hitler came to power on the wave of nationalism sweeping the country, and used that undercurrent of dissatisfaction with the post-war settlement to their advantage. As is well documented the construction of the autobahns and the government's drive to re-arm were large scale work projects to reduce their over inflated economy. Eventually, this dark spectre of German rearmament began to plant fear in their near neighbours and a high level of discomfort in the British Government.

Many questions would be raised as a result, such as; how far would German rearmament progress and what ultimately, would be their potential as an armed nation? And from that state of preparation, what would be necessary in order to have an effective deterrent to a historically threatening power?

In 1933 just after Hitler had come to power, and sensing an era of change ahead, the Committee of Imperial Defence, made an analysis of the private armaments industry, their conclusions were stark. Only one firm providing armaments from the last war had remained in business, BSA is listed as 'Not engaged on armament work.' According to the report there had been a reduction of forty percent between pre-war armament production as of 1907 and post-war production as of 1930, from private firms. As there were no obvious threats posed at that time, and Hitler's plans to re-arm were three years away, the government proposed a nationalised scheme for the production of armaments. It was dismissed because of a comment that had been made by Vickers and ICI, who felt it was impossible to remain on constant armaments work because:

"Large technical staffs cannot be kept in idleness, and the upkeep of empty, or practically empty factories is heavy."

By February 1936, the government was becoming acutely aware of the unstable international situation as the minutes report:

"...in view of the altered international situation, important and extensive measures should be taken during the next 3 to 5 years to modernise our national defence."

It was at this point that the government decided to bring in the 'shadow' munitions factories to help to meet demand, those factories which had been turned over from other things in the previous war, such as engineering firms, to support the production demand then. They also realised that it was imperative to collaborate with the 'professional' armament firms, for the fears were that the demand would far outstrip the supply. It was at that point that a need for an improved air defence began to be raised in their collective thinking. They predicted at one point they would require in excess of a thousand aircraft, and that demanded skilled labour and facilities to produce what was then considered a great number.

Later that year in October, a Royal Commission reported back to the cabinet their findings from their investigations into 'The Private Manufacture of/and the Trading in Arms'. This commission had been formed to investigate the need for a 'general state monopoly' for armaments manufacture. In their opinion there was 'moral objection to the industry', and some felt that manufacturers were capable of war mongering in order to gain lucrative contracts. However, it was acknowledged that apart from Farnborough there were no 'manufacturing resources' in existence for the RAF.

It was considered to be an unjustifiable cost to keep factories in operation in times of peace, whereas, the private producers were able to diversify (as Kynoch's and BSA had done), when arms were no longer necessary. As there were government factories in existence by that time, through the post-depression measures, it was proposed that these should have areas devoted to scientific and technological development. Overall, it was considered more conducive to keep the private industry, but restrict government officials from connection with such firms (a criticism that Neville Chamberlain had been faced with by Lloyd George because of his uncle's control of Kynoch's), and also restrict excessive profits of the industry via taxation.

The same month, Viscount Swinton, produced a report to the cabinet which was going to significantly place Birmingham and Coventry, in the heart of the most sensitive production processes of the war. The document was entitled:

"Note by the Secretary of State for Air on the policy of his Majesty's Government in relation to the Production of Aero-Engines".

This document outlined the proposals for the 'formation of the Shadow Aero Engine Scheme' which had first been proposed in April 1936. It had been decided that the urgency of the problem needed special attention and some considered solutions. There was a realisation that under normal circumstances such research and development could take at least five years. There was also a fear that unless enough firms with the specific knowledge, skill and equipment were recruited and then retained that the demands of production would not be achieved. Initially, four firms had been involved in 1929 to undertake the project under the organisation of the then Lord Nuffield (William Morris).

The 'Shadow' concept, was either a private manufacturing firm that was brought into support munitions and aircraft production, or a factory where production could be dispersed to (should the need arise), to complement or *shadow* production from the *parent* company.

By October 1936, Nuffield was expressing concern that supply and demand could not be reached, Wolseley Aero Engines Ltd, had been involved with the process, and from the documentary evidence it appears that Nuffield was trying to negotiate a stand-alone contract for Wolseley to supply the government with these engines at that time. The government had declined his offer, and decided to 'substitute the programme' for shadow production to an expanded and modified plan, thus, increase its capacity for the production of engines and airframes. The invitation went out to; Austin, Daimler, Rootes, Singer, Rover, Standard and Wolseley. The government realised that the scheme would require expansion of factory premises and equipment financed by the shadow scheme, with a caveat that if required 'in the event of war' they would 'turn to aircraft production'. The plan was that the Bristol Aeroplane Company would expand the production of the aero engines via the shadow partners, who would contract to make 'a different group of parts' of these engines and then final assembly would be undertaken by only two factories. Nuffield was reluctant to participate and sent a representative from Wolseley, however, Lord Austin agreed to chair the group to consider the proposals.

The group reported back fairly swiftly and made it clear that the proposals made by the government were impractical for several reasons; the amount of plant and equipment (and skill) required to repeat the same manufacturing processes in each factory would be prohibitive, and the Bristol Company would face problems overseeing the same operations at each site. The committee proposed to make individual sections in each factory, that would then be finally assembled in one place. They proposed to run a test of 2,000 engines to prove the scheme.

It was difficult for the politicians to accept the division in such a way. The whole concept of shadow, was to alleviate production problems of 'bottle necks' should enemy bombardment put a factory out of action. However, Austin put the arguments of the group convincingly, and from an economical and business position, it was the most practical solution. Of course, it would lead to a very concentrated geographical area of production, that would be extremely vulnerable.

It appears that Lord Nuffield hedged his involvement, initially withdrawing from the scheme because he wished to have the government buy certain items of machinery and accommodation from him, the government declined this proposal, but then Singer withdrew from the scheme, leaving the government no alternative but to accept Nuffield's plan.

All would have been well, if the Managing Director of Wolseley had not resigned and in the ensuing interregnum, the new management based at Morris Motors realised that they could not devote their time and facilities to the scheme. It is widely known that Nuffield had been suffering ill health for some time and the misunderstandings were probably created by the lack of a firm hand on the tiller. The shadow scheme commenced without either of Lord Nuffield's firms, but he was to re-emerge with the development of the Nuffield Factory at Castle Bromwich, where the Spitfire was to be manufactured, eventually managed by Vickers.

The Cabinet Conclusions of that month record the dissatisfaction with Nuffield and his decisions, but draw attention to a letter sent by Austin on behalf of the group supporting the government's proposed shadow scheme.

By February 1937, the Royal Commission of the Private Manufacture of, and the Trading of Arms, reported once again to the cabinet. In this report, two things are of particular interest, the first is an understanding that private enterprise has the energy and the drive through competition, to develop the necessary technologies, and that any government owned facility would not generate the same competitiveness. Further, there was a frank admission of the country's fragility facing a new war:

"A nation like the United Kingdom, which is a small military Power in peace, but may need to become a large one in war... must foster an export trade in armaments... in order to maintain its productive capacity."

Later that month, the feeling of real impending hostilities were beginning to emerge in the cabinet conclusions. There was a full acknowledgement that the development of the German air force was posing a real threat to the country and that it was important to match any perceived threat with an equivalent defence force. They had even begun to assess sites of German vulnerability.

Reserves for the war effort had been assessed and found lacking, it was considered there had to be an increase by '225%' in order to reach the level required. There was a reason to be confident (with added caution), as the minutes record:

"Fortunately the "shadow" factories had been a great success, but even if a firm like Austin was fully equipped and jigged, it would take six months from the word being given before it could be in production: and that was apart from the risk of war damage. The only alternative was for the Air Force to go slow during the first six months of a war."

It was becoming clear, that it was necessary to reach a decision quickly, in order to be in a state of readiness if required.

The issue of reserves, versus potential, was a difficult one. Whether to have actual stock which may become obsolete if kept for a considerable time in stores, or to invest heavily in the potential to produce quickly. Manufacturing in any industry required investment and skilled labour, again a costly exercise if it were not to be used, but the investment needed for engineering particularly (and enabling a skilled workforce to be available quickly) was very expensive. It is probably at this time (and because of this dilemma) that the feeling of a looming war began to be generated in the public consciousness and discourse.

The government were still proceeding with the idea of a deterrent rather than an active defence, they considered the shadow factories as a deterrent. But, there was concern that the enemy could deliver 'a knock-out blow' within days of war, and this was changing the resolve of the government towards a more pro-active approach to defence, indeed, would 225% be enough? Within these conclusions, there was a realisation that expenditure on defence could reach £1,500 million over the coming five years, and some now believed that would be insufficient to meet the defensive needs of the country.

In October 1937, Viscount Swinton oversaw a comprehensive review of the Air Force, in consideration of the present (and estimated future) strength of the German Air Force. It had become clear that the Germans had exceeded their planning and production targets, leaving the UK woefully and inadequately defended. The German plan was to produce 1,620 aircraft and also they had at their disposal 750 bombers. All estimates were expecting these totals to be more than doubled by the end of 1939.

Swinton forecast that the present needs of the RAF, for only 1,736 aircraft, plus 1,022 bombers, could only be filled by the summer of 1941 and that was based on three assumptions. Firstly, that all the present shadow factories would be in continuous full production, secondly, that there would still be 'large scale use' of the sub-contractors, finally, that a second airframe factory was erected. The ministry had requested previously an increase of 700 more aircraft and 600 more bombers, which was rejected. However, with the recent estimates that had come into their possession of German potential strength being almost double for aircraft and just under that for bombers, the ministry repeated its request but this time for 595 more aircraft and an additional 400 bombers.

The Minister for the Co-ordination of Defence, Sir Thomas Inskip, placed a further report before cabinet in December 1937, adding weight to the arguments. In his opinion, the first issue which they needed to address was the raising of revenue if the total for defence of £1.500 million over 5 years was exceeded because of conflict, an increase of taxation and loans were the only possibilities available. There was a frank admission, of the understanding of German air potential and that they had the ability to 'deliver a knock-out blow'. As such, the RAF defensive preparations must take 'a place second to none'. This had shifted current opinion away from the emphasis on home defences, towards counter attack, as possibly, the best form of defence.

The potential of production from the shadow factory scheme, would fall short of the requirements, and as such, it was essential to finance the building of more factories in order to address the new demands. Four months later, Inskip followed up his report with a statement on defence to the cabinet. In this he was quick to note the co-operation of all involved in making preparation and meeting demands of all the armed services. Regarding production capacity he states that:

"The six shadow factories for the manufacture of engines have already begun production. One of the two airframe shadow factories is expected to begin production in a few weeks hence and the other later this year. Other shadow factories for airscrews and carburettors have also started production, and a shadow factory for bombs is on the point of doing so; these factories are additions to the programme as first conceived…"

The word had been given, the country was preparing for the war which was not far away, it had been a confluence of many factors that had led to this point and all seemed inevitable now. But as the planning and discussion gave way to the hard, cold, reality of war, would all these debates and assumptions be adequate to meet the challenge?

Austin was awarded a contract to produce the Fairey 'Battle' aircraft in 1938, by the end of that year they were producing 30 per month but that was insufficient and they were under significant pressure. Towards the end of 1938, and although facing extreme challenges to fulfil the Battle contract, the government approached Austin to contract for the Stirling bomber, as is clear from the documentary evidence Lord Austin handled much of the correspondence himself, for as he wrote in his letter to the Air Council in early October:

"I do not know whether you know of the arrangement made between the Air Ministry and myself at the commencement of our aeroplane efforts. It was agreed that all correspondence relating to the Aero Factory should be addressed to me so that I can deal with it and save any oversight and delay.
Yours sincerely,
Austin"

As ever, he was hands on and made sure that all aspects were dealt with. The new 'Short Plane' as it was known was considerably bigger than the Battle, and further modifications were needed to the Austin Aero factory to enable production. Lord Austin, after careful negotiation secured a further £13,300 by the end of the following year for extensive alterations to his premises. However, their problems with Battle production (several engine modifications had been required) had proved a hindrance, with accountancy problems, as a government auditor had wryly noted:

"These people are hopelessly behind with their aircraft accounting and have practically thrown up the sponge."

Added to this, there had been negative publicity in the national press, due to men being idle during the change-over period. But, considering the demands that were now being expected of them and facing enemy bombardment in 1940, they were as efficient and effective as any other shadow operator of that time. Longbridge at the war time peak was employing 32,000 people and manufacturing a complete multitude of war reserves, and Austin Aero produced its quota of aircraft. This was no doubt due to Lord Austin's immense capabilities as an engineer and entrepreneur, unfortunately he did not live to see the end of the war, dying at home on the 23rd May, 1941.

Rover did well from the shadow factory scheme. Their first factory in Acocks Green, built under the shadow agreement, was used to produce the parts for the 'Bristol Hercules' radial engines. This factory started producing in July 1937. The government realised there were further production needs, and approached Rover to build a second shadow factory. This time 65 acres of farm land were requisitioned near Solihull. This factory was to employ 7,000 workers, and manufacture the complete engines and be three times the size of the existing Rover shadow factory.

The Supermarine Company in Southampton, had originally been contracted to produce the new aircraft called the Spitfire. Supermarine failed to deliver, and Sir Kingsley Wood, took up Lord Nuffield's suggestion to build a factory at Castle Bromwich, to produce 1,000 aircraft. Nuffield was suffering from bouts of ill health and associated problems, and by the time Chamberlain's government fell in May 1940, they had spent £7 million and not one aircraft had been produced. The new Minister for Air, Lord Beaverbrook dismissed Nuffield and placed the whole operation in the hands of Vickers, who were eventually turning out 300 planes per month, 13,000 in total were built there.

ICI Metals Ltd. (formerly Kynoch) and BSA scaled up their production and staffing to meet their burgeoning order books. By 1943, the Witton factories of the original Kynoch's were employing 20,000 people, in total, the company had '27 factories on 20 separate sites employing 50,000 people'. Despite being bombed severely during the blitz with many incendiaries, relatively little damage was done, and production was unaffected. Witton produced a complete range of ammunition, from detonator caps, through to large shells.

The BSA had an impressive production rate during World War Two, being recorded as producing nearly fifty percent of all the small arms required by British forces. At the height of hostilities, the BSA had 67 factories under its control, including shadow factories and dispersal units and was employing more than 25,000 people. It possessed 25,000 machine tools. More machine tools were destroyed the night of the Small Heath factory bombing than in the whole of Coventry during their blitz. Machine tools, equal war potential, and this did create considerable problems not just for the BSA, but also for the national war production. The BSA is credited with the production of:

"...nearly half a million of the Browning machine guns... one quarter of a million service rifles; 400,000 Sten guns; machine guns, cannon, anti-tank rifles, and gun carriages, ten million shell fuses; over three and a half million magazines, and 750,000 anti-aircraft rockets."

Lucas turned many of their standard components that they already produced over to wartime production, and adapted some components to operate other things, 'Starter motors were adapted for the electrical control of tank Gun Turrets'. They were also contracted to produce many objects specifically for wartime use:

"...including Gun Turrets, aircraft wing sections, primers, fuses, anti-aircraft shells, bombs of various kinds, control and release mechanisms and metal pressings."

Towards the end of the war the government had contacted Lucas, to undertake research work into jet propulsion engines. At the commencement of the war, Lucas employed 28,000 people, by the end that had grown to 40,000 (mostly women).

With the extra demands and contracts which were continually put to Lucas by the government it was necessary, to increase their production capacity through the shadow scheme several times. This was often done by adopting dispersal to other parts of the country such as Lancashire and London. They were sub-contractors to the new Rover shadow factory, which required a substantial increase in their production capacity.

The Cadbury family were Quakers, and by virtue of that fact, opposed to war, however, they did contribute to the war effort allowing Lucas to take some premises in Bournville under the shadow scheme.

In February 1944, the approach was made by the government to Lucas for their research and development expertise towards jet engines. Lucas requested the addition of 50,000 sq ft. to be added at the Shaftmoor Lane factory, in the form of a 'pre-fabricated A.1 hanger' Lucas realised this space had post-war value, and agreed to meet £48,000 of the costs to install additional services.

Lucas suffered a considerable amount of disruption during the raids, as did many firms. It had effects on sickness, absenteeism and lateness, and ultimately morale. They became the subject of a Ministry of Home Security study on morale of factory workers, along with other companies such as; ICI Metals Ltd (formerly Kynoch) and Cadbury. It revealed that during the period before the Essential Work Order and 'stay-put' orders that came into force there were significant losses of personnel especially during the November blitz. However, once the Ministry of Labour had established their schemes (and the bombing was less) the workforce settled and became one of the most productive companies of the war.

The shadow scheme brought much development and expansion to the big Birmingham producers, which enabled future prosperity for those companies concerned. As is often the case, the charisma at the top leads the company because of their drive, and their personal belief. Post war, Nuffield acquired Austin creating, Austin-Morris, which led on to other things. Lord Nuffield died in 1963, like Austin, without an heir, so their titles died with them, and with their demise came the end of a great era of manufacture and development for Birmingham.

BIRMINGHAM

Thou mighty city! Stretching toil-worn hands
To grasp the sweet green pasture at thy sides;
Defiling with they breath the pleasant lands,
Building great factories filled with surging tides.
Of men and women, toiling for their bread;
What dost thou gain by all this strife for gold?
Spite of thy wealth, the grey and skull-like head
Of poverty is seen within they field.
The "workshop of the world" they call thy name,
And thou art proud to own thy title great;
Be heedful lest thy wealth becomes thy shame,
Scarr'd by the sin and misery in thy gate.
Thou "Forward" be the watch word of thy town,
"Upward" would be its glory and its Crown.

Alice D Braham from E. Cadbury
– Women's Work and Wages (1909) page 6.

Chapter 2

DAISY'S STORY –
'THE DANGERFIELDS'

I met Daisy Burrows (nee Stanford) in May 2008, she lives very quietly in a suburb of Birmingham surrounded by her photographs of family, and fading mementos of times gone by, a real 'Aladdin's cave' of memories. We sat down to chat with a cup of tea and the morning TV burbling away in the background.

She told me that her family first lived in Hamstead Village in Great Barr where she attended the village school. Her father was working in the colliery on the railway siding, her mother was working at Lucas's and in the happy home were Daisy, her sister Gwen, her mother (Emily), father (Samuel), her mother's two sisters and two brothers, and her maternal grandparents, all was good.

Tragedy was not far away though. A young man started working on the railway sidings, shunting the trains, and in his inexperience he managed to wedge Daisy's father between the buffers of the trains, leaving him very badly injured and an invalid for the rest of his life, requiring care at home. This was to fundamentally change many things in the Stanford household.

While Daisy's mother had worked at Lucas, she had also looked after the children of a very sick woman with whom she worked. After her husband had his accident this led her to take up fostering children as a way of making ends meet. This enabled her to care for him at the same time. Daisy left Hamstead Village School and subsequently attended Canterbury Road Girls School in Perry Barr. Eventually on a Friday at the end of March in 1937, she left school aged 14 and started work at Kynoch's in Witton, the main site in Witton Road. This was the norm at that time for a person not expected to enter a professional occupation which would require more schooling followed by a stint at university.

"At first we was making Lightning Zip Fasteners you know."
She comments enthusiastically;
   "on the sewing machines like, first on the hand machines and then on
   the mechanical ones you know…"
She reflects;

"...In 1939 when the war started they moved us on to what was called The Dangerfields you know... that was making the ammunition, the bullets and like, you know, that's why they called it 'the dangerfields' because it was dangerous like..."

Daisy continued full of stories one after the other from that suddenly, very dramatic time, I had to pull her back to the beginning of it all before 1939. She met her boyfriend Frank (later to be her husband) in 1939 when she was 16 just before war broke out. Her Aunt Evelyn (Emily's sister) had a boyfriend called Ted, and Daisy and Evelyn used to go out 'courting' in a foursome with Ted and Frank.

I asked her what it was like for her and her family on the 3rd September in 1939;

"I was at home you know, with me mum and that like, 'cause I helped with looking after me dad... and I thought 'oh God'... he's going to be called up like, Frank you know..."

"Did you hear it on the wireless?" I enquired;

"Yeah, yeah we heard it on the wireless, all sitting round like you know... that war had been declared, I always remember Chamberlain saying..."

She disappeared into her memories of that time, the whole family, sitting around the wireless waiting in anticipation for the news that everyone knew was coming, but nobody wanted to hear. All the young men that they knew, were going to be called up, and the young women were in dread of the consequences. Daisy was the eldest, but at only 16 it must have seemed such a fearful prospect to know that all your male siblings and friends are to be called up, only having the reflection of the carnage of the Great War for comparison of what might be...

And they were all called up as fast as that, Frank into the RAF. He had worked at The Hercules Cycle factory before the war, and was skilled, and became an air mechanic "stationed all over the place" as Daisy puts it, even spending some time in Northern Ireland. It was boys like Frank that kept the planes in the air, a role that became vitally important as the war progressed, especially during the 'Battle of Britain'.

And what of Daisy and the rest of the family during this time? Daisy had moved over to war production at Kynoch's, but unlike the well-paid more glamorous shadow factories, dotted around Birmingham, Daisy worked in a smaller operation which had to do its bit for war production. A place where the standards and rates of pay were perfectly acceptable for the time in general engineering firms, but quite inconsequential against their much grander cousins. I asked her what she was earning when the war work started, came a sniggered reply;

"Oooh not a lot... we got about 20 something... and then 30 something... you got a bit more on the nightshift than the dayshift... we started off on about 10 shillings... but I used to have to give me mum most of that."

To earn that money they did twelve hour shifts 6pm – 6am, 7 nights per week. Daisy opted for 'mainly nights' probably because it paid more, but it was the most dangerous time for factory workers when the German bombers were abroad, especially during 1940 – 1941. Many workers feared night shifts especially after the bad raids on the BSA factory in Small Heath in August and November 1940. Where Daisy worked was particularly dangerous, Kynoch's was one of the only factories in Birmingham that made the shells, and filled them on site.

They did not get the lavish entertainment laid on for the workers at the shadow factories, every day and night, or even the decent meal supplied every night as in a large factory canteen. Once a week the company used to put on a show at midnight, in what was effectively the night shifts dinner hour. One particular night rather than just a CEMA violinist or singer, they were thrilled to find Joe Loss and his band waiting for them at midnight:

"...oooh it was beautiful it was... after the singers he said 'come on you can all get up and dance now' and everyone was getting up and dancing on the floor, you know."

Meanwhile, Daisy's mum continued to foster and was begged by a woman at Lucas's to adopt her son Reggie;

"...Because I don't want no one else to have him".

And indeed when the lady died Reggie was adopted. At the same time, there was a house for unmarried mothers in Trinity Road. A young woman from there who was due to have her baby, approached Daisy's mother with a view to having her adopt the child because the matron had recommended her as the best person. The young woman came from an area near Cadbury's, she lived with her grandmother, and had become pregnant by the married director of a firm over there. The grandmother felt such shame, that she was unable to have her granddaughter in her home displaying her condition to all the world, and had her duly dispatched to the home for unmarried mothers to await the birth of her child, this was not an unusual occurrence at that time. The child arrived, a baby girl, for whom Daisy chose the name, Sylvia Susan, who then became Daisy's adopted sister.

Probably the worst time of the war was approaching for Birmingham, the bad blitz of 1940. A time Birmingham Corporation was totally unprepared for and in the event found itself lacking in all the essential services and organisation that was required to get the city through such an horrendous ordeal. It was indeed the darkest of times, with fear gripping the city and morale was at an all time low. Daisy was just 17, she was living in a house full of women, with an elderly man (her grandfather) and an invalided and very sick man (her father). She was the eldest, and so much responsibility fell on her shoulders. As her father used to say she was the eldest girl and he was not letting her marry until she was at least 21. She had to give her mother her money (what paltry salary she got) it kept things going for everyone. Then the horror started! In mid-August a summer's eve the skies opened, and the bombs began to fall. In late November the night of the BSA bombing was followed by rumours of employees not being allowed to evacuate and cowering in the basement to shelter as the upper floors fell in on top of them. Many incendiaries, fell on Kynoch's and despite the risk of explosion, Kynoch's carried on manufacturing throughout, with their ARP, working hard to help extinguish the fires as they happened. Through these three months of terrible raids, the people of Birmingham suffered!

Daisy lived and worked in the inner ring of the city and was caught up in the full horror of that dreadful time in a heavily populated area, so much so that, in Daisy's own words;

"...this one time I was on the day shift... and on the night time there was this big air raid... up Lozells we had them big land mines dropping... and it was only just up Chain Walk across from where we lived... and the next morning I went into work and of course I said 'good morning' and the one young girl standing opposite me, and she looked at me and went aaaww... and she fainted!"

What had actually happened was a house that was lived in by a cousin of Daisy's opposite in Hampton Road, had taken a direct hit, killing the young lady, her husband and their three children, the youngest one was just three weeks old. They had not had time to evacuate to the shelter and had taken refuge under their stairs. Daisy's work colleague had been told that it had been Daisy's house, and of course was very shocked to see her alive, but presumably very glad too. It is very difficult to imagine the fear that must have gripped these young girls, for that's all they were, as they tried to go about their business doing their 'patriotic' duty. How must she have felt night after night, on the 'graveyard shift' with bombs falling all around? Not just in danger of taking a direct hit as many had, but working in a factory where the bullets she helped to make were actually filled on the premises by the men. The stock of explosive chargers and gun powder must have put them under constant risk of an explosion, and they all must have realised this. Many women do report becoming almost immune to the bombings and the noise in the latter years of the war, but by that stage they were older and had been through a considerable amount of bombardment. In those first dreadful raids of 1940 when Birmingham fell to its knees, it must have seemed so dark and truly horrific for girls in their late teens. Knowing the chaos going on all around her, and understanding the risks that she was enduring working at Kynoch's, Daisy reflects:

"We was really lucky there… it's unbelievable really."

Daisy carried on stoically, as they all did, and life continued on at an artificially accelerated rate because of the instability of war. Although her father had forbade her to get married until she was twenty one "She was his eldest girl and he didn't want to lose her" (as she was the eldest one, she brought much needed financial support into the household). However, he did allow her to become engaged to Frank at the age of seventeen and a half. Their courting became quite a dangerous activity.

Frank came home on leave, probably sometime early in 1941 and together they went to 'The Futurist' picture house which used to stand in John Bright Street, to see 'Gone With The Wind', which hadn't long been on general release in the UK. All was well until just before the end when the air raid warning sounded. Under normal circumstances if the picture had been midway through the customers would have been given the option to remain in the cinema rather than evacuating to the shelter. On this occasion because the film was almost complete, they had to leave. They started on their treacherous route home through what turned out to be an intensive bombing raid. Initially they had thoughts of going to the nearest shelter as the ARP was directing them to do, however, trying to get home seemed a better idea, and as the buses weren't running they had no other option but to walk. As they walked they kept getting met by another, then another ARP warden who would try and direct them to the nearest shelter, but relentlessly they hurried on the whole three and a half miles to Hampton Road. Every time they were challenged by a warden they would say they were going to a shelter but they would continue on their way, dodging the bombs as they went. After all you could cower in a shelter and still get hurt, so why not chance your luck and make it back to where you feel most at home?

And then there was Amy's in Chain Walk a popular haunt for the young couple who wanted a fun night out, or on other occasions the young air trainees used to put on a show, and Daisy and Frank would be invited to that. Like many of the young people of that bleak period of history, the best escapism was the dance band, and the excitement of the jive and swing. Not a place for single girls unless they wanted a reputation, but for a young couple in love just the thing to make an exciting Saturday night, some would carry on dancing even when the raids were going on. The austerity that came with the ration card, could seem a million miles away, with a dance band playing the latest Benny Goodman or Artie Shaw. All moaning aside, even rationing had its good points according to Daisy;

"We really appreciated everything being on rationing… we used to walk everywhere, and we were healthy."

I should think these evenings of light relief were few and far between for Daisy, as by her own admission she worked 'mainly nights', probably to keep the money coming in, 'save up till you have got enough', had always been her philosophy and she had a big bottom drawer to fill for when she would eventually get married, and that came around sooner than she thought possible. On the 10th October 1942 her father allowed her to marry Frank she was nineteen and a half, maybe the futility and fragility of life during war had made him realise that his daughter should have a shot at happiness.

Her colleagues at work thrilled her by making a presentation of a pink bedspread, she said she thought it was 'so beautiful' and she had 'never seen anything like that in her life'. Daisy continued to live at home with her mother and father for the duration of the war, probably not daring to have children until she had some room. In fact she did not get her first proper house until her first son (who was born in 1947) was twenty one.

Tragedy was not far away. One day, towards the end of the war the telegram that everyone dreaded receiving arrived. One can only imagine the horror that went through Daisy's head as she received it from the postman, but it was not for her, it was for Aunt Evelyn, informing her that Ted had been killed in action somewhere in Germany.

Daisy's experience of housing in post war was not uncommon, and it was a result of the intensive devastation, which went greatly unreported to which Birmingham had succumbed. There was a massive housing shortage post war and you had to take what you could get. Daisy, her sister, and her husband, found a less than ideal solution, but it was a solution. They squatted in the Nissen huts in Perry Park, in what had been a prisoner of war camp. As Daisy describes it, there were no facilities, no running water and she would have to walk half a mile to the main gate to catch a bus, and as for toilet facilities… they were outside too. When she was pregnant with her first child in 1947, and subsequently seven years later with her second child, that was a long walk, just to catch a bus to the maternity hospital. Well before that time, the council had caught on and were charging her five shillings a week for the privilege. It is hard to imagine now, trying to look after a small baby in a tin hut with no facilities, unless you live in a third world country, or a township in South Africa, but even in war-torn Brum.

Daisy's highlight and probably her biggest missed opportunity came just before the end of the war. Frank at that time was stationed just outside Derby and attached to an Australian squadron, as a 'thank you' the 'Aussies' decided to throw a party for all the wives and girlfriends of the British air crews. Daisy had to catch a train from Birmingham New Street to Derby, where she was met, and taken on a bus to the air base. Frank was there and escorted her into the party, it was a spectacular affair, quite a lift after the grey, darkness of the worst of war. The whole place was decked out in fabulous decorations and lights, and a dance band played, and everybody had fun. In the middle of all this razzmatazz was an immense table topped with a creation of superlative magnitude, the Australian chef had created a complete replica of the airbase as a cake, complete with planes!

War brings many hardships and difficulties, but it also brings many opportunities and tough decisions. People are exposed to places and choices, that would never have been granted to them in normal civilian life and Frank was no exception. During the party the Australian squadron leader approached them both, he had been so impressed with Frank, both as a person, and a conscientious worker, that he offered to sponsor them over to Australia, should Frank decide to go after the war. The dilemma for Frank and Daisy must have been profoundly difficult to resolve, this was the opportunity for a real fresh start in a country that had not been bombed, where by all accounts, there were limitless opportunities and rewards for people as hardworking as they were.

When it came down to the wire, the decision was a relatively simple one for Frank. He had lost his own parents when he was young and Daisy's parents had been so good to him, he couldn't possibly let them down and leave them, not with Daisy's father being so ill... so they remained.

Daisy and I finished our chat, and the TV still murmured away in the background. She stayed sitting in the same house that she moved into in 1969 and where Frank succumbed to his heart attack twenty three years ago, only four months after taking early retirement at the age of fifty nine from British Rail, with whom he had served since leaving the RAF. All the photographs of her memories that hang on the wall, the people in her story, are there as silent witnesses, but all is now quiet, no bombs, there is running water and electric lights, all is peace. As she says;

"I am not going to move again until they carry me out in a box!"

FOR DAISY

You blew me away baby,
You blew me away,
In that dress you wore,
You blew me away,
In that dress you wore today.

Let's go dancing baby,
Like before, in that dress you wore,
Let's go to 'Amy's', or the 'Palais de Danse',
You blew me away baby,
Let's take a chance.

Let's skip the light fantastic,
Let's take a lovely trip,
Let's do something really wild,
You blew me away baby,
In the dress you wore today.

Chapter 3

THE MUNITIONS MARCH TO WAR

"I am speaking to you from the cabinet room of 10 Downing Street. This morning the British Ambassador in Berlin handed the German Government a final note stating that, unless we heard from them by 11 o'clock that they were prepared at once to withdraw their troops from Poland, a state of war would exist between us. I have to tell you that no such undertaking has been received, and consequently this country is at war with Germany."

The Right Honourable Neville Chamberlain, Prime Minister – 3rd September, 1939.

When those words were spoken, the ladies who are the subject of this book, were all girls and young women. They had listened to the talk of war for some time, and had probably been aware of the terrible prospect for a year. They had personal experience within their families' living memory of the horror of war, with most having close male relatives who had fought. Five of them were already working in one or another of the Birmingham factories, that would prove so vital to the outcome of this Second World War. One lady patriotically joined the effort immediately, two were employed in reserved occupations which became reclassified in 1941, and the last was conscripted from many miles away when the call came.

The words spoken that day are probably more poignant to people of Birmingham, as Mr Chamberlain was one of their great sons, his father having been the industrialist, politician, and social reformer, Joseph Chamberlain, who had been a major driving force in Birmingham's industrial and social regeneration. Arthur Neville Chamberlain, had first been a businessman and then strove for local politics in Birmingham, becoming Lord Mayor in 1915. Eventually, he became M.P. for Ladywood in Birmingham and after spending two decades gaining much experience in the cabinet, he became Prime Minister, after the Abdication Crisis which proceeded Baldwin's resignation.

Neville Chamberlain, shared much of his father's social reforming interests, and although he considered himself a Liberal Unionist, he had an 'outlook... similar to that of the Fabians', with the interests of the common people, at the forefront. He knew Birmingham, it was his home city, he knew its capacity for engineering and manufacture, its importance to the productions of munitions and armaments, the ingenuity and hard-working determination of its people.

Birmingham had a long pedigree in engineering and the allied metal trades and was the key centre of manufacturing, but unfortunately had a history of the exploitation and 'sweating' that accompanied it. The Fabians and reformers took interest very early on and worked tirelessly to improve the lot of the working people, and particularly women, who were in the majority of the employed workforce. Drake (1917);

> "In 1866, a single pen factory in Birmingham engages, according to good authority, no less than 2,000 women. Meanwhile the competition of cheap 'female labour' causes the despair of the men's trade unions."

Drake continues to highlight that women were essential to economic prosperity of the engineering trades in Birmingham and the numbers of women employed in these areas, had swollen to:

> "...170,000 by 1914; although female labour was confined to 'purely automatic' or boys' operations..."

These operations were on 'every variety' of mechanical process from; 'press, milling, drilling, grinding, polishing, screwing, gear-cutting', performing light repetitive tasks, passing from one skill to another, seamlessly (Drake, 1917). The women were kept under the scrutiny of men, who also kept control of the skill, the tasks were demonstrated and then the women set to work by a male operator. As Edward Cadbury (1909) noted when surveying working practices in the factories of Birmingham:

> "In the first place, it is not skilled work, i.e. in a week at the longest a girl has learnt all that she ever will learn about her machine."

Inevitably, with this limited knowledge and experience, with continuous repetitive monotony, on machines which were poorly maintained and guarded, accidents would occur. Cadbury (1909) was only too aware of this;

> "The chief element of danger lies in the nature of the machinery; in greatly varying degree there is always some risk to the hands, and hundreds of Birmingham women show maimed and scarred fingers, as a result of their service in the press shop."

Unfortunately, women were vastly underpaid for their services, the trades unions had a strangle-hold on the interests of their male associates, the employers would have no desire to anger the vanguard of skilled male workers, and as a consequence, paid women a fraction of what they paid the men. As Cadbury and Shann (1907) noted, women were paid less simply because they were women, and their apathy to organise themselves and fight for social change prevailed, limiting their advancement. They found that in many cases women were happy to receive 'half or a third' of what a male colleague would receive for the same undertaking, even piece-work rates were adjusted downwards when remunerating female employees (Cadbury and Shann, 1907).

The First World War was not the first experience of large scale munitions production in Birmingham, the previous conflict of the Boer War had stimulated many ammunitions factories to fulfil government contracts. The Chamberlain family had particular interests, with Neville Chamberlain's uncle, Arthur Chamberlain being the Managing Director of Kynoch's in Witton. At one stage, Lloyd George had accused Joseph Chamberlain of profiteering from war, by securing preferential contracts for the family firm, in fact he was always suspicious and contemptuous of Neville Chamberlain as a result.

Without a doubt it was the First World War that elevated the position, and wages, of female workers in munitions factories. The sheer weight of numbers required for the fighting forces, in terms of weapons and ammunition, and most importantly the male fighting foot-soldiery, meant that women were left as the only source of manual labour. This is where the dichotomy of skilled labour, and unskilled labour, first arose and necessitated some radical redefinition of what would become 'women's work'. This would re-emerge again twenty five years later. As Wightman (1999) explains, the 'ceaseless requirements of war' forced the government to re-organise the skills base within engineering manufacture. More and more men were being taken for the frontlines depleting the skilled workforce, unskilled men had to be upgraded to 'tool room' work and setting, leaving women to fill the void that they left in ever greater numbers.

To avoid recognising their contribution in equal pay, thus angering the unions and male union members, a redefinition of 'women's work' of their undertakings was required, Wightman (1999):

"The electrical firm of British-Thompson-Houston in Willesden gave an example of its 'women's work' as any miscellaneous light work which is fairly clean and does not require great strength."

This explanation of the tasks of women, allowed employers to leave rates of pay untouched and keep women on rates lower than that of men, except for those women who had to be upgraded to take an 'unskilled' man's job as a 'dilutee'. 'Dilution' was the process of taking in men and women to fill vacancies, who were then given limited training, to undertake the 'automatic and semi-automatic' tasks (Woollacott, 1994). Women faired better towards the end of the First World War, munitions work relative to other women's employment was highly paid, because of the dangers of TNT poisoning and explosion, and for the first time a social class who had previously been limited to the aspiration of a downstairs maid in domestic service, could afford independence in society unthinkable prior to 1914, but it was not to last.

As the war came to an end, public opinion fuelled by political interests swung against these women, who had largely been hailed as heroines for their efforts during war time. It was in no one's interests to have women continuing to hold 'men's jobs', by which time many had become very skilled. There were going to be returning men, with interests in re-establishing their working lives, and their home lives. Men worked and were the bread winners for families, women could not work in the same jobs, and take away the pay of the working man.

Besides anti-working-women propaganda in the press, the government took a series of actions to force women back into their place in society. They allowed them to have out-of-work pay eventually at the rate of '20s. a week (compared to 24s. a week for men)', which was reduced to 15s., girls under eighteen received considerably less. This was to force them to take other work (Woollacott, 1994). This for women who had prior to the war according to Woollacott earned between:

"…10s. and 14s. a week. By the end of the war, women in the munitions industries were earning on average, between 30s. to 35s. a week, often with overtime and bonuses on top – roughly a threefold increase."

Regarding the sudden loss of employment, Woollacott (1994) notes that:

"In Birmingham, by 11th December there were estimated to be 10 times more women unemployed than men."

Dismissal followed by the vastly reduced income, had in many cases the desired effect, to return the working classes back to their service roles to the upper class. Women in some cases had their out-of-work pay stopped completely for refusing to take wages of 15s. or even as low as 3s. a week. In one particular case, Woollacott (1994) has found that out-of-work pay was refused to a woman:

"…who turned down a live-in domestic service position because her husband was expected home soon."

Women were once again returned to their lower status, although Birmingham remained as the main centre of manufacture for the UK, and needed a high proportion of low-paid female workers in order to function. Nationally and internationally, the world went into recession and this forced many firms to limit pay still further in an effort to stay in business. For many to have employment at all at a time of high unemployment was a bonus, and if you had a job you hung onto it even if your pay was vastly reduced.

Neville Chamberlain's relationship with Birmingham was always apparent and many of his national social reforms, were built on his experiences of reform in Birmingham, which he then enacted nationally at this bleak time. These included the passage of the Factory Act 1937, to improve the conditions and limit the hours that women and minors could work. He was Chancellor of the Exchequer in the early thirties and oversaw the economic recovery, for which he received many plaudits and also caused controversy for introducing E.P.T. raising revenue from excessive profits in industry.

It was at this stage that he could be considered as responsible for much of the city's post-depression regeneration, for nationally he introduced a policy of rationalisation. This was done by the purchasing of old factories and mines, followed by their reconstruction as new factories, 'shadow factories'. He realised that the international political situation was very unstable, and that the United Kingdom, could only stand as a strong nation, if it was seen to be a strong military power, as Herr Hitler had regenerated Germany. Chamberlain realised that from a position of military strength, Britain could keep aggressors at bay and that if a war were to come it would be one that would be waged in the air. As a consequence, he invested heavily in the development of the RAF at the expense of the other two services, defence spending on the RAF 'rose from £16.78 million pounds in 1933 to £105.702 million pounds in 1939' (Levy, 2006). Aircraft production was centred on the cities of Birmingham and Coventry, in the new factories built by; Nuffield, Austin, Rover and others. As the push to rearm drove on, more and more of the cities' population found themselves gainfully employed building new technologies using new technologies, machine tools. These machine tools were absolutely vital to arms and aircraft production and required individuals of great skill to design, build and assemble them, and a new factory could not function without many of them, another field that Birmingham engineers excelled in.

Some co-operation was required from the unions to changes in working practices in order to accommodate new government directives for rearmament, Boston (1980), raises the issues the union had to acquiesce too:

"...in March 1938 the government assumed powers to direct industry to manufacture what was necessary for rearmament. On the following day,

23rd March, the TUC leaders were invited to No. 10 Downing Street, where they agreed to relax Trade Union restrictive practices in the engineering industry."

Whereas, under the Factory Act 1937, women had been banned from night shifts, given only limited periods of overtime and allowed to work for a maximum of forty-eight hours a week, by 1939, females of sixteen or over would be permitted to work up to fifty-seven hours per week, and this would be critical for war production (Williams, 2002).

The tensions in Europe emanating from Germany's aggression towards its neighbours and the coveting of once possessed territories, was rising steadily year on year from the mid 1930's. Chamberlain knew that Britain was militarily weaker than Germany, and needed time to reach a feasible capacity for defence. He was aware that near European neighbours were vulnerable and nervous as a consequence, and that a balanced approach to diplomacy was better for all. By the time he reached 1939, he had been Prime Minister for nearly two years; and at this point Hitler had invaded Czechoslovakia. Chamberlain used a speech given in Birmingham on 17th March to communicate to the Third Reich his challenge against their apparent moves to dominate Europe. It was inevitable that once Germany had invaded Poland, any chance of peace through appeasement had gone.

The 3rd September, 1939, was by all accounts a very grey day in Birmingham. Eileen heard the announcement over the tannoy of the BSA Small Heath factory where she was working a Sunday shift. Evelyn and Win heard it and got on with things. Win had a small daughter to care for and Evelyn was expecting her first baby. Daisy, Iris, Jenny, May and Kathleen were upset, as were their families sitting around the wireless at 11 o'clock in the morning, but being young and naïve to the horrors of war, to some extent they let it wash over them. Iris Cooke, was having her 17th birthday which had turned into a pretty miserable affair. Those that were not already working in a factory, would soon be called upon to do so, faster than any of them had thought possible.

Initially, things were quiet in Birmingham, they entered the time from September 1939 to April 1940 known as the 'phoney war'. Some factories were already very busy and had been for a few years producing the required arms and weaponry, the BSA being by far the biggest producer. Austin Aero and Rover were undertaking their government contracts for the RAF. The smaller producers such as Collins and ICI Metals Ltd. (Kynoch's subsidiaries, companies such as; Lightning Zip Fasteners) were soon turned over to arms production. There were already shortages, as the call up started, skilled and unskilled men were leaving their occupations in droves, the cabinet became aware of the impending crisis as early as 31st October, 1939, when the Supply and Production report from that month was already reporting deficiencies in orders due to the loss of skilled men from their roles.

By January 1940, things were moving on apace, the Minister of Supply reported the establishment of an Advisory Committee in Birmingham, to monitor requirements, he also reported further relaxations for the working restrictions on 'women, and boys over 16 years of age, engaged in the making of small arms ammunition'. Total expenditure on munitions, explosives, tanks and vehicles from August 1st to December 30th, 1939, had been calculated to be £17,976,000. In the same month a Supply and Man-Power report was circulated around the cabinet with a note foreword produced by the Chancellor of the Exchequer, regarding the acute problem now facing munitions production, he wrote:

"4.(iii) Means should be found to open out the peculiarly acute 'bottle-neck' created by the shortage of skilled labour through the adoption of dilution (including the introduction of female labour) and the more even spreading of the available skilled labour through the whole of the engineering trades."

The report forewarned that there was a predicted shortfall of 1.2 million workers by July 1941 although there were 1.3 million currently employed. The total population was given at that time as 44 million. The report considered that although women were 'more suitable than men' for some processes, that for many 'the employment of women is not practicable'. It estimated that both in general engineering and in aircraft manufacture, women totalled less than 10 per cent. of the workforce, and although a recruitment drive was vital, that 'special inducement' such as 'high wages' must not be given as this would affect the export trade. The report did recognise that training would be vital, but that with a shortfall of 1,000 machine tool makers, it was important to raise semi-skilled men, and fill in the vacancies left through dilution. On the 18th January, 1940, the Minister for Labour (Ernest Brown) promoted the idea of the adaptation of Government Training Centres to train women. The cabinet joined forces in the suggestion that their ensuing speeches around the country, should be used as platforms to:

"...stress the need for change from one occupation to another, as an essential part of the war effort."

Things began changing significantly, both for Birmingham and Neville Chamberlain. The war came to Birmingham in April, 1940, when the bombing started, at the same time there was a failed campaign of the British forces to free Norway from the German invaders, followed by the invasion of Holland, Belgium and France.

There was a loss of confidence in Chamberlain's leadership. He had shortly beforehand, made an ill-timed speech to the house, where he spoke of Hitler having 'missed the bus', by not having persecuted his threatened aggression against his neighbours. Once things had deteriorated he was forced to attend the House of Commons for the 'Narvik' Debate on the 8th May, 1940, where he was taunted by chants of 'missed the bus' and told by Leo Amery that he had 'sat too long for any good you have been doing, depart', a reference to the speech made by Oliver Cromwell to the 'Long Parliament' some three hundred years previously (Gardiner, 2004).

On May 10th, Chamberlain offered his resignation to George VI and recommended Churchill to succeed him. The new war cabinet, that Churchill had reduced from 9 to 5 ministers, with Churchill as Minister of Defence (Gardiner, 2004), very quickly assessed the situation they faced. It had become very apparent that since the German bombardment of the cities had finally started, air superiority was the only way to save the country from invasion. With the imminent and predicted fall of France, Britain would be facing the aggressor alone, the production of aircraft was essential if we were to stay free as a nation. They knew at this point from the evidence that they had, that the most sensitive sites strategically were the cities of Birmingham and Coventry, and these areas would pose the greatest vulnerability to attack, which could be the end.

With the collapse of France and Dunkirk, it was August before the cabinet was able to assess the munitions situation effectively. Herbert Morrison wrote a report entitled, 'The Munitions Situation', in his view the problem that the government faced at this stage was an over production of munitions, combined with a lack of storage facilities. It appeared that the assessment of needs had been based on the 'siege conditions' of '1914-1918', and although the ammunition was definitely required, storage was posing an insurmountable problem:

> "To show the scale of the problem... will produce 38 million of complete rounds of ammunition in 1941... give a grand total at the end of next year of 48 million rounds... storage accommodation must therefore be provided... At the end of next year we shall be producing 3.7 million rounds per month but must have the manufacturing capacity sufficient to provide 8.3 million rounds per month."

They were caught in the dilemma of the need not just to maintain the present factory workforce, but to increase their numbers substantially, and at the same time trying to limit the over production of ammunition. Another labour issue which was becoming burdensome was that of the needs of the technically highly skilled aircraft manufacture, and despite the fact there was now six million more people than during the previous war labour shortages were crippling production.

He also pointed out in this report that automation was not necessarily the answer to the problems faced by the government. He reported a visit to Stewart and Lloyd's Shellshop, near Birmingham, where there was 'a wonderful display of machine tools – some of them taking several cuts at once', but on the occasion of this particular visit hardly any women were to be witnessed working there. In his opinion it was better:

"If you could make the same number of shells in a shop fitted with general purpose lathes and employing workers to five times the number, it would be a wartime economy though the shell might cost a little more to do this, and use the skilled men for making tanks and guns."

The turning point came after Ernest Bevin, who was the Minister of Labour under Churchill asked, Sir William Beveridge to undertake a thorough survey of man-power, this was offered to the cabinet in November 1940. The main conclusions highlighted the waste of man-power that war causes, through inappropriate use of personnel; that incorrect location of new factories now required a substantial transfer of labour (particularly skilled labour); a problem that would be difficult to address because of the immobility of the British workforce. That the acute 'super skill' shortages had to be addressed; that peace time economy is not the same as a wartime economy and should be approached differently; that the state should take control of national recruitment and wage issues to address shortages; and that Employment Exchanges had to receive greater powers. The most influential suggestion was that of registration and direct transfer of labour was essential, while recognising that women and dilution were not being used effectively and that the Women's Services would be competing for their recruitment. Added to this, the problems with lodgings in certain areas (Birmingham was given as an example), and wages that varied dramatically from £5 to £16 per week (men's rates), there needed to be a complete rationalisation.

Beveridge recorded that in his opinion:

"…obstacles to dilution arise as much from the reluctance of employers as from resistance of the men."

He considered it was relatively simple to employ women through dilution, but the skilled tool setter, tool maker shortage had to addressed as a matter of the utmost importance. He felt that was easier to mobilise women to transfer from other parts of the country than it was to mobilise men, but that consequentially the government must do something to alleviate home sickness, through adequate provision of lodgings and wages. Incidentally, there must be some control of wages set by employers, as he recognised that the larger factories were able to offer larger salaries in an effort to poach staff, he found that:

> "The high earnings of certain limited classes of armament workers are undoubtedly a source of weakness in our economic organisation to-day. The main trouble, however, is not high earnings, but inequality of earnings; there are many cases of low or reduced earnings to set against £10 or £12 earnings of some munitioneers."

He identified that 'provision' had to be made to assist married women, with issues such as childcare and other 'household duties'.

From this Bevin drew up his plan towards his Total War Economy.

As Boston (1980) writes:

> "Bevin's plan was to utilize women to the maximum. Single women with no ties were directed to move into men's jobs; childless married women were moved into single women's jobs; married women with young children and even grannies were expected to work even part-time."

Within a few months Bevin had put together his plan, but he did have some obstacles which were unavoidable. In the previous summer an agreement on women's wages had been reached with the unions that allowed women to rise incrementally to a level of 44s. in women's work on munitions. The dilemma that then faced an employer was whether or not to transfer her on to a man's grade, thus having to find more women to draft in to fill her position. He was confronted indirectly by a member of the Women's Advisory Committee (Miss V. Holmes) to the Ministry of Labour, who many of the male staff considered to be a group of interfering 'feminists'. She wanted to know why it could not be possible to employ the women on the most skilled work that they were capable of undertaking, and paying them commensurate with the task, she had been firmly told by the Deputy Secretary that the unions had reached these agreements, to which she replied:

> "It seems probable that women munitions workers had as much say in agreements on their wages as Czechoslovakia had in the Munich agreement... they did not exist in large numbers at the time... were only in the process of being called into being... there were no strong independent women's unions."

The ultimate reply which came from the minister was that in his considered opinion it would be 'uneconomical' to elevate women, leaving gaps in the workforce, and that for the firms concerned it would cause a 'dislocation in production' which is why he could understand them not supporting this idea.

According to Boston (1980) the registration process was undertaken from April 1941 until October 1942, all women aged twenty-one to forty-five were registered and later that was extended to those 'up to the age of fifty'. As she acknowledges (Boston, 1980):

"Although registration was not the same as conscription, the distinction was fine."

Women were withdrawn from non-essential occupations in their thousands and interviewed at Employment Exchanges with the motive to transfer them to munitions work. Those that had not already moved themselves into the Land Army or other Women's service were left with little or no option, unless they could prove domestic responsibilities. As the shortages continued throughout 1941, occupations were re-registered as non-essential that had once been considered essential in an effort to fill the shortfall of labour. This did have negative consequences on some sectors of industry, the textiles trade reported a huge loss in staff, due to women leaving before they were drafted, older women towards domestic responsibility and the younger age groups choosing to volunteer for essential work rather than waiting for the Employment Exchange interview.

Jenny was transferred early from Sunderland, she had her interview because she left it too long before attempting to apply for telephony work, she asked for a 'sit-down' job, and got her travel warrant to Birmingham, where her lodgings were not the best and her salary was not the highest. Iris walked into the Austin, when 'work got slack' and she felt that she ought to be doing something important. May, who had been working for a brewery (officially deemed the Ministry of Food), was reclassified and called up for Rover (Solihull). The only bonus for these ladies was that their salaries were considerably better than those who had been in the industry since before the war.

In the Munitions Production report for the period of January to July, 1942, there were some causes for celebration, Bevin's plans had come to fruition. They reported that in the UK machine tools had risen by 170,000 to 940,000 and that was because they had 24,000 more men, and 13,000 more women. Win was working at such a firm, H. C. Wards in Birmingham making machine tools, as was her mother (as she had in the previous war).

There had been an increase of 519,000 personnel to munitions (men 148,000 : women 371,000), however, they were stressing the need to transfer even more personnel before the end of 1943.

It was it seems a never ending problem, to recruit and provide the much needed labour force to feed the war effort. Those that were there worked very long hours, the women received considerably less pay than their male colleagues, and they had their lives changed for ever, as Wightman (1999) explains the effort was incomprehensible:

"Between 1939 and 1943 an extra 1.5 million women entered the 'essential industries'. In engineering their numbers rose from 97,000 to 602,000 or from 10 to 34 per cent of the workforce. The industry had never seen such a huge and compulsory influx of workers."

MUNITIONS WAGES

Earning high wages? Yus,
  Five quid a week
A woman, too, mind you,
  I calls it dim sweet.

Ye're asking some questions -
  But bless yer, here goes:
I spend the whole racket
  On good times and clothes.

We're all here today, mate,
  Tomorrow – perhaps dead,
If fate tumbles on us
  And blows up our shed.

Afraid! Are you kidding?
  With money to spend!
Years back I wore tatters,
  Now – silk stockings, mi friend!

I've bracelets and jewellery,
  Rings envied by friends,
A sergeant to swank with,
  And something to lend.

I drive out in taxis,
  Do theatres in style.
And this is mi verdict
  It is jolly worth while

Worth while, for tomorrow
  If I am blown to the sky,
I'll have repaid mi wages
  In death – and pass by.

Madeline Ida Bedford, "Munitions Wages" in Scars Upon My Heart: Women Poetry And Verse Of The First World War, ed. Catherine Reilly (London: Virago, 1981) page 7 and 8. Quoted from On Her Their Lives Depends: Munition Workers in The Great War. A. Woollacott (1994).

Chapter 4

JENNY'S JOURNEY

"The Sunday morning that war started I was at work, I managed a sweet and tobacco shop at that time. Of course we worked long hours then, from 9 o'clock in the morning till 9.30 at night, this included Sunday work as well. This particular Sunday I remember seeing a newspaper boy go by with a big poster saying that 'war had been declared'. Shortly after the siren sounded, and I suppose everyone thought there was going to be a raid immediately, people were running up the road to find shelter, however, I just stayed put, then the 'all clear' sounded. The raids were to come in earnest later in the war. One night, the Victoria Hall had a landmine fall on it, blasting out windows all round including the shop where I worked. I arrived to find the shop windows out, sweets scattered on the pavement, Binn's (department store) was burned down. I remember having to step over the fire hoses, as I went to work. Even the tea and sugar, I had on the shelf in the back of the shop, to make a cup of tea had disappeared, these are just some memories among many during the war."

These are Jenny's own words written for a local Birmingham newspaper a few years ago. She is a very eloquent lady who comes from Sunderland, and was one of those many who were handed a rail warrant and conscripted into munitions work, from other parts of the country. As she says, they were so broad where she came from, she had to practise saying Birmingham, and when she was asked by locals in Sunderland where she was bound for, she used to say 'the Midlands' rather than having to say Birmingham, or as they say up there 'Bormingum'.

Jenny Bellenie-Tullock was 23 by the time war broke out and had already worked a few years in her home town as is reflected in her letter. She has memories of a blitzed-Sunderland which adds colour to her story. Her parents, Annie Bellenie and Edward Tullock had a very close family and already had much experience of the Great War. All five of her mother's brothers; Joe, Jim, Harry, Ben and Bill had survived the war and come back, quite an achievement for a family of so many not to lose at least one.

Edward, Jenny's father, had been a professional soldier and was wounded quite badly at Ypres, he lay in the trenches, and only survived by licking the ice off his moustache for three days. When the stretcher bearers eventually found him and the battle was still raging, he told them to hide in the hedges every time they came under fire, and to leave him on the ground as he had already been shot.

Jenny's mother Annie, had worked at the bottle works, and this is where she had met Edward who by that stage was working as a glassblower, he moved to Scotland and tried to get Annie to go too, but she refused. So there was nothing for it, and he returned to Southwick to marry her. Annie had tried working on a farm, as a housekeeper for a while, but she missed the company of the other 'lasses'. Jenny was born in the 'downstairs of a four-tenanted place', where the tap for drinking and washing was in the outside yard. She had a brother three and a half years older called Jimmy. Little Jenny's main job was to help her invalided father to put his special orthopedic boot on. Jenny contracted Scarlet Fever at the age of ten, and she was sent to the hospital for a while, during that time her younger brother Edward was born.

When it came time for Jenny to look for work, her mother was adamant: 'no rope works for you'. The rope works was considered the worst place. Jenny had ambitions to work in a shop, and she also liked minding children. Initially, she became a young nanny for a shop keeping family, then by word of mouth she got a job in her first shop where they couldn't afford to pay her stamp when she turned 16. Then she kept house and walked the dog for a retired schoolteacher, she worked very hard cleaning for Miss Wilson for three years, before finding her too difficult to work for because she always expected more. Following this she moved to work as a relief shop girl for a difficult shop keeper, Mr Marlee. Although, Jenny found him to be generous in some ways she also found him to be quite demanding, expecting her to be in two places at once. One day Jenny had enough and 'put her coat on and walked out' however, realising that she was such a hard worker he asked her to return, and gave her a rise. This ability to move jobs and frequently change was normal for the time. Eventually, Jenny ended up in the sweet and tobacco shop, where she felt happiest because she was her own boss. This was the beginning of Jenny's war and her long journey in life.

She knew war was coming and there were rumours that they may be expected to go elsewhere as Jenny says:

"They were rounding up these girls."

Her one brother, who worked in the fire service suggested that if she was working for the Fire Service as a telephonist that they would not conscript her, she was slightly reluctant not having a telephone in the house, and thought she would 'hang on' a little longer at the shop.

She lived near the shipyards, when the bombing started this was another major target for the Germans, as Jenny remembers:

"My father used to stay in the house... as you walked down our street, you could see the big crane and that's what they used to bomb... they used to machine gun Stoney Lane... and we had no shelter and we made friends with the lady over the road, Mrs Grey... but she went with us to a big house at the top of our street called West House... and we used to run up there because you'd had pyjamas on and you'd just put trousers on... they were Salvation Army people and they had a big shelter... one particular night we were told we hadn't got to go in there, we had to go in the wine cellar... and it was terrific they must have been so near, me mother was so frightened she scratched down my face... eventually people started going out to have a look because a plane had been shot down... and I could see the plane on fire..."

Jenny suffered many bad raids in Sunderland, and her brother Jimmy being in the fire service was always a worry for her mother. Just like Birmingham when the raids were on, public transport stopped, and Jenny can remember when she was working at the paper shop having to walk back through the raids. On one occasion, she can remember having to walk back from the shop where she had been working, and there was chaos all around her because of the raid. She had to cross over Monkwearthmouth Bridge, a bridge that bears the legend, "Nil desperandum, auspice deo" (never despair, trust in God), how very apt! She struggled on, when she was nearly home she was stopped by an ARP warden, by that time the raid had got so bad that she had to 'dodge into a service shelter' for cover. She recalls the shelter was terribly dark and the raid was very heavy. She recounts her fear in the notes that she wrote for me about the events that followed;

"Three bombs were dropped all round it and the earth shook, and I thought this is it! But when it stopped the lights went on, and who should I be sitting next to, but my cousin Billy, my Auntie Jenny's son. He put his arm round me. Someone started to play some music. The house behind was empty that night no one killed, the pub in front and the house next door, the same, so no one was hurt."

Just before Christmas 1941, Jenny got her 'call up' for the BSA factory in Hall Green in Birmingham, she did not want to go, because she imagined Birmingham to be a smoky city with lots of factory chimneys. As she says, although the BSA Small Heath had been bombed:

"I knew nothing about it because they didn't divulge anything..."

She was ignorant of those events, for if she had known she would have probably not have gone. Her quiet father saw her off on the train with her rail warrant, it was a long journey. A journey where she could have made friends with many other girls in the 'same boat', but she didn't think to look down the train for other unfortunate conscripts. She does not remember much about her arrival, as it was pitch black and she was exhausted. She was taken to a hostel in Grey Street, where she slept well, and remembers going to breakfast and being met with a girl crying at the breakfast table, Jenny felt nothing except shock. Then the coach came to transfer her to her digs, which were spread all around locally in private houses, in Jenny's own words:

"I went blithely on the coach and I was pleasantly surprised, we were taken to Hall Green, near the Robin Hood... but we had to go along Solihull Lane all along there... and the girls was clinging together... anyway about half way along, (the liaison officer said) 'one girl wanted only' and she patted me on the back and said 'that's the spirit' but it didn't feel like that..."

Her first landlord and landlady were Mr and Mrs Loins, they had a daughter living at home and a son in the army. The next morning was another 'first' for Jenny, her first day at the factory. Once again it was dark, she was in a very foreign city, probably totally disorientated with all the travelling and she had to go and stand outside the Robin Hood pub and wait for a special coach to pick her up, and then:

"I was following girls with green turbans on, because you couldn't see you know... actually this was built on farmland... a nice new factory."

Jenny was set to work on a training section for a fortnight rubbing down small parts of rifles on emery cloth. During her very first day, Jenny had an accident. During a break she had been watching a girl clean down another machine with a blower, Jenny was not wearing eye protection. Unfortunately some swarf became lodged in her eye and she was taken to the infirmary, where the nurse was very apologetic because she could not get it out. It set up conjunctivitis in her eye, and recurrent eye problems for the rest of her life. They decided to give her UV treatment at the time, they may have felt she was very pale and needed the boost. When she got back to her digs, her landlady was shocked, at the state she was in.

As if Jenny had not got enough to contend with, her landlady told her two weeks after she had arrived that she had to find new digs, because her son was coming home on leave, and she needed his room back. So, on Christmas Eve she had to move to new billets with Mr and Mrs Evans.

After Jenny's initial period of training, she was moved to working on the body section of the rifle, filing the body. This was possibly one of the factories used for dispersal of the Browning Rifle, after the BSA suffered the various calamities. She was watched carefully by two foremen who announced to her one day:

"We think you're a big enough girl to go on machines."

They moved her onto a drilling machine which she liked, and she had never done anything like that before, the only draw back was they made her wear a long rubber apron, and as she was drilling the suds used to run down into her shoes. She says:

"It was what you call a two drill... you what you call reamed it out, slipped it into what you call a jig... and you drilled... you did one for there and one there..."

But Jenny's eyes were wandering onto bigger and better things. She saw another girl on a milling machine, and she liked the look of the operator and she started talking to her. She turned out to be another girl drafted in from Newcastle, Betty Percy, who had come down with a friend, Isa Kirkpatrick. The three became great friends. When the two girls from Newcastle were moved onto a larger machine together, Jenny moved onto the mill.

The BSA looked after them well. They had a nice canteen, where they were given a good meal everyday, and entertained by concerts, generally put on by works people. As Jenny reminisces:

"There was one particular lady called Conny and she used to get up and sing and eventually the machine next to mine, I do not know whether the girl had left, or been moved, but Conny was put on that machine."

At the digs that Jenny had moved to, she was told to call her landlord and landlady 'mam and dad'. The Evans had two daughters and a son, and they used their spare rooms to billet four girls who were on compulsory work orders. There was Jean Patrick from Scotland, and Jesse from Scarborough (she was on permanent nights). Then there were the Scottish sisters, Nan and Mary Mulligan. So five including Jenny, who would 'swap' about with the beds, with the girls on nights. The Evans must have been doing very well, because they took most of Jenny's earnings as board, over £2, and this must have been the same for the others. For that, they used to get two slices of toast for breakfast and an evening meal.

Jenny was on a fortnight of days and a fortnight of nights and earning, £2 9s a week, she felt very well off, she had only been getting a pound in the shop. Of course, with her landlady taking so much there was not much left, but Jenny was very good at saving and as she had no access to a social life, or shops really, there was very little to waste her money on. Later on, Betty and Jenny used to make trips home up north when they could.

It was about this time she met Phil, he worked on the barrel section of the factory. He was only working there for six months to recover from a hernia operation before he got his call up. He had been seeing someone else home on the coach. She was with her friend Nan Mulligan who knew Phil, on the coach, as Jenny explains:

"…I remember this hand coming in the coach and helping her down… and then he helped me down because I was lodging with her… he saw us home like that… but I didn't know him and he didn't know me until he saw me next day, and I realised he was on the barrel section."

Phil got to waiting for her, on and off the coach, but Jenny never thought much about it, for she had several boyfriends in Sunderland. When she first got to know him, he was working on the first operations on the barrel of the rifles, which were rusty and he always had brown hands. A figure of much amusement to Jenny's friends who would squeal with delight when they saw brown marks on Jenny's legs.

On one occasion he asked her to stop and say goodbye before she left for the evening, she duly obliged, obviously a very popular move with the whole of his section, who passed by, cheering. Another time, after refraining from eating cakes from the tea lady that used to come round, Jenny was shocked to see a young girl who worked with Phil coming towards her, with a tin lid complete with doughnut, and a verbal message 'Phil sent you this'.

Phil was called up for the RAF and served down in Maidstone, where there was quite a battle. Then he served abroad and he was not allowed to say much about his whereabouts or what he was doing, he would simply say, that he was 'in the mountains'. He was sent to Arnhem, and he flew over Holland, and at some point he was presented with a cigarette case by a Dutch family. He was on the Beaufort guns and was made a 'leading aircraftsman'. As Jenny remembers, he was allowed to write two letters on one he would address:

"…Mrs Rose Hurle (Phil's mother)… (she laughs) and for me he used to put Mrs P…"

In later years when work slackened off a bit, they moved her onto government view, where she had to inspect the finished rifle, which meant she moved around quite a bit and spent a great deal of time in the men's section, but at least she was able to sit down after spending three and a half years standing to do her job. Her recruiting officer back in Sunderland had asked her if she was a cripple, when back in 1941 she had asked for a 'sit down' job, it was not something you could ask for. When she changed to the 'viewing' she decided she might like to go back home to Sunderland, but 'Phil put a stop to that'. He got 'special leave and a special licence' to marry Jenny. Not something that was particularly popular with his family, she was not a Brummie, she was an incomer, 'a stranger in the camp'.

Phil had been born in Cherrywood Road in Bordesley Green, but his family now lived in Hall Green. Jenny had to go to tea, but managed to offend his mother by saying to Phil quietly, that she thought his mother talked funny, which he then repeated very loudly. Which is quite amusing really, because Jenny used a few phrases local to Sunderland. As a Brummie would say 'duck' she would say 'henney'. As she says they were known as the 'mak and taks' from Sunderland, because they would make ships and take them. She hated being called a Geordie.

This faux pas made her wedding a bit of an afterthought with her mother-in-law who went back to work, rather than taking the day off. The occasion itself was a wartime affair, with whatever could be pulled together at that time, as Jenny remembers:

> "We didn't have a wedding as such... but this Conny I was telling you about... when she heard I was getting married... she brought me this lovely blouse, it was white satin and hand embroidered... and I had some comfortable shoes and that... and I got myself a suit... and I had my horseshoe and a bunch of flowers and that... but there were no photographs."

They were married at Birmingham Registry Office in 1945, on special licence, her landlady Mrs Evans was a witness along with Jackie Ward Phil's friend. Phil stood to attention, and Jenny just slipped her hand into his. After a hurried cup of tea, with her new sister-in-law, they went off to their honeymoon at his Aunt Alice's pub, The Red Lion in Leominster. There Jenny was met by Phil's Uncle Fred, the manager of the local Co-op, and Uncle Albert who was the manager of a local men's outfitters, they were there as the welcoming party along with their families. Aunt Alice was able to provide a lovely meal which became the young couple's reception, away from the chaos of war-torn Birmingham, it was made even more romantic by the oil lamps, and candles. On their return, they had to live at his mother's house, and as a consequence they did not have their first child for four years.

While he was still in the RAF and when he was stationed up north, Phil was complaining that he was not getting enough food, particularly breakfast, so when Jenny used to visit him she used to bring scones from her mother's to feed him.

She had little time for a social life, and as she said the shops were not that good around Hall Green. Her weekends consisted of 'picking the swarf out of her fingers'. So it was quite a treat when Phil used to come and take her out. Once he took her out on a tandem, but told her off for not pedalling, she had been so used to going on her brother's motorbike, she was not used to peddling.

She once bought a nice dress in Hall Green, which she took to be cleaned. It was a time of rationing and clothing coupons and a nice dress was a much desired commodity. As a consequence when she went back to collect her dress the manageress knew nothing about it. That was not the only time she became the victim of light fingers. Once when she was still staying in the digs, her whole pay packet went missing. She didn't kick up a fuss, but she had her suspicions who had taken it, she just made sure that she never left her handbag lying around again. Luckily, being a canny girl, she had saved and had enough to meet her board for Mrs Evans.

One of her highlights was a particular visitor who came when, in Jenny's own words:

"I was working at a machine and someone said there's General de Gaulle, but he didn't come up our section but he just walked... tall he was... he just walked down the bottom..."

There were hundreds of girls working there and very few men, and in Jenny's opinion most of the girls were from Scotland and very broad speaking. One particular girl, did not seem to understand what she had been set to do one day, and stood by her machine and talked to Jenny, she was then challenged by a man from the office, Jenny recounts:

"This young chap came from the office, young chap, tall... 'haven't you got work to do?'... and she looked at him and said 'I didna' ken?' and he walked away bemused."

She often wondered what must have gone through his head as he walked away. But if any girl did not fit in on their section, the foreman had them moved, to keep the peace with the ladies.

When the war was over, married women were discouraged from staying on, as the men were brought back, Phil being one of them.

Houses were in short supply, and Phil's sister now had intentions to get married and as was customary, the daughter took priority when married to living in her mother's house. So Jenny and Phil managed to find some rooms in Alum Rock. Jenny fell pregnant, and was unable to be booked into the hospital, and was not allowed to give birth in the rooms, she became very distressed about the whole thing, and cried a whole day while Phil was working. Phil's mother came to the rescue and told Jenny that she could have the baby at her house. Eventually, after a considerable amount of effort the young parents managed to find an old, well-built house in Tyseley, which they managed to 'fix up'.

Jenny tried various jobs while her daughter Jane was at school, at Lucas and Bakelite, but they were mainly assembly operations, and not the skilled jobs that she had been used to doing. After the war there were many women who wanted to work back in the factories, according to Jenny, because they had all this skill, and the money had been so much better than they could earn anywhere else.

Jenny made a very long journey to come to Birmingham, not just the train, but a journey from a northern to a Midland culture, and a dislocation from all her family and friends. After all these years she is still here, because she fell in love and made her life here. But as Jenny reflects, the hardest thing for all these girls was leaving all their friends behind, and in some way, the hardest thing for Birmingham was to accept such a large influx of 'others', all those young ladies, who were not given the option, but had to come and assist Birmingham in the 'war effort'.

FOR JENNY

Are you all right pet?
Do wan' some more?
A cuppa' tea will see you throu'
Will help you win the war.

Me? I ken many tha' nays,
I ken were I came fra'
I tak' the train fra' Sunderland,
And ended up in Brum.

To mak' the bombs and shells see,
They needed women just like me.
So if ya' had na' useful job ta' do,
Ya' got the warrant, they wanted you.

So on the train, ooo! it was a long way,
I came fra' home to here, Bormingum,
And they put me to work £2 per week,
And the landlady, tak all fa' ma' keep.

But then I met ma' man, ya' see,
And he took a strong liking to me,
So we married before I went away,
So in Birmingham I had to stay.

Chapter 5

KATHLEEN – CIGARETTE CASES AND BLACK-MARKET SUGAR

Kathleen's story is one that was repeated all around the central part of Birmingham during the war. As with Daisy, she was not as fortunate to be working for one of the larger government owned factories, she had been working for a small private firm, which had to undertake wartime contracts, so the salary was paltry in comparison and the hours and working conditions were long and hard.

Her family lived fairly centrally to the city, in Ledsam Street, just up the road from Belliss and Morcoms. Her parents' names were Lillian and Edward, she had three elder siblings; Betty, Joan and Ted, and three younger siblings; Madge, John and David. She had attended Osler Street school, leaving at 14. As was the way then, she was able to pick and choose where she worked. Initially, she tried to work for Lewis department store in the centre of the city, but she did not get on with that because she disliked working Saturdays. Then she tried her hand at dressmaking for a lady in Broad Street, but she could not get to grips with that either. Finally, she ended up at Five Ways working for Kunzles, as she recalls:

"They were Swiss them were, and did chocolate and fancy cakes… up at Five Ways and then the war started."

That must have been a very happy and care-free time for Kathleen, and indeed to one moment be making chocolate and fine cakes for a Swiss chocolatier at 15, and then find yourself a year later at war must have been a massive shock. Before the war broke out, Kathleen made a move of work again this time for more money, because although Kunzles was nice to work for, the pay was not marvellous:

"…it was like what I says, my sister was working at Collins down Hockley Brook… they were doing cigarette cases and compacts right… she was getting more money than me… I was getting 11 shillings at Kunzles, and she was getting £3 more… so I moved over there…"

Then came that dreaded Sunday 3rd September, 1939. As she says, 'we were just all 'on edge' sitting around the wireless waiting'. Kathleen is honest, not really knowing the horror that war could bring, and having the wisdom since, at that time she did not really let it affect her, she was young, she says it would be different now. Collins like many small firms moved over to munitions work. It was a family firm run by three brothers, quite a large private firm, in the heart of the metal engineering quarter of Birmingham. She was one of only 20 women, who had a charge hand (a foreman), training them and monitoring their work. She was moved over to the manufacture of detonator caps and was paid at the piecework rate:

"…we used to put 'em detonator caps in a tin… and then they'd weigh them see…"

And making the munitions:

"…and there was little lathes and we did detonator caps and we had to do it in suds…"

This was Kathleen's life for the next five years, arranged in shifts:

"And we also did, worked shifts, fortnight about… you know… so we'd finish on Saturday… at 1 o'clock… then you go back on the Sunday… at 6 o'clock… I think it was 8 till 6 then…"

And that two weeks days, was then followed by two weeks nights, the same as the others, no time off and if you did take time it was without pay. During the day shift, they got a reasonable meal of mainly vegetables in the canteen, at night there was no canteen available. They were given at 12 o'clock, 'music while you work', which they made a little bit more interesting, as Kathleen says:

"…and we used to have on tu'pence or thre'pence… it wasn't much… and you'd pick a song… and the first song that came out, you'd win the money…"

Throughout the duration of the war, Kathleen remained living with her parents. She had been born in Lee Bank, and had been one of seven, she says:

"I was the middle one… I had two sisters and a brother older, then there was me… then there was my sister and two brothers… I only have one brother alive now me… well we lost one sister just after the war because she had TB, we had lost a lot of friends then, she was 28…"

That is a very sad reflection of the times, war and disease caused families to lose siblings as a matter of course, and Kathleen as expected, recounts this tragedy in a 'matter of fact' tone. Life before Kathleen's arrival had undoubtedly been hard, her brother can remember the tough times of living in a back-to-back house, but by the time Kathleen was born things had improved somewhat for the family, as she recalls:

"It was a big house… ten roomed… by the time we'd cleaned the top to the bottom… we had to start again, we had our own toilet…"

She tells me her parents had married young, and as was the custom her mother had stopped work. Her father had worked at a familiar place in this book 'the Austin'. He was a foreman there, quite senior, before the second world war, but suffered the negative consequences of factory work in a government shadow factory with the onset of war, she remembers:

"…he was white collar then they called it… you know the blueprints… and then the war started and they was on piecework… and the people underneath him were getting more than him…"

As a consequence it was essential that Kathleen gave her mother her keep, and it was the majority of her income as was the expectation of that time, she recalls:

"Whatever you earned you give your mum £3… coz even if you went on holiday you still gotta pay…"

In the early days of the war, when Collins had just moved over to munitions, Kathleen tried to burn the candle at both ends in an effort to maintain a social life, she says:

"Yeah, what we used to do (she laughs)… we used to work at nights. And then a pair of us right… we used to go skating… at the old rink up at Springhill… I think it caught up with us in the end… we just couldn't do it…"

She recalls, on the night shift she might find herself putting her head down on the table and grabbing forty winks. Once she experienced difficulties with her foreman, when her work was weighed light, yet she had produced more than her friend, but Kathleen stood her ground and got her pay. On the whole, they were well looked after at Collins. Like many other families, they tried to carry on as normal, with basic Christmas celebration; roast chicken and paper chains, though her mother used to have to cater for many, as the relations would descend on an already large family.

Within the year, the bombs were falling and life changed in many ways, Kathleen's two youngest brothers were evacuated to Bromyard, but not for the duration, as the youngest one kept writing home, although he liked it he was terribly homesick. Where they lived they had an Anderson shelter, but as Kathleen recalls, the requirement and the usefulness did not always achieve what it was meant to because:

"there were five of us… and me mum and dad… and by the time me mum got us in the shelter, the 'all clear' would go…"

Apparently, this was a common complaint of many large war time families, that the inhospitable atmospheres of these water-logged, dark places, meant many gave up using them and risked other means to shelter their families. They were particularly fortunate having a cellar as a good alternative and certainly was well used before the Anderson shelter, as she recalls:

"...we'd got a cellar, and at the top end of Ledsam Street they were like police houses right... and I always remember a little lady, I mean she was older than me... and she come running down the street... cause they told you, to get in the cellar, right?... 'we haven't got a cellar! We haven't got a cellar!'... you know, but we never went into the cellar actually... you just got to get on with it didn't you?"

Like many round the city, whether it be foolhardiness, misplaced bravery, or desensitisation to constant raids, they would very often take advantage of their skylight, with its vantage point of a spectacular view over the city of the raids and dog fights.

She remembers how bad it was the night of the BSA bombing, for that was a bad night for most of the city, and where she lived was particularly hard hit. She recalls two tragedies from other raids, that have stayed in her memory. There was the sad case of the young couple from Gestion Street, who were sitting on a bench saying goodnight when a bomb fell near by and blinded her, Kathleen had been reminded of this by seeing the lady three years ago recalling her story on the television. Kathleen quietly muses:

"Then there was another incident... in the bad raids... and there was a couple getting married on the Saturday, in Friston Street, and they were saying goodnight, and they were killed... mmm... and they buried them both in their wedding things..."

Socialising for Kathleen during the war was very restricted by her shift work and when she could get out the options were the 'pictures' or to go dancing 'six of us in the afternoon' to the 'Palais De Danse', and in the blackout that could be interesting, but still safer in Kathleen's opinion than venturing out today, she says:

"...do you know the Tower Ballroom... well there was me brothers, and all of us and there was thick fog... and we used to always go have a drink, shandy, in the Hyde Pub... opposite Osler Street school... and we used to follow each other to the 'em... I think we had a torch... I don't remember because we had to keep them down... but we all went onto the dance but you are young then... I mean you wouldn't do it today... I mean today, you can't go out on your own can you?..."

She remembers, once walking to work as the weather was so nice, of course being on a night shift on a summer's evening meant that she passed all those, dressed up for their evening out. On another occasion when out dancing in Birmingham, during the time of the blitz, Kathleen reminisces:

"...and during the raids we used to to erm... the YMCA on Broad Street, dancing... and then this one day, there was a raid starting and we thought 'oh' and we carried straight on..."

Many did carry on dancing, or continue watching the film they had gone to see, the endorphin release and escapism from the general mayhem around, helped to get them through.

Kathleen's family opted for a little help from the black-market to ease the shortages caused by rationing, as she recalls:

"Well what a... we had some black-market sugar... (she laughs)... we had a big bag like that... but they wrapped it up that much... I think we got more cardboard in it, than actual sugar... black-market".

That was that, you were never sure what you would get and the provenance and the quality were always questionable, and of course if you were caught, it was illegal. Other supplements came courtesy of Kathleen's elder brother, he had joined the navy and despite getting pneumonia after his training in Scotland, he still managed to get a good posting to Australia, as she recalls:

"...and he was there quite some time... you know he used to send us nylons... and he got in with these people, which they still keep in touch like... and they used to send us food parcels..."

Kathleen's war ended, and she went back to making cigarette cases and compacts at Collins, her normal progress through life of meeting someone and marrying young, had been interrupted by war. Some time after 1946, she met her husband, while attending a wedding in Shakespeare Road. He had been in the army, but had actually been shot in the face, narrowly missing his temple. Even so, he continued in the war, and did not get demobbed until the end of the war against Japan in 1946. However, it did leave indelible scars, as Kathleen says:

"Affected his nerves, like, you know..."

When they were courting, they were able to go to The Hippodrome, a much favoured haunt of Brummies. Kathleen remembers seeing a very famous lady there:

"...Mary Poppins... Julie Andrews... her mum and dad was on, and she was on with em... and they parted afterwards her mum and dad."

Even though it was some years after the war when Kathleen eventually married (she was 27), the housing shortage still caused difficulties, and her story is similar to others:

"When I got married I still lived at home... we had the front room... and we had one room upstairs, well you couldn't get a place could you..."

And she feels strongly that this initial hardship and struggle, built more solid marriages, she says:

"I think that's why them marriages break up… they want too much at once… no when we first got married we used to have Co-op cheques… and then you bought your bed linen… then when I had the children you bought their clothes with 'em… you know you couldn't afford much anyhow, £1 a week you bought a lot…"

Kathleen moved to the Northfield area for 49 years, which had undergone some improvements as she says 'it was a lovely shopping centre', but she was a victim of the 'Austin' syndrome, the prices in the shops were artificially high, because it was assumed that everyone worked there, and even if you did, 'not everybody that worked at 'the Austin' got the money'.

Although, her youth and 'matter of fact' approach got her through the war, she does reflect that it was very hard, when at the time she had no idea of what she was about to face, Kathleen is ever honest, and what was possible then, would not be possible now, as she says:

"I don't think I could go through that again… as I said when you're young…"

FOR KATHLEEN

When the lights come on,
And the darkness is gone,
What joy here will be?
For all to see.

When there's no more sirens,
Deep in the night,
No more bombs and noise,
Only joy and delight.

When the days of summer,
Rejoice with the sun,
And echo with children's laughter,
So filled with fun.

The food will be plentiful,
And tasty too.
Pleasures will be bountiful,
For me and for you.

When the lights come on,
And the darkness is gone,
It will feel like heaven,
For everyone.

Chapter 6

'COVENTRY'S HAD IT!'

Everybody is well aware of the severe bombing that Coventry underwent in the early part of the war, a point raised most eloquently by Brian Wright the chairman of BARRA (the Birmingham Air Raid Remembrance Association) in his foreword for Professor Chinn's book 'Brum Undaunted'. This was as much due to its location, which was known to the Germans as the industrial heartland of the UK as to its commercial capacity as an engineering capital. What went largely unreported was the destruction that Birmingham suffered, which to any person visiting the city even now, is all too evident. Where once stood old Victorian housing are swathes of concrete replacements, put up in haste in the following decades, to meet the drastic housing shortage, and to try to rebuild a shattered city. As a consequence, like Coventry, city planning was not always sensitively carried out and the city that first emerged was rebuilt for the vehicle owners, one that could be driven through and by-passed quickly, rather than for the urban dweller. Many of these hurried concrete edifices are thankfully now being replaced by a more people-sensitive plan, that in recent years has seen the opening up of the canal sides, and the other hidden treasures in the city.

I remember as a small child being driven round the city in the late 60's with my father, and questioning the piles of rubble still apparent post war, especially in Tyseley, Small Heath, Sparkbrook and Greet, and being told it was what remained of the bomb damage, and some reference to not moving it in case they still found bodies, quite gruesome if untrue, for a seven year old to take in. Indeed, the reconstruction of Birmingham did take some considerable time and this proves the point that the devastation had been substantial.

In this chapter, I will examine a document found at the National Archive, which describes in detail some of the effects suffered in the continual bombardment of Birmingham, and the factors that exacerbated an already difficult situation, causing an acute housing shortage that had long-term repercussions for the city and its people.

My father and mother had been out on November 14th 1940, trying to celebrate her twenty first birthday, he was on leave. They were driving just south of Birmingham avoiding the city, and from where they were, they could see a stark, orange, glow on the horizon, it was Coventry some 10 miles away. They were stopped by an ARP patrol, all roads to Coventry had been shut off, no one could get in, or out, as the ARP mournfully reported;

"Coventry's had it!"

That was the worst night of the Coventry blitz in which according to Chinn:

"Within a square mile, 80% of buildings were destroyed and 568 people killed."

The report that I examine was produced for the Home Office. The title is Birmingham Social and Economic Survey, dated 11.3.42, it is stamped <u>MOST SECRET</u> and the section that particularly attracted my attention is entitled Morale. The focus of the survey is the effects on the populace, both civilian and industrial, from the sustained attacks of August 1940 and November 1940. In other words at the same time as Coventry was undergoing the hammering. The document makes no reference to the earlier raids on Birmingham, which had actually commenced in April, but concentrates on the later (more intensive) raiding.

Unlike Coventry, Birmingham as a chief centre of munitions production had been 'D' listed, it had a Defence Notice attached to it, effectively enforcing a total press blackout. The only reference that could be made anywhere in the British Press could be to 'a town in the Midlands' having suffered any raids, or attacks. This was to protect the strategic importance of the city, and keep the essential flow of munitions and weaponry that the city was so famous for, coming out in train loads to service the forces.

In the introduction, the authors are critical of four major factors that, in their opinion, led to the substantial loss of faith and the subsequent demise in morale of the city. They point to; (1) poorly organised Civil Defence Authorities; (2) a lack of 'preparedness' and poor state of mind of the population, to withstanding 'heavy... enemy aerial attack'; (3) the 'awareness' of the people 'of the effects of a sustained blitz attack on a neighbouring city'; (4) and finally, the 'weight' and 'duration' of attack.

They criticise the authorities for not taking affirmative action sooner;

"...the city of Birmingham had not made the necessary preparations to cope with either a sustained or heavy attack from the air."

The authors point to a lack of planning and forethought for what the effects of a blitz on Birmingham could be, a point supported by Chinn, quoting Tiptaft:

"Although Birmingham Corporation appointed a special committee to deal with the government's proposal, its overall response was dilatory."

However, this could be accounted for by the sheer expense that they incurred, again Chinn, quoting the Birmingham Mail (1940):

"By January 1940 the city was spending £5000 a day on A.R.P. totalling the huge sum of £1,800,000 a year, a fifth of this amount was met via the rates."

The 'rates' referred to being what a householder paid in tax to the local council, or from the working man's pocket.

The document that I quote from makes no mention of cost, merely the lack of preparation and forward thinking, as such, the accusing tone of the report continues throughout, they find the city lacking in its planning, and is said to have made a major contribution to 'a false sense of security' among the people which was soon shattered when the bombing started in earnest. As a direct consequence the author claims that this led to civilians inadvertently contributing to the 'dangers' and 'hazards' faced by the authorities when they were trying to assist.

The report claims that the first heavy attack took place in August 1940 and was mainly concentrated on the Tyburn Road and Ward End area of the city. This caused near riots, as bombed out residents took over the mess rooms at the Hockley Depot and the mess room of the Social Club at the Tyburn Road Transport Depot. This was as a direct result of the tardiness of the authorities in dealing with; in the first instance, feeding, but also, clothing, money grants, billeting and alternative housing. This response of scared people who had nowhere to go, had lost everything they had, and saw that no one was taking action to help them, is understandable. It is a description of localised chaos, which would have quickly been passed round other areas of the city, via word of mouth.

In the days that followed, there was more organised action of the populace making demands for 'a more effective ARP policy' which judging by what was recorded elsewhere, had been a very 'hit' or 'miss' affair, with bad interrelations with other services. There were also calls for an 'organised evacuation of women and children from target areas', something that one would have assumed would have been a chief consideration when initial defence plans were being drawn up.

The report does make a slight defence for the authorities, claiming that the combined factors of the speed of change of Government Civil Defence policy and the sudden 'military collapse of France' may have exacerbated the situation, but it goes on to criticise the corporation for not reacting quickly enough between the August and November raids. On reflection of these initial raids and the authorities responses, it is not surprising that the effects of the subsequent, more devastating, attacks wreaked havoc on the material infrastructure and the state of mind of the population.

The report continues to examine 'The Defence and the Organisation of the City' in some detail. In their view, the 'active defences' of the city were not enough to cope with the weight of the attack in November, there were simply not enough retaliatory measures in place to make any impression on the incoming German bombers. It was commented by an un-attributed individual or individuals, about the 'ease' with which 'enemy raiders' had made their attack on 'Coventry earlier in the month', probably a reference to the night of the 14th November. In other words, did nobody see this coming? Birmingham was wide open to the same fate to which Coventry had succumbed. As such, people did agitate for better shelter protection for both the 'civil and working population'. After the November raids, people were commenting on the 'ease at which enemy reconnaissance plane' were making, virtually unchallenged, daytime sorties over the city.

The report criticised the authorities for not making adequate provision of shelters for the population, nor making available the material and manpower, to construct, or repair. The Civil Defence authorities, in their opinion, were poorly organised, and too slow to recruit, with an over reliance on volunteers. A point highlighted in Douglas (2006):

"Ninety percent of wardens were part-timers…"

The most damning criticism is levied against the 'Public Assistance Committee' which was set up specifically to help those in need. The report claims that the council had known 'for some considerable time' that there was a desperate problem with emergency housing, and this was being made worse by;

"…the movement of a certain section of the population from houses in the inner wards to empty properties in the outer wards."

This appears to be a veiled reference, to a forced migration of poorer, scared, people to the outskirts, effectively taking possession of empty properties by 'squatting'. This added to the acute housing shortage which had been caused by the existing housing stock having been severely damaged, in the preceding August raids. As a consequence of the council's inactivity to address the situation adequately, there was 'no central organisation' to deal with people who were made homeless, with a complete lack of hostel accommodation and mobile canteens. It seems the corporation made little effort to communicate effectively with the population, further, it devolved much of its responsibility to Estate Agents demanding they release their housing stock to re-home people. Most detrimentally, there appears to have been a lack of cooperation between certain sections of the Civil Defence Authorities, and there was no overall response by these authorities for deploying 'either persons or public bodies endowed with a sense of civic responsibility'.

The report goes on to highlight the raids and the effect on 'Social Morale' and in this section there is an initial reference to commentary and action made by the Birmingham Labour Party, particularly using its paper the 'Town Crier'. It notes that in this paper, there is a reference to the 'muddle' the ARP first made on the 27th September and that by the 2nd of November the paper commented that there still had not been enough action to address this. The report then examines Police Reports from the same period to further illuminate their findings, one of the main complaints from the general public on 6th November had been the lack of use of headlamp masks on the main 'arterial routes' the public fearing that the lights were actually acting as;

"...guiding lines for enemy aircraft."

This caused so much concern that the Regional Transport Commissioner decided to take a night time flight to observe the situation for himself. Unfortunately for him, this coincided with one of the big November raids forcing his aircraft to have to divert and it landed;

"...in a distant part of the country after undergoing considerable hazards."

Crime, particularly juvenile crime, was reported to have increased during this period and a sharp rise in 'lootings' had been recorded, with two thirds having taken place since the 20th November. Places of entertainment, were said to be closing early, due to the perceived 'lack of support', and a few enterprising coach firms were;

"...advertising motor coach trips into the country nightly."

The report states that the lack of information and communication perhaps helped to accentuate and promote myth and rumour. For instance, when meat supplies became low during the December raids, the population attributed this to the 'loss of merchant shipping'. Additionally, after large raids, casualties were high, and this led to a 'depressing' effect on morale;

"The bombing of the BSA works, where casualties were high, proved very disturbing to public opinion and it was, and still is, believed that all the casualties were neither recovered or accounted for".

The authors of the report claim that, in their opinion, the rescue work was hampered by a lack of qualified personnel to assist, and the sheer weight of devastation caused put immense strain on the already stretched rescue services. The report quotes, Alderman Grey, the Deputy Regional Commissioner as having written his records regarding the 19th and 20th of November;

> "...that the rescue personnel in Birmingham are suffering from the strain caused by having continuously to handle so many mutilated bodies. The men are said to be going 'crackers'."

This understatement in context of the gentility of the time is hard to imagine, but we have to remember that we had never experienced enemy bombardment in any previous war. No one could have imagined the consequences of what the blitz could bring, and how high explosives and incendiaries could maim and disfigure, extinguishing civilian human life in the process, particularly, the elderly, women and children. The shock and grief caused to even hardened veterans from the trenches of the Great War, must have been simply heartbreaking.

Further criticism is levied at the authorities for not taking advantage of all the willing volunteers who wished to assist in the rescue operations, because;

> "...there was not in existence any machinery at the disposal of the responsible authorities to make use of such help."

This fact must have further depressed the morale of people who felt both helpless and powerless. The feelings of anger generated through the inability to assist your friends and neighbours when they were in trouble, or even the unsuspecting, unknown victim, must have been immense and insufferable at this time .

On the 19th and 20th of November, the Labour Party made a stark warning to the council, there would be a 'break down' in the existing arrangements for rescue and recovery, because they were quite simply inadequate. Following the raids on the 21st and 22nd November they were proved right, when hundreds of bombed out victims were forced to take refuge in the rest centre in Garrison Lane. Worse still, they remained 'without food until 4pm the next day.' As Chinn highlights:

> "Nearly 2,000 houses were smashed to pieces and thousands more were damaged seriously."

On the 23rd of November the Labour Party sought guidance from Civic House, and were informed that there was no one of significant authority in attendance to make decisions, both the Regional and Deputy Commissioners had gone to visit Coventry.

Catastrophe was one step away, the city's water supply failed, and the military had to be used to bring in water from Yorkshire, and still no official communications came from the corporation to the population, it was left to the Labour Party through the use of loud hailers to inform the city's residents.

The shamefully inadequate Public Assistance Committee, in whom the general public had totally lost confidence by now, only had two offices open city-wide and as no communication had been imparted by any authority, as to where victims should go in order to get assistance, the information was slow to pass round. As a direct consequence, people were left to 'wander aimlessly around the city'. This led to the Labour Party offices (then in Corporation Street) being 'besieged' by desperate homeless people, who simply did not know where they should go, or what they should do. This situation was further aggravated by a complete lack of flexibility on behalf of the Public Assistance Committee, who, due to a lack of organisation, simply would not stay open to manage the crisis. In fact, the Housing Estate offices insisted on continuing their practice of closing on the dot at 5pm everyday. On Saturday 23rd November, after one of the most horrific and sustained periods of raiding, the PAC offices closed at 12 noon, and told those waiting who had sought relief and not received it, to come back on Monday morning when they reopened.

The report records that people were quite simply left to 'fend for themselves', sleeping in shelters and finding food where they could. There is no evidence of figures, or statistics compiled at this time by the corporation, the victims were simply left unnoticed and unrecorded.

The report continues to express the concerns of Canon Guy Rogers who made strong comments regarding a large shelter in his parish at New Saint Street Market (originally constructed as a car park), he is recorded as having condemned the facilities as being 'wet' and totally inadequate. It was said to have been able to accommodate several thousand people, yet there were no amenities; it had neither a canteen nor any provision for food. It was left to a volunteer group from 'The Society of Friends', who took it upon themselves to provide 'cocoa' for the cold 'shelterers'. There were no medical facilities, a difficult situation further accentuated by the few occasions when pregnant women had to be 'conveyed in haste' elsewhere to get the necessary assistance.

Another area where records failed to be kept was on the nightly migration of people out of the city to seek refuge, but as the report ascertained, the traffic flow was noticeably high.

As I have already alluded to, one of the primary causes of Birmingham becoming such an 'A' list target for the Germans, was the manufacture of munitions, and the various other engineered components necessary to keep a country at war. It is unsurprising then that the report chooses to focus on the raids and the effects on 'Industrial Morale'. The authors commence this section by stating on record that the evidence is 'credible'. It documents that initial raids of August 1940, created some 'alarm' among the workforce, primarily, at the inadequacy of the early warning arrangements. The system of 'spotters' was criticised for being inadequate, and confidence was only restored when factories were allowed to appoint 'spotters' from within their own workforce. There was a feeling of 'unease' created because of the relations between ARP's and the factories. This difficultly was somewhat appeased when a visit was made by the Government Minister for Labour (Ernest Bevin) on the 16th November, he managed to allay fears, and gave assurances that solutions would be found.

There had been a sharp fall in morale, stimulated by the attacks on Coventry, and the workforce was naturally scared that they were not being adequately protected by those in authority. The fear was further perpetuated, by the fact that areas of special or significant risk would not be defended properly. It is noted by the authors, that despite all of the above fears and grievances, work/production never stopped, and this is credit to the workforce. There had only been one threatened stoppage made on the 27th of November by the Corporation Women Transport operatives, who were fed up with the 'abusive' language and behaviour that they were receiving nightly, from desperate passengers trying to get home before the raids started, and the buses stopped.

Managers had reported that during times of distant gunfire the workforce were showing signs of 'sensitivity', and it was said that;

"...certain sections of the workpeople attempted to rush the gates."

This was particularly noted at ICI, Witton and the BSA in Small Heath, however, later strong 'local leadership... asserted itself' and evacuations became 'both orderly and effective'.

One incident that was serious enough to merit being recorded, as a case, concerned the BSA in Small Heath which after a period of bombing in the early raids, workers protested about the length of time it was taking to pay their wages, they blockaded the factory entrance and are reported as being 'ugly, and menacing';

"The authorities were powerless to control the temper of several thousand workers and relief was only gained when an air raid alert was sounded which heralded the approach of an enemy reconnaissance plane."

Following the workers' action, Sir Bernard Docker the Chairman of the BSA, appealed directly to the Chancellor to reduce the EPT, in response a dividend of seven and a half percent less income tax, being levied. Sir Bernard Docker is quoted in the Birmingham Gazette as saying 'the workers also serve who stay and work', as the authors record;

> "This admonition was delivered to several thousand workers who did not return to employment at the Small Heath works after the heavy raids on the 19th 20th and 21st of November."

In summarising their report, the authors praise the steadfastness of the Birmingham people for withstanding such a damaging time. They comment that the November raids were much more detrimental to the morale of the civilian population than the earlier raids. They criticise the authorities, who despite having knowledge of the earlier raids and reflecting on what had happened to their close neighbour, Coventry, did not commit to affirmative action, or indeed make adequate provision for civil defence. As a consequence, the authors consider 'the demands of the people during this period were quite rational.'

In their opinion, there was no evidence of widespread panic across the city, though they do comment that the nightly exodus of city-dwellers was still in evidence after the raids in April 1941. They reflect that due in some part to the attitude of the factory workforce, confidence soon returned after the November raids. Their final comments warned, that had the public transport provision, failed during that time;

> "...the consequences may well have proved grave and far reaching."

There is an addendum to this report, in the form of an eye witness statement of the nightly migration of city people, in this a Bridge Engineer called Mr Farrington, is recorded as expressing the concerns that;

> "...others found shelter in sheds, barns and even ditches... moreover... that the morale of the inhabitants had been strained almost to breaking point, and that the raiding had ceased just when the serious effects might be expected to manifest themselves."

According to the Birmingham Air Raids Association on their memorial, the 'city suffered 365 air raid alerts and 77 actual bombing raids'. The most intense part of the bombing took place between, August 1940 and April 1941. In the greater period of August 1940 to April 1943 there were 2,241 reported civilian deaths and over 9000 casualties (BARRA memorial). According to Chinn, the majority of bombs fell in an area of 14,960 acres, in which quoting from Black;

> "The raids destroyed 12,391 houses and destroyed tens of thousands more;... 4,863 fires were reported."

And:

"The *Luftwaffe* dropped 5,129 high explosive bombs... scores of thousands of incendiaries... about 2,000 tons of bombs..."

The civilian death total is possibly higher as Birmingham was home to many itinerant workers, who may not have been identified as known at the time of their deaths, which brings me back to piles of rubble still around Birmingham in the late 1960's, and a corporation that failed to compile or keep adequate (if any) statistical records, at that time.

GONE

Black, cold and dark,
It catches on your throat,
You choke, in the black smoke,
All around is nothing,
I feel nothing, I am nothing,
Noise is distant, like a long forgotten thought,
A memory of my past, that didn't last,
A melee of sounds with no order,
An image of horror like no other,
All has gone, all that once was,
Has gone, an absolute destruction,
I am nothing now, I am no longer,
Don't look, you will not find me my dear,
I was, but am no longer here,
I blinked and that was it, you see,
That was all there was of me.
So rest now, all is rest,
All is calm now, all is calm,
Don't fret my dear, all is done,
I am no longer, I am gone.

Chapter 7

EVELYN'S ELBOW AND
THE PEANUT FARM

"I don't know whether you ever heard of a T.B. elbow?" Evelyn enquired quizzically.

"Eh... n-no?" Comes my stumbled, caught-on-the-hoof reply.

"Nor me, but still... I can remember having my arm on a frame... and I went to Uffcombe Open Air School in Moseley... and that's where I met Dorothy..."

This is the same Dorothy that had just died three weeks earlier with whom Evelyn had been friends for eighty years: the same Dorothy who was in some part responsible for Evelyn's marriage. This is my introduction to a lady who is remarkably fit and able at ninety one years old, who looks and acts at least 20 years younger. She is strong, and she reflects on the loss of her best friend with amazing stoicism.

Evelyn Cookson (nee Eustace) has a remarkable self-confidence and self-assurance: she maintains a strong desire to retain her independence from any outside interference. She lives in a very tidy house, with a few select photographs and objects displayed. You can see that Evelyn likes things to be 'just so'; very much 'a place for everything and everything in its place'. Her story, as I am to find out, spans the whole of the war, with her moving in and out of employment, due first to the marriage bar, then pregnancy. Those closest to her add to the rich texture of her narrative, enhancing the stories that Evelyn now recounts with unstoppable enthusiasm.

Evelyn had been born some 15 months before her father (William) finally came back from the battle of the Somme and the Great War, and the letter that Evelyn's mother (Elizabeth) had sent to inform him of Evelyn's appearance, in the chaos of that dreadful time, had never quite reached him. Whether it was humour or genuine surprise, his reaction on first setting eyes on Evelyn was to ask whose daughter she was.

Prior to this, Evelyn's elder brother (who had been eight and a half at the time of Evelyn's arrival – 16th December 1917) had been very much the man of the house. So much so, that this little man had to cook the Christmas dinner single-handedly, however, he did once get into the wrong queue when sent for margarine, and came back with a bag of potatoes instead!

Evelyn was one of a family of eight: she was number six. Her mother had her hands full and she was a working woman (as a polisher in Icknield Street), especially while her father was away fighting in the war. Hence, elder siblings were drafted in to assist with the care of the younger ones. It was a life of juggling to make ends meet. Once when Evelyn was young, she was sent to the local grocers' shop to make some purchases for her ever-busy mother, and as usual her mother had asked her to put it on 'the tab'. However, the grocer Mrs Evans decided that the ten shilling bill needed paying and sent the bailiffs round. Evelyn was duly despatched to her aunts to borrow the offending ten shillings. Her aunt ran a small general store and was a canny woman: she lent the ten shillings, but charged two shillings and sixpence in interest. Despite this slight lapse in the household budget, her mother was a frugal woman and always said that it was important to save for your old age. As Evelyn remarks with a long forgotten sentimentality:

"We were clean but poor."

Her mother's philosophy, as Evelyn recalls, was simple but profound:

"Keep a good table and a clean bed, and remember you reap what you sow."

So Evelyn got tuberculosis of the elbow. TB as a condition now is so rare, but still strikes fear into those who knew how debilitating and, in some cases terminal the disease could be. I had never realised that a joint or bone could be infected, until researching Evelyn's story. How the symptoms became manifest, or detected, Evelyn cannot remember, but she does remember being sent to the open air school. She was 9, and as her family lived at that time in the middle of Small Heath, she was considered to be a city dweller, and as such necessitated full-time boarding on a weekly basis at the school. That's where she became friends with Dorothy. Dorothy was a day boarder as her parents did not live in the heart of the city, but things were soon to change for Evelyn.

Her family were lucky enough to get a house in Liddon Road (off Tavistock Road) in the village of Acocks Green, a very rural location, and as a consequence there was no need for her to attend Uffcombe anymore and she started at Hartfield Crescent School (now Ninestiles):

"...when lo and behold, I hadn't been there long, but who should walk in the classroom? It was Dorothy... and from then on we were friends... and we married two friends... Dorothy married my husband's best friend."

At 14 Evelyn left school, and started work as a trainee French polisher, and she was good at it, but the fumes began to make her ill. Every morning her mother would give her a packed lunch, which she then wouldn't eat, so her mother gave notice to Evelyn's employer, who was quite disappointed by the sounds of things, at losing such an enthusiastic, hard worker.

> "…I left on the Friday and I said to my mother 'I am going to get my own job now' because school had got me that job, and I went to the BSA and started as a 'lacer' lacing bicycle wheels…"

That's when Evelyn's first stint at BSA began. It was 1931, she was just turning 15 and she began work making bicycles at the BSA as a 'lacer'.

> "…there's three jobs on bicycle wheels… there's doing the hubs and 'lacing' them, then there's a 'puller up'… and a 'trewer'… you usually went from 'lacer' to 'puller up', then 'trewer'… but I went straight from 'lacer to trewer'…"

The three roles are easily defined, a 'lacer' inserted the spokes into the hub, the 'puller up' used their jig to tighten the spokes as a first operation. The 'trewer', made the wheel true, by balancing the spokes so the wheel was perfect. Then the men would insert the bicycle wheels into the frame, and the rest of the bicycle was assembled, in the production line.

The BSA also brought Evelyn an active social life: she joined the cycling club, which used to meet at Meriden every Sunday. In the evenings, Evelyn and Dorothy used to visit 'The Green', with its picture house 'The Warwick' and the Public Hall for dances.

A young man called Chris who was a mutual friend with both the girls, for a time thought he was 'sweet' on Dorothy. He was not keen on dancing, as Evelyn comments he was a bit 'straight' and he would arrange to meet Dorothy outside. Dorothy was not interested and gently tried to let Chris down by avoiding him. Chris soon realised that his real affections lay with Evelyn, whom like Chris had no love of dancing, soon they became romantically involved. She remembers fondly their courting, which sometimes took place around 'The Swan' at Yardley the half-way point between their homes, and the pictures in 'The Green', when she was allowed to meet him.

She would never let him meet her on a Sunday; that was her day to herself with the cycle club. Chris was a determined young man, and wanted to show Evelyn how keen he was to see her and take part in her hobby, so one Sunday, he joined on the back of the cycle rally. Evelyn was very surprised when the cycle leader noticed this strange young man in all the old attire sitting astride an 'upright' ('sit-up-and-beg') bicycle. Evelyn was very touched by his enthusiasm to be with her, and even more so, as the following week he turned up on a tandem!

She admitted to be 'going with him' when she was 16; she was engaged at 17; and they were married on the 16th April, 1938. Consequently, due to the 'seasonal' nature of bicycle manufacture, where only single girls were kept in gainful part-time employment during the summer 'lay-off', and the marriage bar that was in operation to married women, she got 'the sack' in June, and had to report to the Waverley Road Labour Exchange to sign on.

When she was first married, she had been renting two rooms in Hay Mills, but Chris was taken ill and sent to convalesce near Blackpool. Evelyn took it upon herself to find somewhere nicer to live. She managed to rent some rooms in Mary Road, Stechford, from an elderly couple from Bristol. She had French windows into a kitchen, the rent was steep at twelve shillings and sixpence, but it was found, and she moved in and Chris had somewhere better to come home to and continue his recovery. Just before the war, Evelyn decided it was time to rent a house, and the only place she could afford was back in Small Heath, near the BSA, in Bolton Road. It had rot and bugs, and her mother desperately tried to persuade her not to take it, but Evelyn, as stubborn as ever, decorated and that was that.

When I asked her about the impending war and the thoughts that everybody had, she made a very considered response, and said:

"People talked about it… but we didn't expect it… because Chamberlain went out (Munich), and he come back, and he was a 'man of peace'… and he made a solemn promise that we weren't going to war… but we had been talking about it since I got married… everybody said there was a war coming… twenty five years after the last one…"

When the 3rd of September 1939 came, with the grave announcement that we were at war with Germany, the Eustace family sat tearfully around the wireless, and became very much a family at war. Her brothers were enlisted in the army: one became a Company Sergeant Major, the other a Regimental Sergeant Major. Another brother enlisted in the Navy, as did Evelyn's husband Chris, and later her younger sister's husband. The same sister eventually joined the NAAFI (because she didn't want to work night shifts in the factories and would have been compelled to do so, had she not joined the services), and throughout the duration her father assisted as an Air Raid Patrol Warden. Later in the war, her younger brother in the Navy was married to a young lady in the RAF.

For the first part of the war: 'the phoney war', they didn't really know a war was on, apart from the 'shortages':

"...we used to try getting things like tea and sugar and hoard them I suppose... that's when I stopped using sugar actually..."

Evelyn had been re-employed as a 'trewer' at the BSA in November 1938 at the Waverley works, but left before her daughter was born in 1940. She had been living but a 'stones throw' from the Golden Hillock BSA factory, in Bolton Road, since 1939, where 'everyone knew they was making munitions'. Chris was mobilised to Scapa Flow, 20th July 1940; the same day that Evelyn gave birth at the Sorrento Hospital in Moseley, making him a few hours late reporting for duty. His first leave wasn't until his daughter, Christine, was four months old.

By this time the bombing had started, and Evelyn was living in the thick of things. The BSA and the raids that it suffered, there was almost constant enemy bombardment of the sites, with significant consequences on occasions. She was living two doors down from her sister-in-law, with no shelter, and the munitions railway at the end of her garden:

"...we could stand on our back step and watch the enemy planes machine gunning the munitions trains..."

Her sister-in-law had a cellar and Evelyn used to sit with her and her husband, with her baby in her arms, while the raids were going on. In one of the bad raids earlier on that year, Evelyn had just said goodbye to her friend from two doors up the street as the raid started. The bombs fell thick and fast that night, and one fell particularly close, so much so, that Evelyn had feared it was going to hit her sister-in-law's. After the black smoke had cleared, it became apparent that it had landed very close, on this young girlfriend's house who was the same age as Evelyn. The young lady was found with her husband, sitting at the top of their cellar steps, killed instantly!

In the bad raid of the 19th/20th of November 1940, Evelyn had been loaned a shelter by a neighbour who had moved out to Solihull because she couldn't take the bombing anymore. When the raid was at its height and the high explosive shells had hit the BSA Small Heath Works, the shelter door flew open, as a man who had fled in panic from the factory fell in through the door:

"...it wasn't just the bomb that killed a lot of them... it was people rushing to get out... they had to seal it if I can remember right... they couldn't get the bodies out at the time and it was sealed up..."

Her mother couldn't take the strain of Evelyn living in such a dangerous place with her granddaughter, and pleaded with her to come home. Finally, Evelyn agreed and moved back to her mother's with her baby, putting her

Daisy & Frank.

Frank Burrows.

Kynoch Ltd. Witton Works, Birmingham, 1920.

I

Edward Tullock (Jenny's father).

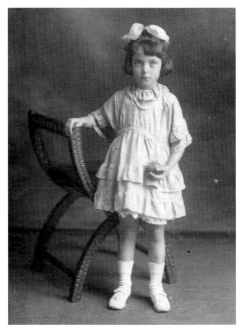

Little Jenny.

Phil Hurle.

Jenny Hurle.

Kathleen (left).

Kathleen's wedding day.

Chris Cookson.

Evelyn & Christine Cookson.

HMS Indomitable.

Eileen Slater (right).

Eileen Slater.

Francis Smith.

Eileen & Francis Smith.

CITY OF BIRMINGHAM
EDUCATION COMMITTEE

SCHOLAR'S LEAVING CERTIFICATE

THIS IS TO CERTIFY

that

Eileen Slater

has attended the

Tindal St. Senior Girls

School

for _____ years, *3* months

and is legally exempt from attendance at an Elementary
School, having reached the age of 14 years as defined by
Section 138 of the Education Act, 1921.

Standard completed *Working in 1st Age Group* Punctuality *Ex:*

Percentage of Attendance *98* Conduct *V.G.*

Eileen's leaving certificate.

Eileen at the Leopold Street Brass Foundry circa. 1934.

Iris & Eric Clarke.

May (second row 5th from the left).

May & Suei (in her mother's wedding dress).

John Charles James jnr, May's eldest brother.

Den Allen (left).

May & Den Allen.

Iris Lodge (2nd left back) in a show at Hercules.

The Mayor in the audience at Hercules.

Iris & Sam Lodge.

Woman on milling machine – courtesy of the Imperial War Museum.

Night shift workers on lathes – courtesy of the Imperial War Museum.

*Woman on pillar drill – courtesy of the
Imperial War Museum.*

*Shell production – courtesy of the
Imperial War Museum.*

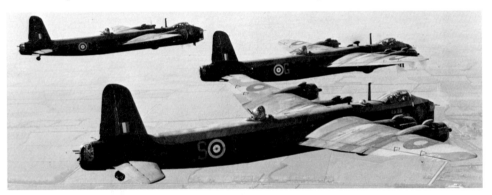

Stirling bombers in flight.

THE ABSENTEE IS HITLER'S UNPAID ALLY

Shell production – courtesy of the Imperial War Museum.

Woman using a riveting gun – courtesy of the Imperial War Museum.

Production line of women on centre lathes – courtesy of the Imperial War Museum.

General De Gaulle making a morale visit – courtesy of the Imperial War Museum.

The Minister for Labour, Mr Ernest Bevin – courtesy of the Imperial War Museum.

Queen Elizabeth the Queen Mother – courtesy of the Imperial War Museum.

King George VI – courtesy of the
Imperial War Museum.

Prime Minister Winston Churchill
(circa. 1943) old postcard.

furniture in storage. Evelyn, and her daughter, her mother and father, her grandmother, and her elder sister all shared a three bedroom house. Her grandmother slept in the recess in Evelyn's parents room. It was about this time, with her baby four months old, that they were appealing for those women who could not be ordered to work (because they were either too old, or nursing) to help out in the factories. Evelyn offered two hours a day to the 'bosses' canteen at Lucas', in between breastfeeding: 'I couldn't get home quick enough'.

When her daughter was a year old, Evelyn's mother offered to mind her, so that Evelyn could go full time. This was at the time that, in order to protect a consistent level of workers employed in the factories, there was a ban on moving between factories, once you were employed by one. Evelyn did not want to go full time at Lucas' and had aspirations to work round the corner at the Clay Lane, the Rover aircraft factory. Indeed, the factory had offered her a better job with more money. On returning to Lucas to ask if she could leave, they enforced the no-movement rule against her, and she was stuck with going full time on the manufacture of gun turrets at Lucas, Shaftmoor Lane, Acocks Green. She worked there from 1941 until the end of the war and was very much the victim of her own success.

She worked in a team of six women, all in the same boat; their husbands away fighting. The foreman set them a task to sort themselves out into roles: to drill a steel ring without splitting it. Evelyn was the only one who managed to complete the task successfully, and she ended up stuck in a job she found both 'tedious' and 'boring' for the duration of the war.

She was paid two pounds and ten shillings, but she didn't have to give her mother very much, and she had her ten shillings pension from Chris. They were lucky being at a larger factory: they were fed reasonably well, and they had 'music while you work'. They used to sing songs, both mornings and afternoons. Being women with men in the war they were never far away from tragedy. One of the young women in Evelyn's team was married to a young man in the RAF, who got shot down and received horrific facial burns. He became so disfigured that when he was eventually medically discharged from the RAF, his young wife found the extent of his injuries very difficult to live with, but she came to terms with it eventually.

In June 1942, Chris' war became entangled with Evelyn's. Evelyn went into work that day and noticed that everyone was very quiet with her. Quite disconcerted with this, she enquired as to what was wrong. It was then that she learnt the other's had been listening the night before to the infamous 'Lord Haw Haw' the NAZI sympathiser, and 'anti-British propaganda' exponent. He had made one of his many pronouncements to destabilise the war effort: that the 'HMS Indomitable' (Chris's ship), had been hit with the loss of all hands! Evelyn, in shock, remembers her foreman Alf 'tapping' her on the face, and going off in a haze to collect the soap from the office to wash her hands (another effect of rationing, soap having to be kept in an office and handed out when needed). Her foreman took her home about three o'clock that afternoon, where she was reassured by her mother not to believe it, until she knew for sure.

That night, Evelyn and her mother sat around the wireless waiting for 'Haw Haw' and to Evelyn's relief, he retracted the statement that it had been the 'Indomitable' that had been hit, announcing it was 'HMS Informidable'. Well that was that, as Evelyn says; she was 'as right as rain' after that and she thought nothing of it, even though she never heard from Chris for a further four months. She just carried on as normal...

In fact, it had been the 'Indomitable'; it had been part of the 'Pedestal' convoy travelling near Malta. Chris was Fleet Air Arm and part of a team of six loading bombs onto the planes. He had just taken time for a break and had been down below for five minutes, when a water launched torpedo of 1100lbs hit the side of the ship, killing sixty men, five of them being Chris's team. Malta had been particularly badly affected by the war by 1942, and there were not the facilities or the protection to make substantial repairs in safety. The ship's crew had no other option, but, to offload the dead at Malta and make temporary patched repairs. They were then towed by tug across the Atlantic, to America.

Eventually, Evelyn received her first communication from Mrs Bassett, an owner of a peanut farm in Virginia:

"...she could write to me and tell me what he couldn't you see... and telling me not to worry and he was convalescing on their peanut farm..."

From this a friendship was formed through correspondence between the two ladies either side of the Atlantic. Mrs Bassett had two sons who were medics in the US forces and implored Evelyn to move out to Virginia after the war, writing that it would be very good for Christine, Evelyn's daughter. Evelyn did try to pursue this suggestion with her husband after he was demobbed, but because of his experiences of the racial segregation, he was not prepared to make the move. He recounted a story of an evening's visit he had made to the cinema to Evelyn:

"He couldn't understand why one half was completely full, and the other half was empty, so what does he do?... sat in an empty seat... and he hadn't sat down long, when the usherette came and said 'excuse me but you can't sit here and he said 'but why I am comfortable enough?'... and she said 'no... this is not your side... you have got to go over to the white side'..."

Chris served in Africa and was awarded the Burma Star when he served in Penang, but he could never come to terms with the way coloured and blacks were treated. He used to say to Evelyn (in her words);

"...I have travelled all over the world, and if I can't live in England, I can't live anywhere..."

As with the other ladies I have interviewed, Evelyn has her fair share of humorous anecdotes, particularly with regard to the funny things in the raids and the blackout. Once, early on in the war, before Chris got his call up, they had gone out to 'The Grange' cinema on Coventry Road. At that time Evelyn used to suffer from terrible chilblains. In the middle of the picture she asked Chris to get her some ice cream and Chris reluctantly obliged. In the midst of this, the air raid siren sounded and then panic ensued, especially as Chris had just stood on Evelyn's feet, to which she let out a piercing scream. In the confusion and chaos, a passing man who thought Evelyn needed help from 'a molester' offered to assist her. A very tearful Evelyn replied;

"It's alright, it's my husband... he stood on my chilblains."

On another occasion, one of her sisters had been caught in the blackout and was trying to find her way up Liddon Road by 'feeling' the fences. A young man saw this young woman struggling and stopped to assist. After enquiring if she was alright and did she need help, his look of interest turned to humour, as he shouted back at his friend;

"...it's alright... it's only me sister."

The utter cheek of younger brothers!

The funniest story that Evelyn told me, actually describes the blackout definitively. One night, Evelyn and her sister Betty went to the 'outdoor' on Gospel Lane to buy their father some beer. On their way back, it was so dark that Evelyn managed to walk into a lamppost and bumped her nose. So black you couldn't even see the end of your nose, quite literally!

So the war eventually ended. Chris was demobbed on Christmas Eve 1945, and upon his return he tried to make a go of it, working for himself as a window cleaner, unfortunately not successfully. They both ended up working at Triplex Glass; Evelyn worked in the accounts office. They had a son, and their first house was a 'pre-fab' on Bowood Crescent (off West Heath Road). When I asked Evelyn did she ever think about what she was doing, that she was making weapons to kill, her reply was considered and measured;

"...there is a war... and you'd got to get it finished..."

All that scrimping and saving and making ends meet has never left Evelyn; it has become manifest in her by years of 'doing without', during and before the war 'waste not want not' and 'count your pennies'. A mentality that caused her to lose out on buying a mobile home, because every year she saved up, the price went up still further outstripping her savings. Her war time frugality, much to be admired is a point of humour with her family who know that is the way to get her to take Sunday dinner 'leftovers' home, is by threatening to throw them away.

FOR EVELYN

We will get on, we have to you know,
That's the way it is, for all of us,
There's no point brooding, no tears should show,
No scenes, no weeping and no fuss.

We are made of sterner stuff,
We have faced these fears before,
When all around was bleak and tough,
We battled through that war.

And now again we face our foe,
And our boys go off to fight,
Of panic there will be no show,
No fears through any night.

We will just get on, you see,
Because that's what we have to do,
To win this war it must be,
Like this for me and you.

Chapter 8

THE CATASTROPHE OF THE BSA

This is the title given to part of a report that I unearthed during my research at the National Archive, and it describes in some detail the aftermath caused by the high explosive bomb that fell on the Small Heath works in late November 1940. It is the one incident most talked about by the interested historians, however, it is only part of the story as became clear from the information that now rests at Kew.

From numerous other sources, what has become most apparent to me is the lack of clear information, and the general confusion that was caused by this devastation of Birmingham. Reports and information can appear contradictory, and this does perpetuate the myths that surround the incident even to this day.

Carl Chinn's book 'Brum Undaunted' (2005), gives the most illuminating personal accounts of rescue from the November blitz, and has helped me to clarify my own picture and understanding of the more sanitised, non-emotive, government reports. The account in Chinn's book underlines the chaos and pandemonium that the rescuers faced, and outlines the immense bombing that Birmingham had already been subjected to in the three months prior to that dreadful night.

Professor Chinn describes the militaristic build-up that took place in the years prior to 1940, both from the international-political dimension and from the national-local rearmament push, from the mid-1930's onwards. He uses the written and verbal accounts of those who were involved, combined with local newspaper reports, to evoke an image of a city battling through, and eventually emerging victorious.

The BSA features in his account as it does here, because it was, until quite recently, an untold story due to the press censorship that surrounded the main centre of munitions production for the UK. BSA was the most significant manufacturer of precision fire arms, and many sources cite that they alone were responsible for more than 50% of the total firearms production for World War Two. The Birmingham Small Arms company, Small Heath had been founded in 1861 for "the production of interchangeable arms". Birmingham was recognised as the gun making capital of the UK, so it is no small coincidence, that a large production manufacturer would capitalise on the skills and expertise, and the availability of raw materials to which Birmingham had access. However, to make limited runs of anything requires skilled and semi-skilled operatives, once mass production became the norm, semi-skill could give way to assemblers. With the advent of the Great War labour became even cheaper by replacing male semi-skilled and non skilled workers, with women dilutees. These women were there to perform production line tasks for which they had limited training and as a consequence, they could be paid considerably less than the men they would temporarily replace. For that was always the plan, women would fill in while the men were away fighting, but were later then forced back to domestic service, or the home. Additionally, the marriage bar which prohibited women from working after they were married, allowed for the freedom of the employer to hire and fire at will.

This is something that emerging industries on that scale had to have the flexibility to do, for the depression of the 1930's had led to a downturn in industrial capacity. This was then followed by an urgent requirement to rearm and build aircraft, hence, the emergence of the shadow factories in Birmingham and Coventry. These firms, were bright new enterprises led by industrialists and receiving preferential contractual support from the government. A private armaments firm such as the BSA, although responding to the call of the government to shift its production from bicycles and motorbikes, back over to armaments and engines, was not so favoured contractually. I have found evidence to confirm that when contracts were not forthcoming the workforce suffered various contractions, and this would almost certainly be the semi and non-skilled staff.

The main BSA factory at that time was situated in a densely populated area of the city, it was flanked on one side by the Great Western Railway and on the other by the Grand Union Canal. If you lived around there and you were a young unmarried girl, you could get a job. It had several sites in Birmingham and several sites in Small Heath. By the time war broke out, the main Small Heath works was already producing a range of armaments from the; Browning gun, Bofors gun, to the Lewis gun, Besa gun and 40mm shells. Whereas its neighbouring site at Waverley Road was still producing bicycles. Eileen worked at the main factory, and Evelyn worked at the Waverley Works, both women lived within a stones throw from the factory.

That was the way it was, girls left school at 14 and somehow found themselves at the factory gate on the Monday morning looking for work.

There was also a transient population of itinerant workers, who could find work at the BSA if they needed a job. Obviously, they retained a core of highly skilled men, who in turn worked with gangs of semi-skilled men, but the proportion of unskilled to skilled would be as expected, considerably higher.

The majority of the factories consisted of old buildings, built before a time of health and safety, these were busy places, dirty, noisy, producing highly machined metal items, which required the use of suds on lathes, and machine oil. The range of machine tools had to be capable of reaming out a barrel on a Browning gun, to machining a 40mm shell. They were on average at this point manufacturing 1,700 Browning guns per week and employing a workforce in Small Heath of 2,000 people and War production was on a rapid increase as Ernest Bevin, the then Minister for Labour pushed towards a 'Total War Economy' (Appendix 1).

The UK had been at war for 11 months and had prepared accordingly. Barrage balloons and Ack Ack guns were placed at key points around the city. Chinn describes the evacuation measures that were put in place to remove vulnerable youngsters from danger and then the forced repatriation, when many parents already impoverished, could not meet the 'means tested' contributions. There may well have been a feeling of general complacency around the city, following from the corporation's inadequate investment in the essential services, protection, fire and rescue. So, when it did come, when the bombing finally started it must have taken the people by surprise and then instilled them with fear. Very quickly, by the 13th August the bombs began to fall from the sky, raids were almost continuous for 2 weeks, lasting anything from 3 to 8 hours per night. Then on the 25th August according to Chinn (2005);

"the city centre of Birmingham was attacked by 50 bombers."

In that raid the Market Hall was destroyed. Incendiary bombs were being used extensively in these raids, a factor which was going to place a great strain on the city and its woefully inadequate fire and rescue services. The following night the attack was even more prolonged and the Luftwaffe concentrated on trying to hit a major target, the BSA. In doing, much of the civilian area surrounding the factory suffered as a consequence. According to D. H. Stevenson DHO (Air Ministry Birmingham) in his report to the Chief of Air Staff, 28.8.40;

"Birmingham had been attacked by enemy aircraft for three consecutive nights culminating in a fairly heavy attack on the night of 26th-27th/8. In all 445 HE bombs were dropped, plus a large number of incendiary bombs."

On the night of 26th August the Rifle Mill at the factory was totally destroyed, which stopped the production of the Browning rifle immediately. Fortunately, there was no one working in that part of the factory that evening, though the fact that it was unmanned probably led to its total devastation, for the one canister of incendiary bombs had been used which in Stevenson's opinion had been far more effective than the high explosive bombing;

> "…most of our factories are old-and incendiary attack presents by far the most serious problem."

For even though according to the sources he investigated he considered that the factory fire services were 'well organised and equipped', it is of no use if the factory has been locked up and no one remains on watch; he made this a recommendation of his report. When he compared the damage that had taken place at the Nuffield factory from high explosive bombs on the same night, to that caused by incendiary bombs on the BSA, he concluded that the effect of HE were 'much more local and easier to deal with' whereas in his opinion;

> "It would be impossible, however, to repair the damage done by <u>the canister of incendiary bombs</u> to the BSA Rifle Mill for many weeks to come."

Another very important factor that he raised in his report is the delay of the alert. Apparently in the incidents that he had investigated, bombs had fallen into the factory workshops before the alert was given and had fallen again after the 'all clear' had been sounded. This appears to have been common practice at this time of raiding, in order to 'maintain production' for as long as possible, however, it was having a very negative effect on morale according to Stevenson. Not because the workers were particularly concerned for their own safety for as he indicates later;

> "After all the English workman is pretty good in a game of chance and will be able to calculate "the odds" from experience."

The concerns of the workers were driven by fear for their 'folk at home', because the alert was proving too late for them too, a problem that had been reported by others in Chinn's book. Stevenson suggested that these alerts had to be more effective to counteract the negative effects they were having on morale, which was leading to a lack of faith in the works ARP unit. He also made a suggestion that shift changeovers needed to be reorganised so that they didn't coincide with the raids, leaving the workers who had to take immediate cover in the shelters, 'sleepy and unable to work the next day'.

This first really bad raid on the BSA had caused immediate production problems, but with all munitions and engines factories the 'shadow' principal was the key to its success, according to the BSA records;

"Instructions were immediately issued to proceed with dispersal."

The term 'dispersal' was a very clinical word for clearing up and moving production (and manpower) to alternative sites as soon as possible. The dispersal arrangements for the BSA consisted of 26 alternative factories, 12 of which were dedicated to producing the Browning gun, there was a factory in Redditch which was 'fed by about 15 independent contractors'.

So critical was this process that although there was a substantial drop in production initially, after five months the BSA was back up to full production in alternative sites. They calculated the loss of guns made (between the August and November raids) to be 35,000, yet the BSA insisted that;

"...there was never any question of aircraft being actually short of guns."

Within that raid of 26th August 1940 according to the company documentation, there were 570 machines destroyed (including machines used for other gun production, such as anti-tank rifles), the estimated cost of replacement and repair was calculated to be £283,000, but much worse was to come.

As Chinn points out, raiding didn't stop it was continuously happening every night, and as more raids took place they caused further damage to the city, and piled more pressure on the already badly stretched fire and rescue services. According to Chinn, in the raids between August and September 1940 'over 100 Brummies were killed'. On some nights during this period and until November there could be in excess of 200 fires blazing each night. Then Coventry happened on the 14th November, as Chinn recalls;

"Within a square mile 80% of buildings were destroyed and 568 people killed."

It seemed the German Air Force had turned up the heat, and the neighbouring city was their next target. Chinn (2005);

"...at 7.17pm on Tuesday 19 November when the first of 350 planes dropped flares and incendiaries, lighting up their targets..."

There followed a raid of nine hours duration, where the Germans;

"...discharged more than 500,000 kilograms of bombs (nearly 450 tons), some of the heaviest calibre."

The next part of the report is stamped 'Most Secret' and was written for the Department of Home Security, to relay the horror that the police and others were faced with at the BSA, as the authors point out the value of these reports are that they were 'contemporary records' of the time, rather than 'recollections' given by works 'officers... some twelve months after the event'.

"In Message to War Room 20.55hrs 19/20-11-40
"H.E. on B.S.A. New Factory, Small Heath Casualties reported.
"Police Officer's Report
"At 21.40hrs (1) a bomb fell on B.S.A. works in Armoury Rd, known as 'the new building'."

At that point hell was breaking loose all over the city and within close vicinity to the BSA, battering the already shocked civilians who had sustained raids for weeks and months. Within the building itself, which was a six storey factory of relatively modern construction 1,500 employees had been working that night. The first to respond was the works ARP who valiantly tried to assist, which explains the 45 minute discrepancy between the war room message and the police report, something that was later indicated in the Home Security report, at that point the sheer enormity of the disaster forced them to call in the local ARP for help.

Another important factor which hampered rescuers was the break down in communications, according to Birmingham Economic and Social Survey, the special section entitled BSA the Small Heath Factory, both the internal and external telephones systems had already failed prior to the disaster. Relaying the tragedy to the central authorities must have posed some considerable problems.

High explosive bombs of 1,000lbs dropped through the roof and then detonated, causing the supporting walls to fail, the building at that end collapsed. The structure had been breached so severely, that as debris fell through the crater left by the explosion so did the heavy machine tools from these upper floors. From the evidence in the survey 6 bays of shop 83 and 4 bays of shop 84 were completely destroyed, at that time it was estimated that 750 people were working in that part of the building.

"(83) and (84) shops both received direct hits from what appear to be 500kg H.E. As far as can be judged after the lapse of time, bomb on (83) detonated about first floor and that on (84) about second floor level. Six 20ft bays at the south end of (83) collapsed..."

According to the evidence and oral accounts, the alert had sounded and the employees were ordered to the shelter, there is some dispute here because in the final report for Home Security, the investigators found that, the ARP shelters for the works were situated across a bridge to the other side of the canal, and there was considerable reluctance during raids to cross that bridge and use the shelters, additionally;

"...a considerable proportion of workers later preferred to remain at work, seeking local cover when danger was imminent."

This accounts for those workers who decided to take temporary shelter on the ground floor as had become the norm. Which is actually stipulated in the report later;

> "Rescue work was difficult and prolonged (for a period of two weeks) due to the fact that these workpeople had taken refuge in the basement of this section of the factory (which had been set aside for this purpose) and were crushed and buried there in."

With the collapsing building, the falling debris, combined with the sheer weight of the heavy machinery those sheltering below had limited chance of survival. According to the police officer's report the situation was further exacerbated by an ensuing fire, which was probably due to the oil impregnated timber flooring, at that point;

> "The works Investigation Officer stated that between 150 and 200 people might be trapped inside under the debris, since they had taken shelter on the ground floor."

It is hard to imagine a disaster of this magnitude in peacetime, with the fire and rescue services being called to a site with limited communications, and as it would turn out, a limited water supply. Only to find a collapsed building with the possibility of many people trapped inside, and no heavy lifting equipment available, further no way of ascertaining if any time-delay or unexploded devices may remain and an extensive fire having broken out. But the situation was far more serious, there were bombs quite literally falling everywhere, the smell of pungent coal gas, the sounds of screams, shouts, bells ringing, massive explosions, the ground shaking, the risks taken that night by those involved in the rescue effort were incomparable to any peacetime event, yet, as they are recorded by officialdom they lose much of that sense of fear and confusion. Here follows a chronological order of events as recorded in the Home Security report taken from police records;

19/20
> "0010 hrs Fire under control
> 0210 hrs Rescue parties not yet arrives – services of same urgently required.
> 0245 Rescue parties now in attendance.
> 0310 Main First Aid Party returned to their depot…"

At 06.15 hrs it is reported that;

> "…between 75 – 100 persons remain to be accounted for… To that time also, no fatal casualties had been recovered."

Then there are the various comings and goings of rescue parties, who were quite literally called in from all over the country, on the 20.11.40 at 13.45hrs:

"One dead body recovered".

On that same day later in the afternoon the Coventry Road Rescue Party stood down;

"...stating that no further operations could be taken by them until a large crane capable of lifting heavy girders arrived."

All the 'BSA services remained on the scene' and an hour later they had managed to recover two more bodies. They continued tirelessly the next day without success with raiding continuing the night of the 22/23.11.40 according to BSA reports.

"...a number of bombs fell including a number of incendiaries. Both (8) and (10) shop received hits from what seems to be a 50kg H.E. Fire followed, but whether it was the result of the H.E. or further I.B.'s is not known. It is stated that the timber floors were heavily soaked with oil in these shops."

Bombing was so heavy that evening that the Waverley Works, the Tyseley Works and the Radax Works all suffered direct hits and buildings were either completely demolished, or gutted by fire. As Stevenson had warned three months early, incendiary bombs posed the biggest problem. Now the factory rescue services were stretched to their limits, already trying to cope with a rescue mission, with very little lifting equipment which they must have known by then was pointless, but more fires were breaking out around them. It is at this point that Birmingham was quite literally pushed to the brink. The water supply failed and the fire fighters on the premises of the BSA were forced to pump from The Grand Union Canal for two days, to the extent that by;

"...the morning of the 22nd November, the canal was practically drained, and that a follow up raid would have found them without water."

There is absolutely no doubt that if raids had continued on the same magnitude for the following night, or nights, it would have broken the city through fire, there were so many fires raging around the city by that point with limited fire services to deal with the disaster and now no water to douse them. Fortunately for the BSA that was the end of their intensive raids, it gave the rescuers respite to actually undertake the urgent task in hand. The police reports from the 25th November, 1940, states;

"BSA. 23 bodies recovered, 60 still missing, 100% production held up chiefly by lack of water and power."

And with the first account of the disaster;

"When the bombing commenced, the employees went to the ground floor instead of to the shelters. The rear block, six storeys high, collapsed, bringing all the machinery with it."

By the 28th November, 1940 the last Police Reports state that;

"<u>BSA</u> 'Power now in order – still without water.'"

And;

"All those employees thrown out of work through bombing are now being offered employment at other units of the firm."

Further that;

"The work of recovering bodies from the debris is continuing – approximately 50 persons still unaccounted for."

Bearing in mind, this was 10 days after the disaster, and that as far as it is possible to tell, 25 bodies had been recovered, there seems to have been some confusion as to how many may have lost their lives. Reports had ranged from a 150 – 200 trapped, and the works seemed to offer very little in the way of accurate recording.

Although the figure now given by many sources is 53 having lost their lives, the actual memorial website can only record 52 names yet the Home Security report is categorical in their statement;

"54 work people were sheltering on the ground floor of these premises all of whom were killed by falling debris."

So why is there such confusion even to this day? There are several possible explanations, the first is given in the initial police report which records that;

"The police were unable to ascertain the exact number of person's trapped as a number of the workpeople had gone home."

We have to remember that the place was in total chaos there were bombs dropping in close vicinity on civilian housing, many probably dashed to check on the safety of their loved ones. However, 10 days later there were now accurate figures available from the works itself, this is something that researchers were struggling with when trying to gain general data from the BSA for their research (for the Home Security report). It seems that records were poorly kept, and that as a consequence they had very little idea of exactly who and how many were missing. As the report's authors note with frustration, with a number of essential working practices, such as; accidents, absenteeism, production-per-man-hours etc, 'no reliable records can be found'. Further, if we assume that the BSA did employ a proportion of itinerant workers on short time, it is more than possible that no one knew exactly how many were there, and bodies don't necessarily remain intact, or identifiable, in bomb blasts. This uncertainty and inaccuracy did lead to rumours and speculation.

The factory was shut down, 2000 people laid off, 1,600 machines destroyed, but the BSA was the main producer of arms, so the immediate concern was dispersal, a process in which they had already been active some months previously. However, this process had its fair share of difficulties, in the first instance it seems that government procedures may have caused offence. A memo dated 27th November, 1940 and addressed to BCAFF, which appears to be an official communiqué from a member of the Air Arm, asks a senior government official to accept the local managements suggestions for dispersal rather than conducting full investigation for in his opinion it is;

"...impossible to insist on normal procedure in a case of a factory where they are still digging out the men."

Dispersal was planned as in April but on a much larger scale, which encountered a number of problems according to the Home Security report, due to limited assessment of viability in the first place, such as;

"...difficulty in securing a rapid removal was due to an acute shortage of skilled labour."

And in the first instance;

"other difficulties experienced by the BSA after dispersal had been fixed, arose from the lack of selectivity of suitable sites, factories and workshops."

"Furthermore, personnel and local labour requirements had not been borne in mind."

It sounds as if too many things were taken for granted in locations chosen for dispersal. The accessibility of the right kind of labour that was afforded in Small Heath, was not so easy to source, and because there were problems arranging transport to convey personnel from Small Heath, the problems were further perpetuated. The organisation at this level was open to some criticism in the report, for it appears that those that found themselves elevated to that position for the process, did not always possess the appropriate skills, 'initiative or determination.'

This report then concludes by examining the working relations and atmosphere between the management and employees, the findings are not as one would expect of a factory of this size, but do go someway to explaining why they were so dependent upon an employment structure of unskilled and dilutee labour, because the pricing structure pre-war had been fixed to 'peacetime' as well as 'piece work rates', which meant of course pay in the first instance was low. Then with the outbreak of war, and 'shadow' factories offering higher than normal salaries, those that came in later were getting paid more than those before even some, semi-skilled and skilled workers. This did a great deal to disenfranchise and this acted as a disincentive to those already in employment, as a consequence, a large number of those in employment even pre-war were women.

That is not to say the BSA did not try to offer the facilities to their workers, there was a good works canteen according to the report, where they tried to offer 'mealtime concerts and entertainment', not always successfully as it turns out, as bands found the transport costs too prohibitive, even if they waived 'fees and expenses'.

At no time did the report suggest that the 'workpeople had attempted to hold up production' because of 'grievance', but this was a workforce that did not feel that it had the ear of the management. The suggestion therefore was that the subsequent dispersal and after effects of the disaster could have progressed more smoothly had their been a greater cooperation between all concerned.

Even today the rumours persist that not all the bodies were recovered, even among those employed there. That it was such a mess at that time, with the continual German bombardment, that the premises were sealed for some weeks until there was greater opportunity and resources to deal with what remained. At the time of writing this report, over a year later, the authors comment that;

> "The knowledge of the disaster amongst the other workpeople was depressing in the extreme, and rumour as to the extent of the disaster and casualties had a disturbing effect on (local and) public opinion, and which is not yet allayed."

Further that the;

> "Operatives were and still are unwilling to work near the place and no inducement offered by the management for night shift workers had any effect for some considerable time."

This section of the report concludes that unsurprisingly there was a considerable reluctance amongst the workers to 'undertake' night shift working, in fact 'out of a total of 1522 men, and 357 women' they could only find 38 people willing to do so.

After those awful November nights, it is a wonder anybody came back at all, this just goes to point to the stoicism and determination of the Birmingham people to carry on through all adversity. Just as a final point to consider the report on its last page points out that 'two of the 50 person shelters' that they would not use for the difficulties faced crossing the bridge during raids had 'direct hits' but fortunately no one was in there at the time. So would these poor souls have perished wherever they were?

THE 'BLESSED' SHELTERERS

Are we safe in here,
Do you think my dear?
I hear that bomb that fell,
The one that sent us straight to hell.
500kgs of power and might,
That detonated in the middle of the night,
The one with our name on,
First we were here, and then we were gone.
We sheltered where we thought we should,
We covered our heads with our hands, like we could.
We heard them dropping, one after another,
Sometimes nearer, and sometimes farther.
You hear the scream, as they swish down,
To kill the heart of this god forsaken town.
Bang, bang, bang, and boom,
We cower in this tragic gloom.
This metal mayhem that falls on our heads,
One minute we were alive, and now we are dead.
We made those things for our own boys,
Those hard-nosed, unforgiving, toys.
But that's on them and not on us,
We cowered in the gloom and dust.
Are we safe in here, do you think my dear?
I can hear our bomb getting ever near,
Will it be quick when it comes do you think?
Will it be seconds, or minutes, till it ends?
Will we be together, through all, as friends?
I am scared, are you too?
Of this? There is nothing we can do.
Soon it will come, that one for which we wait,
Soon it will come and make contact with our fate,
Are we safe in here...
Do you think my dear... ?

Chapter 9

EILEEN – HE'S MY SWEETHEART!

Eileen Smith is one of the most cheerful souls that I have ever met, she laughs and smiles with every phrase she utters. A person with a more pleasant disposition would be very hard to find. When I first met with Eileen back in May 2008, her daughter was there, who had quite a bit to contribute to our discussion. Eileen comes from a family with a strong sense of community, real 'salt of the earth' people. Her story is as individual as the others in this book, but is connected by the same occupation and sense of purpose that accompanied it.

Eileen describes her father, John James Slater known as Jack, as a 'good old Brummie of Balsall Heath born and bred'. Jack joined up for the army under age and his mother 'had to fetch him out' and 'he still went back', and lost his arm in World War 1 at the battle of the Somme, becoming a pensioner as a consequence. He spent much of his time backwards and forwards to Uffcombe Park Hospital in Birmingham for therapy. To this day, Eileen refuses to buy a poppy because of the way her father was mistreated when he tried to seek financial assistance once when she was young, she says:

"…they refused him help and turned round and told him 'you should be ashamed of yourself having kids'."

Eileen was born after he returned in 1919, the first of nine children. Eileen showed me a bit of paper that her mother used to give her father to take with him when he used to go to make claims, his aide memoir to all the names. As another was born, a freshly written name was added to the list, Eileen still carries this dog-eared bit of paper in her purse to this day.

This place that she held in the family, probably accounted for much of the strictness that he used to display towards her, although she does say he was always a very lovely man. However, he would never allow her to go dancing or wear makeup, as Eileen recalls:

"I had a lovely dad… he was very strict… I had a back hander from him – I was 17… I met him round the corner I must have been talking to someone and he seen me… and he went (she shows his backhand)… 'go and get that bloody muck off your chops' he says... he used to think 'only naughty women went dancing'."

She had to be in at ten o'clock, every night, even when she was courting and engaged, and her father used to question where she had been.

Her mother Alice Emily Atherall, was from Langton Green, Tunbridge Wells in Kent. She had been in domestic service in Kent, all her family worked on the land, hop picking. She met Jack when his regiment the Royal Warwickshire became attached to the Royal Kents. She had Eileen in Kent, and when Eileen was twelve months old, her parents brought her to Birmingham.

Eileen's family lived in a big double-fronted house in Vincent Crescent. They started by renting one room, from the landlady, old Mrs Cooke, she took in lodgers into all of her rooms. The owner lived in Selly Oak. Her mother, father and five other children lived, ate and slept in one room. There were four or five other families living in the same house. Eileen's Aunt Ada, and her family also lived there. As people left or died, Eileen's family began to take over the house, room by room, sometimes secretly, until finally they had the whole house:

"Mrs Cooke died you see... she died... and me aunt Ada said to my mum... put a little bed in that room, the landlord won't know..."

Eileen attended Sherborne Road School, then Mary Street, Balsall Heath, before finishing her last three months of education at Tindal Street, this was due to a reorganisation of schools in Birmingham. She has her leaving certificate which states that she was an exemplary student. She left, as all children did, at 14 years of age, and started work as an apron maker in a place called The Lockstitch.

Having done other jobs, she started work at Heaths, the brass foundry in Leopold Street, where she had to learn to operate a fly press. These were the days long before the health and safety police, when machines could be old and defective, and safety guards, and cut-off mechanisms, were a thing of the future. As Eileen shows me, she learnt to her cost not to get her hand in the way, for one day she brought the press down on her fingers crushing three of them:

"They was almost taking them three off... but they didn't they put them in splints... and that's how they are deformed like."

She was young and had damaged her hand quite severely. Again, this was a time when claims against your employer were difficult to make, and if you did not work you did not get paid. As she says:

"I didn't claim compensation I was 17... and they more or less... they didn't say... but they more or less, tried to work me out."

Eileen returned after some weeks, but she had lost a great deal of fine motor skill in her hand, as a consequence (and probably because the firm wanted someone uninjured to replace her), they put her on a very delicate operation which she struggled to do, so after a little time she decided she had had enough and left.

Eileen's wage was critical to her family, she was the oldest and effectively the breadwinner, as her father was disabled, she could not afford to be out of work long. Her sister Doris was already working for the BSA in Waverley Road making bikes. But Eileen heard they were taking on at Golden Hillock Road, the main factory (BSA Small Heath), and Eileen decided to go and chance her luck there. As she says wryly, it was known by the locals as 'bloody sore arse'. To her it was 'massive', she says:

"The one I worked at, there was floors and floors, there was thousands worked there."

They gave her a job, and for her first year they put her to work in upper floors making motorcycle parts, but before the outbreak of war (probably 1938) she was moved to the ground floor of the infamous 'new building', to manufacture armaments, detonators, and bullets. She says that the machines were only ever quickly demonstrated, and because she was machining lots of different things, she never knew what she was actually making. But she worked 'funny hours' Sundays and Saturdays, as she recalls:

"All the hours we worked... we used to clock in, clock out... clock in, clock out. But all the hours we worked... I swear I never earned £3! Our average wage... and it was a bloody good job then, was probably around... £2 10sl"

And it was piece work:

"You'd go for your job... and you'd go to the stores and they'd give you your work... might be nuts and bolts and stuff... you'd take 'em back and weigh 'em, god knows what... and they used to just book it down and just a few paltry shillings you earned for that like..."

As was the custom at that time, she used to give her mother all of her money, and her mother would give her back pocket money to spend.

The day that war broke out, as Eileen remembers was a very sad day, she had turned 20 at that time. She was at work, and by this stage there were in her estimation hundreds of women working there, and an announcement came over the works tannoy, Eileen repeats it clearly;

"We are now at war with Germany."

Even working in a place where everyone knew they were making weapons and rearming, nobody wanted it to happen, and nobody was happy about it when the announcement came, as she remembers:

"Oh it was a sad day... and I think some of the girls was crying... because we knew what it meant you see."

Then of course the phoney war lasted for nearly a year and then the bombing started.

She talks of the 'only pleasure they had especially after the war started' because they 'were frightened to go anywhere else', was Eileen and her 'good friend Winne Preston from Monica Road', catching the bus outside the BSA to go to an afternoon's performance at the Birmingham Hippodrome, she recalls with glee:

"We used to queue up in Hinge Street... ready to go in the afternoon performance... we used to go up in the gods, you know right up in the gods there... we used to see all the old variety acts and... oh lovely... we see them Wilson, Betty and Keppel the once... we used to love them... all the old ones... Sandy Powell 'can you hear me mother?' and that was the enjoyment... and that was all we got because of the blackout... couldn't see a thing..."

The November blitz has a particular place in Eileen's memory for it was her building that collapsed with the bomb, and it fell onto where she should have been working if she had been on nights.

"Do you know what? If I'd have been working that night... I would have been killed! My machine I was working on was buried!"

But one of her father's strict rules was not to allow his girls to work nights, combined with the fact that the factory had never asked her to work nights, a fortuitous act for Eileen, who but for that twist of fate would not be here now. Of course that shut the factory, and during that time of closure, rather than being 'dispersed' as many workers were, Eileen was told to report to the Labour Exchange in Bottleville Road everyday, until the factory re-opened six weeks later.

Eileen has many good memories of her time at the BSA. She says they were an extremely good humoured and generally a happy bunch of girls who worked there. She particularly remembers Annie MacGliesh who was a Scots lass. They used to have 'music while you work' and they would often join in, dancing in the aisles. As it was the BSA, which had suffered from attacks, a number of high profile visitors went to meet the workers in order to lift morale.

She can remember Churchill coming:

"Churchill didn't come in the factory, we were all... if we wanted to let outside, the whole of Golden Hillock Road, when Churchill come... in his car..."

But the old Queen Elizabeth (Elizabeth Bowes-Lyon), was much more accommodating:

"We had a surgery like, a proper little surgery... we used to have to go like across the courtyard... and that's when we all went there, when the Queen Mother come..."

However, for her the best visit she recounts is:

"Oooo he was a handsome man, he was... can you imagine who it can be? General De Gaulle!... ooo he came right along the... coz I worked then on the ground floor, so as he came through the big main entrance and god knows what... ... there he come... and do you know what?... in his uniform... oooh I could see him now..."

She talks of the raids and how they changed things. When coming home she used to have to catch the number 8 bus down to Belgrave Road, and run all the way home down Balsall Heath Road, where her mother would be waiting on the step, with her tea ready in the shelter before the raids would start. On other occasions they would hear the distinctive intermittent rumble of the German aircraft and:

"...they seemed to make their own special noise... them German whatsit... they used to go... uuur... uuur... urrr... and you'd go gawd blimey that's a German one you know, and we used to go oh god, we used to be petrified!... I'd been coming home from work and the sirens had gone and of course, the bus used to put the lights out and that... I got off the bus at Moseley Road and I've ran all the way home, and I've been frightened to death I have... really... scared stiff!"

Small Heath was involved in some of the heaviest raids and consequently suffered much bomb damage, much of where Eileen lived was subjected to incendiary damage, the house opposite her parents was hit. She remembers one sad story of a deaf and dumb family who lived on Vincent Parade, being killed in their shelter, with a direct hit.

She met her 'sweetheart' as she refers to him, on what she calls the 'Monkey Run' and what Carl Chinn refers to as 'the Lane', Ladypool Road. Apparently, there was a bit of a courting ritual locally, where all the girls would walk up one side, and all the boys would walk down the other. This is where she first set eyes on Francis Smith, she was 17. They courted around the Olympia Picture house, and by all accounts, Francis was a 'cheeky bugger he was' and a very lovely man:

"I was sitting there watching and the way they'd built it there were pillars... and these fellas were sitting at the back... and he went... 'can you see miss?'... 'Yes thank you'... I thought cheeky bugger you know then... 'Would you like an ice cream miss?'... I said 'No thank you'... anyway that was that, and when the picture had finished... everyone come out see... they was all behind coming out... he went 'Can I walk up the lane with you?'... I said 'I'm going to meet my friend' which I was... I'd promised to meet her... 'Well can I walk with you' he says 'till you meet your friend?'... I said 'Oh if you like'... so he walked with me and when I met me friend... that was that..."

No it was not. There was a mutual friend of Eileen's called Arthur, who had split up with his girl and asked Eileen to make a double date with him and his brother, Eileen agreed. Then she waited at the appointed time and place and Arthur came but said his brother had been delayed, so Arthur and Eileen chatted, and waited, all of a sudden the 'brother' turned up and it was none other than Francis. He was one of ten, and being a black haired boy much favoured on News Years Eve. Both Arthur and Francis were booked on every New Year with their pieces of coal to let the New Year in for neighbours and friends.

He joined up in 1939, 'Private F Smith 7610580 in the Royal Army Ordnance Corps'. Eileen was given a stern warning by her father, not to mess Francis around while he was away fighting. His war got very interesting, he ended up at Dunkirk, his train had got bombed. He had taken some shrapnel in his eye, and with a very injured friend was hiding in a cornfield, and Francis had blood on his arm from helping him. They finally got away in an old coal boat, with a tin of corn meat between them. He said to Eileen, in Eileen's words:

"...'Do you know Larl' he said... 'we was on the train'... he said to one of the blokes 'that's where I live'... 'I live down there'..."

As the train taking him off to Leicester Infirmary passed over the railway bridges in Balsall Heath going over his house, at the top of Camp Hill in Birmingham.

After his near miss, Francis and Eileen became engaged, that Christmas, and Eileen bought her own engagement ring from Samuel's for £2 15s. He was then posted out to the middle east, where he met his brother Arthur (the one who acted as cupid between the young Francis and Eileen), these accidental meetings across the world seem to be a feature of many the ladies stories in this book. Frank was then posted to Italy before his final posting in Craven Arms, Shropshire. Meanwhile, Arthur ended up in a German prisoner of war camp, Stalag 18a, he was there for quite a time and did make efforts to escape. On one occasion when he was caught in the forest outside the camp, he was challenged as to where he was going and he replied, 'I'm going home'.

Eileen and Francis were married at St Paul's in Moseley Road, 16th June 1945, Eileen borrowed her wedding dress and her veil, friends provided red carnations from the market for her bouquet. A local man played the piano, and her mother 'laid out' the reception and re-iced the cake because the icing did not pass muster. She remembers fondly their wedding and nuptials:

"...we hadn't been in bed five minutes when I come down... and they said blimey that was quick... 'I've only come down for the bucket' I said... because he wants to be sick."

Francis was not demobbed until after their daughter Maureen was born, in March. He went and got a job at the market, doing deliveries on a horse and cart. The only place they could get to live was at Eileen's parents, who gave them a front room and one bedroom to start them off, until they had two small children, with two cots in their bedroom.

Eileen finished at the BSA in January 1945 because she was expecting, and the machine she was using at the time was getting in the way of her bump. Their first house was given to them by the council in Dymoke Street, it was a back-to-back, and it fronted on the street. In 1952 Eileen's youngest infant daughter Angela, became sick with TB and ended up hospitalised for three years. Soon after Eileen was diagnosed with suspected TB, she spent five months in another hospital, leaving poor Francis having to put the other three in a care home for twelve months.

He spent his time between working, on a round of visiting, to his sick child and sick wife, and three other children. They were fortunate enough to have kind neighbours who helped to take care of Francis, who must have been incredibly tired. The three older children were allowed out on Coronation Day. Eileen came out a little while later, the clinic helped her to get a house in the countryside, which was considered better for her, in Dimsdale Road, Northfield. Eighteen months later, Angela finally met her family, just before her third birthday.

Eileen has eight grandchildren, and six great-grandchildren. Her husband Francis died 24 years ago of a malignant melanoma, having worked as a proud dustman, all of his life since leaving the army.

Eileen is a highly philosophical lady and looks back at all of her life with great pride, she enjoyed her time at the BSA for all the difficulties that the war and raids brought, as she says firmly when remembering those times again:

"We'd got a job to do and we had to do it!"

FOR EILEEN

He was my sweetheart,
He was my beau.
We walked down the lane
Together you know?
All those years ago.

He was my cheeky chappy,
He was the love of my life,
We walked down the lane
Together, before I was his wife.
All those years ago.

He said, can I walk you home miss?
And we did you see,
We walked down the lane
Together, before he kissed me.
All those years ago.

He was my honey bun,
He would always be the one,
We walked down the lane
Together, always having fun.
All those years ago.

Chapter 10

CENSORSHIP V. DEFENCE – PROPAGANDA AND NON-PUBLICITY

Censorship and propaganda are two sides of the same coin, they are both about the control of information to the general population. In a time of war, control of that information is seen as even more critical for two reasons, firstly to defend a country from those who could exploit that information to their advantage, and secondly to maintain the morale of the country being defended.

During World War Two, Birmingham was viewed by the government as a particularly sensitive area of the country because of the key role it had in the production of munitions, and it required special consideration for being defended against enemy bombardment. As such, there were times when it became subject to a press blackout even though the neighbouring city of Coventry received considerable publicity during the bad November raids of 1940. For the people of Birmingham this was particularly poignant, because it took more than fifty years for the city to publicly acknowledge the loss of life at the BSA factory in Small Heath through the erection of a memorial to the dead. It has been claimed that this blackout of information was due to the Defence Notice that was placed on Birmingham, because of military sensitivity, but Coventry was equally sensitive, yet this was conveyed differently to the greater populace of the country.

I suggest this was due to the escalating situation at that time, rather than a deliberate attempt to conceal the facts, and that the circumstances when analysed chronologically reveal reactions to events which evolved with political changes and ongoing wartime events. There is a possibility that much of what appeared to be censorship, was also initiated to alleviate the sense of panic that may have become manifest during that time in Birmingham. Nationally, there was a need to keep morale high, and if the facts had become general knowledge this may have depressed the civilian population as a whole, allowing counter-British propaganda to succeed.

Defence Notices were first employed in the Great War, consequently, prior to the second world war the government took these notices as they stood in 1918 and simply reactivated them, however, much had changed in the intervening years and it soon became clear that these notices were in need of some modification. In November 1937, the Ministry of Information came into being, to control press publication and promote the war effort of Britain, by October 1938 it had published revised Defence Notices, one of which was:

"Defence Notice No. 1/Munition Factories

On no account should the name or situation of factories producing munitions of war be published nor should any statement of their output, either its amounts or nature, appear in any published document... No reports other than official announcements are to be published with regard to any explosion or other accident in any factories engaged in the manufacture of munitions of war."

Meanwhile, censorship had to be addressed and clear messages given to all those who would seek to exploit weaknesses in the system. In April 1938 Sir Samuel Hoare, put before the cabinet a paper concerning the Official Secrets Act. Concerns had been expressed in certain sections of the press including the Birmingham Post, that the censorship laws being proposed would be 'an instrument of inquisition and punishment in trifling matters in an ordinary journalists everyday work'. The government responded to this by saying that where 'information disclosed' was in 'itself of serious public importance' that it would be open to 'interrogation'.

By July 1938, there were concerns being raised that radio broadcasts on medium and long wave lengths could be intercepted by enemy aircraft and they could then be used to lead bombers into cities. The government took advice from the Civil Defence Authorities that broadcasting should be discontinued in any region where there were warnings of enemy aircraft approaching, within fifty miles.

By the outbreak of war, it was becoming apparent that the press were not happy with what they saw as inexplicable restrictions on their reporting. The Defence Notices in place could not be interpreted easily, and many feared prosecution for infringements due to ignorance, rather than a deliberate act. A draft document from staff at The Daily Mail came into the possession of the cabinet which expressed the discontent with the lack of clarity of Defence Notices, that, in their view, appeared to have been inherited from the last war when 'conditions were very much different'. The Daily Mail staff felt that these notices would only become important if the war endured. The anomalies which they highlighted, were those regarded mentioning materials and resources such as; oil, coal and gas. Of most concern was that particular notices were not considered, or observed, to be important enough by the Ministry of Information, at that time, such a notice was 1/IT which required the press not to publish any information regarding those factories making munitions. This notice initially created problems because it meant the submission of every advertisement for any staff vacancies to the Ministry, who would of course allow publication. These unintentional infringements were causing serious difficulties for all concerned and action had to be taken.

Proposed revisions to the notices were offered by the Trade and Technical press from Mr Percival Marshall, these journals were finding it almost impossible to publish anything at that time that did not contravene the notices and he felt that something had to be done. In his consideration many of these notices were ludicrous as British Consulates in other countries had been for a long time in possession of these directories and journals, and as such:

> "...the Germans must have in possession trade directories which provide the names and addresses of practically every manufacturing firm of any importance in this country."

In his opinion the absurdities were being created by the censor passing, situations vacant advertisements, yet not allowing publication of technical news or suppressing the names of factories in editorials. The only reason that he could give for these anomalies was that the censor who was dealing with trade articles did not possess enough 'technical knowledge to understand its innocuous character'.

Censorship was being confused with defence notices. Censorship was primarily about inhibiting publication of anti-war sentiment, whereas Defence notices were to filter information that could be of use to the enemy. This became particularly noticeable to the cabinet during early October, 1938, when the 'Stop The War' campaigners were raising counter-propaganda publications which were causing sporadic pockets of unrest. The three campaigns highlighted by the government were; The British Union of Fascists led by Oswald Mosley, who were making anti-semitic and racist statements, The Communist Party, who considered that war was capitalist exploitation of the workers, and the Peace Pledge Union, which at that time was being led by the Canon of Birmingham Cathedral, Stuart Morris. The government decided that the threat of prosecution would be enough to deter explicit anti-war reference for now, as none of the groups had much of a following.

Another issue which was of concern to the Ministry and the Government at that time, was what should be published in the event of an air raid. It was decided to centralise and control the release of this information to the press, taking direct control of all information of what facts should be released, such as; the numbers of casualties, eye witness accounts, the amount of bombardment, and the use of civilian defences, most importantly:

"(a)

No more than a general indication of locality is given. Except in the use of the phrase "In the London area", no reference whatever should be made to the name of any Town."

At the same time the Ministry of Information was suffering from internal power struggles within the cabinet which led to a threat of resignation by the Minister I. Mclaine on the 23rd October, because he felt his hands were tied by the Foreign Office having control of censorship. He felt that there had been a loss of public confidence in the ministry, and by virtue of that, in him as the minister. Consequently, press censorship was passed to Ministry of Information early in 1940. This created confusion for a time as the edited Defence Notices refer to information being passed to the 'censor' rather than the 'ministry', the Defence Notices for a time were replaced by censorship, but were still termed as Defence Notices, as the revisions made in October 1939 show.

Among those particular revisions, the munitions notice was re-worded as following:

"1. Munitions

(ii) the locality, output or nature thereof, or the number of employees of any factory producing munitions...

There is however, no objection to the publication of the mere fact that a particular factory is engaged on work to the order of the Government..."

Another revision proposed was that of publication of royal visits, where it was suggested not to publish information regarding such visits until 15 minutes after the visit had ended. This was in direct contradiction to another statement contained within, of giving the press advanced warning of visits to 'centres of public interest.' A point that Buckingham Palace made clear was impractical because as the Secretary of the Palace stated:

"This I think, covers an occasion such as last week when the King visited Aerodromes, and it was impossible to follow the usual practice of publishing information concerning His Majesty's movements 15 minutes after the time at which the visits was scheduled to end. In other words, when the visit is secret, advance details of the programme will not be given to the press."

Which of course, protected the royal family and meant that little evidence remains of the many morale visits that they made during those years.

In March 1940, the emphasis moved away from censorship of information within Great Britain to active pro-British propaganda against the Germans and within the country itself. This also reflects the change in the balance of power that occurred within the cabinet, as Chamberlain's leadership came to an end and the rise of the coalition government premiered by Churchill assumed power, with the accompanying shift in emphasis. Sir Campbell Stuart head of the Department of Enemy Propaganda reported that 7,000,000 leaflets had been dropped all over Germany and that was despite bad weather which had hampered the operations.

By April, the Ministry of Information had assumed control of the Press and Censorship Bureau and there had been a change in structure which enabled a more pro-active approach to propaganda. The Labour Party was seen to be working in co-operation with the Ministry of the Home Front. Two hundred meetings were held all over the country with union members, including a meeting to night-shift workers in Birmingham. Censorship advisors were appointed in key sites such as; Newcastle, Birmingham, Edinburgh, Belfast and Cardiff.

There was a focus towards de-bunking the information being given by anti-war organisations. The press was given authority to 'attack' these organisations and counter propaganda was being distributed at their various meetings. There were numerous campaigns authorised including; an Anti-Gossip campaign, an Evacuees campaign, 'Plough Now' for the Ministry of Agriculture, and a Fuel Economy campaign. There were two particular campaigns for the Ministry of Labour, one to promote Government Training Centres, and one to encourage the recruitment of munitions workers.

Broadcasting became a major feature of the propaganda initiative, according to a report from the cabinet on May 11th, 1940:

"The BBC now broadcasts 43 foreign news bulletins in 22 languages."

Within Great Britain all of BBC broadcasting was now focused on the war effort. With a complete range of programmes that focused on every aspect of; home, work, political and economic, and cultural life. There were programmes entitled 'The Economic War' narrated by J M Keynes, 'The Supply Front' narrated by Leslie Burgin, programmes that focused on aircraft production and fuel economy, and vast range of cooking programmes, narrated by Ambrose Heath and Mrs Berry.

By the end of May, Churchill's cabinet had assumed control and had been sobered by the strategy document that had been produced by the Joint

Chief's of Staff Committee, entitled 'British Strategy in the Near Future'. This document forewarned of Dunkirk and the serious effects of enemy bombardment on our particularly sensitive cities such as Coventry and Birmingham, cities which had already experienced severe bombing in the raids of April. This report was put to the cabinet on the 26th May, the same day as Operation Dynamo (the evacuation of Dunkirk was ordered, Gardiner, 2004), it stressed that if Birmingham and Coventry fell, the war would be over. Censorship of the press was now considered vital, and the opinions of the previous year had been revised sharply. A memorandum to the cabinet from the new Minister of Information, Duff Cooper, dated June 11th stated that:

"Under modern conditions it ought to be faced that there is little that occurs in this country, including trade, technical and industrial information of all kinds, knowledge of which is not useful to Germany."

It was a mammoth task to undertake a broad censorship of the press in Great Britain. At that time there were 133 provincial daily papers, 11 London daily papers (some with three editions per day), and 760 London, suburban and provincial weekly newspapers. The system that existed at that time with newspapers volunteering information to the centre was proving impossible to administer, because newspapers were not co-operating in making submissions. This had caused a rash of stories which were considered damaging to the war effort. The report gives the following example of an article in the Evening Standard on February 22nd:

"An example of this is the passage in the 'Evening Standards' article on the vulnerability of the Birmingham and Liverpool waterworks."

This article had raised the hackles of the Ministry of Information, which considered in these terms;

"…it is inaccurate, or exaggerated, or misleading, or injurious to public morale."

Hence, the need to curtail the freedom of the press.

Two suggestions were given in this report on how the situation might best be managed. The first was compulsory censorship, where it was thought possible that a new defence regulation could be passed, that would prohibit the publication of any information without first going through the censors. This would have required a fivefold increase in staffing. The second involved compulsory sources, that there was to be no publication of any article which mentioned sources on a defined list. That of course, was already in existence in the form of Defence Notices.

Duff Cooper was charged with putting together a committee to find a solution to the problem. By July 18th, 1940, he reported back that the committee had met, and although they had felt that the best course of action was the compulsory censorship, he had to report that:

"The Newspapers Proprietors Emergency Committee had, however, been unanimously opposed to this proposal."

Consequently, he proposed that:

"A different scheme, whereby all the existing Defence Notices would be slightly amended and strengthened had then been put forward. Under this scheme it would be compulsory to submit to censorship all matters dealt within Defence Notices. Failure to do so would be a punishable offence."

He insisted that prosecutions of breaches should be made, and further he was empowered by the cabinet to put forward a bill that in the event of invasion, he would have the power 'to compel the Press to publish only information derived from official *communiqués.*'

There were further problems regarding the reporting of air raid damage. Duff Cooper put forward a paper to the cabinet in October, outlining. Up to that stage, the Air Ministry and the Ministry of Home Security had assumed control of the release of air raid reports, which had conflicted with the 'ordinary news reporting of events'. In their endeavours to control information where the targets were considered sensitive, such as; munitions factories, railways and power stations; or where the enemy had actually been in ignorance of what they had bombed; or where corrections to enemy navigation could be made, the joint ministries were making exceptions. The exceptions were in cases such as sites where 'special sentiment attaches (e.g. Churches and Buckingham Palace)'. In Cooper's opinion this was creating disenchantment with the general population especially in the provinces, 'particularly big cities', who observed far too much emphasis on London targets and this caused certain assumptions:

"They attribute the non-mention of those suppressed to some sinister desire to suppress details of damage done."

He proposed that the cabinet should make the decision of what the policy should be, and that this policy should be effected by the Ministry of Information in close liaison with the other two ministries. The Ministry of Information could then convey this to the press, at the same time, advising the press of more appropriate ways of conveying this information to the population to avoid 'needless agitation and distress.'

This control was enhanced by a more personal oversight of published information by the cabinet itself. In certain circumstances they intervened to allow the passage of information, or not, to the press. The November raids over Coventry and Birmingham being a case in point, but the unfortunate situation of the November raids overtook these plans. Coventry was severely bombed including of course the cathedral, which created a significant amount of press reporting. However, the government was able to suppress the reports of Birmingham as is evident from the cabinet minutes of 28th November. Duff Cooper had managed to publish an instruction a few days previously, which stated that the press were not allowed to publish for 28 days except in exceptional circumstances, 10 days, however, the 28 day rule would hold fast in the case of military objectives, such as; munitions factories. He was specific that the 10 day exception could not apply:

"...to any works or factory of national importance, damaged to which must not be mentioned in the press."

The minutes of the 25th November, record that the 'raid on Birmingham on 22nd November was: killed 407, seriously injured 429, and slightly injured about 300'. A. Greenwood, the Minister Without Portfolio reported that he had visited Birmingham, and he records that:

"Birmingham had not been given as much publicity as Coventry, but the damage in Birmingham was probably more serious. Munitions productions was certain to be slowed up as a result. He (Greenwood) instanced the damage to the BSA factory. Apart from actual hits on factories, production was frequently held up after heavy raids by the failure of the electricity, gas or water supply."

As Birmingham was at the centre of industries of national importance, editors were left in a very difficult dilemma, did they publish and infringe the statement above, or did they wait?

Within the minutes of the 28th November the position was clarified where:

"*The Secretary of State for the Home Department and Minister of Home Security* said that the matter had been carried a stage further at the Meeting of the Civil Defence Committee on the previous day... In the case of Coventry, it had been agreed that the name should be published, because the raid had been one of outstanding importance, and it was clear that the enemy must be aware that they had in fact, bombed Coventry. It had, however, been decided not to publish the fact that Bristol and Birmingham had been bombed."

In my opinion, it was due to confusion and inconsistency rather than any effective cover-up. There appears to have been so much happening at the same moment, that just for a short while the thread was lost. Coventry was published the country was in shock, Birmingham was suppressed, possibly to diffuse any demoralisation of the population, that not just one of the chief centres of aircraft production had been hit, but both, according to the government's own assessment.

In the same minutes of the 25th November, there is a reference, to the 'Daily Worker', the communists newspaper printing 'libellous' cartoons of Ernest Bevin, he wanted to prosecute and not suppress the paper for fear of repercussions, and the cabinet felt that the communists had got off lightly compared to the British Union of Fascists, it was time for action.

The Home Secretary Herbert Morrison, brought a memorandum to the cabinet on the first meeting after Christmas. Opinion was given that the Communist Party, had been systematically publishing 'matter calculated to foment opposition to the persecution of the war'. it was felt that it was time to suppress the activity of the newspaper, which was printing such things as; the government were failing to build deep, bomb-proof shelters for workers, that the 'spotter' system in factories was about increasing profits for the employers, and that food was in shorter supply for poorer people. One headline particularly raised blood pressures, after the air attack on Birmingham, it read:

"Bombed City – Monument to Government Callousness."

Although suppression was called for, it was felt that this may have negative repercussions for the government, as both the national and international press may view this as gagging. Additionally, there had been no observable deterioration of morale as a result of the 'Daily Worker's' stories, and there had been no incitement against the war effort or 'the handling of munitions'. It would have also meant a suppression of the 'Week' which would pronounce against the government on any act against the 'Daily Worker'. The cabinet needed time to reflect and asked Morrison to bring it to them again in three weeks. At that meeting, it was brought again and this time the decision was taken to suppress the two papers, and take action against several others, in order to display an even-handed approach to the public.

In June and July of 1941, the Communist Party tried to get the decision overturned but the cabinet stayed firm and the papers stayed suppressed. A concern that did not appear to reach the cabinet, but involved high level members was that of an article that appeared in the Daily Mirror in July about workers slacking in various factories around the country. Before the article had appeared the Head of the Board of Trade, Oliver Lyttleton, had attempted to raise similar concerns with the Prime Minister. According to

Lyttleton he had been approached by a group of industrialists, one in particular who had commented that:

"...the slackening off in Birmingham in the metal-using industries was most marked."

Ernest Bevin was asked for his opinions and wrote a long response to Churchill. In his reply, he stressed that he thought it was a self perpetuated story that was being repeated to create a truth, however, in his opinion there was evidence of a lowering of a morale because:

"We have run the food supply too low for the people on these heavy metal industries; their energy has been sapped and no appeals can make up for it... It must be remembered that people have had two 'black-out' winters, very little sun all the spring and it is only recently that I have succeeded in getting employers over a large field of industry to realise the necessity for canteens."

Bevin noted that the complaint had originated in Birmingham, but as he pointed out the Essential Work Orders were now in operation enabling checks to be made as necessary. In his opinion, the biggest cause of apathy in the workforce was probably due at that time to the over emphasis to supplies that were being gained from America.

The story refused to die, and the Daily Mirror published on 25th July, entitled 'Britain is going slow – What will you do about it?' The article referred to several examples of work slackening off over the country, it referenced a factory in the Midlands. The investigations were underway in Whitehall, as Head of the Ministry of Supply, Lord Beaverbrook was charged with getting to the bottom of the article. He dispatched a number of officials to investigate and report back. The factory in the Midlands, had been identified as the Austin's Airframe Factory, in Birmingham. Where, it was alleged there was:

"...a great deal of idle time and that the men spend much of their time in air raid shelters, for which they are paid".

The report in the newspaper, had men complaining that they had nothing to do, and that the kettle was on all the time. The investigator found that the idle time was due to the change over, from production of the 'Battle' aircraft, to the 'Stirling' bomber, which was invariably going to create down time. Actually, there was less shelter time than the general population, as the factory 'spotter' system was particularly effective and enabled the workers to take shelter quite late. The investigator did say that the change of production had brought another change:

"A change of management of that section of the factory produced greatly accelerated results."

Other claims in the article from other locations had been much the same, a factory in Wales where jigs were changed and they were wrong for the wing tips that were being manufactured and assembled, and a factory in Manchester where a female munitions worker claimed that she had not done a week's work since February, and where the Rolls Royce engine production seemed slow. None of which when examined were true, the engine production rate was very good, and the young lady in question was still under her period of training.

None of the stories published stood up under scrutiny, and Lord Beaverbrook made that clear in his summing up, when he said:

"…the statements in the Daily Mirror cannot be justified…"

It was considered nothing to be over anxious about, and none of the Defence Notices had been infringed, so the story was ignored.

The Defence Notices continued to pose problems of interpretation and in 1942, there were concerns that editors were contravening notices by using astrological columns in their respective newspapers to relay that Germany was on the point of collapse, that and other anomalies, caused a further revision to the notices which took place in 1943. In that there was an amended notice concerning munitions:

Amended Defence notice – Trade & Supply No. 84

84. Munitions

(1) No information may be published concerning:

(i) The locality, output or nature of production of any arsenal or stores of munitions;

(ii) The production of supplies for use of the Government by any factory or works, including the locality and number of employee of such factory or works.

(2) No information should be published without submission to Censorship concerning:

(i) any housing scheme for munition workers;

(ii) any very large increase in population of a town or area owing to the presence of munition workers;

(iii) the compulsory billeting of munition workers in any town or area; or

(iv) the application of a Closure or Lodging Restriction Order in any town or area.

These changes had to come into operation to protect the many workers who were being forced to migrate to other cities such as Birmingham, under the Essential Work Orders, like Jenny. The Defence Notices were revised further in 1944 and 1945, but after that they began to be revoked right up until 1949.

There is no doubt that in a time of considerable press sensitivity they were very important not only as guidelines to anxious editors, but also as a control of public morale. Many scare stories could have been written at a time when Great Britain was defensively weak, this could have undermined the great efforts that were being employed to win the war. Some stories could have assisted German forces in finding a small chink into the defences of the country, just enough to turn the victory around to their side.

In the same way, we exploited our own weaknesses to design and proliferate a propaganda campaign for the German people to attempt to destabilise the Nazi regime. In The Home Office documentation there is a report entitled "Effects of Morale on Industrial Capacity" and within that file is a report 'Scope of propaganda in increasing the effects of air raids'. This is the research report conducted a year after the bad raids on Birmingham, and suggested ways of affecting the German people's morale based on the experiences in Birmingham. Some of the suggestions made included; creating rumour about people having been killed in factories and the danger to families living near by; factories being completely put out of action, or foremen keeping workers at production (in raids) in order to fulfil government contracts; that workers should demand full pay even if a factory was shut in the same way soldiers could. The thrust of the campaign seems to have been to create as much feeling of social injustice as possible amongst the civilian population, as these effects had been made manifest in Birmingham during the August and November raids of 1940. It is also known that the RAF took note of how much more damaging incendiaries had been than high explosives, and that was much exploited in the subsequent allied raids on Germany.

In my opinion the press blackout was not necessarily deliberately imposed on Birmingham anymore than it was on any other city. I believe a combination of circumstances came together quite fortuitously as it turns out, for the government, that enabled them to blackout the devastation of the city at that time. For it was probably the most important city, strategically to war production, and if the greater population of the country and been aware of how close Birmingham had come to utter destruction in that November, it could have seriously altered the outcome of the war. Managing the country's morale through the control of information, became a government imperative. Birmingham was not the only city to have such a press blackout imposed on it, Sheffield suffered the same anonymity during the December raids, and evidence exists that this was well reported in the German press, yet only received a cursory mention at home.

Chapter 11

IRIS AND THE ROAD
TO 'THE AUSTIN'

Imagine what it's like to have your birthday the day that your country declares war against another? Imagine what it is like to have a dreadful war within recent living memory, where millions died, from such atrocities as gas attacks, and fear that this time it would be happening to you at home?

For Iris Clarke these fears were real and tangible and the events that happened in September 1939 impacted on her very deeply as they did for all the others in this book. Iris was so moved by the events of that dark time, that she very kindly wrote some notes for me which I have added in her words, which paint a shocking picture. Iris is a very modest lady, living quietly on the outskirts of the city, in a more rural area. She spends her time between, her family, the songbirds she keeps and the many friends that she has made due her very active and creative life. She makes many beautiful things, the beadwork, so delicate and fine, that someone half her age would struggle with it. She has always been a talented seamstress, and paints fine pictures, she has won umpteen awards for her multi-talented works.

Iris recalls with sadness 3rd September 1939:

"I was 17 the day war was declared… I lived at the foot of the Lickey Hills."

What a birthday, I asked her more about how she felt, her apprehensions, she replied quietly and with care:

"It was a day I have never forgotten… well we all sat round listening to the Prime Minister… telling us… well everybody was crying… it was my birthday…"

A day that should have been filled with family celebration and love for a young girl, just turning 17, was a very depressing event. Like other families in this book, that grey Sunday morning they sat round listening to Mr Chamberlain, giving his solemn address to the nation at 11 o'clock in the morning.

She was with her father (Fred) and mother (Agnes), and elder sister (Muriel) and brother (Tom), each with their own fears and dreaded anticipations. Her father had particular fears, he like most of the other fathers mentioned in the book, had served in the Great War, he had been fortunate enough to make it through without physical injury, but he had lost a brother. He at this time was working at the 'Austin' as an upholsterer, or as it is pronounced in Birmingham, the 'orstin'. Her mother was working as a mental nurse, and was noted to be particularly sensitive and caring. She had a moderately sized family, with another daughter (Clara) who had died before Iris was born in 1919. Both of her parents feared the potential gas attacks, as people were aware that it was now possible in the 21 years that had elapsed for planes to carry trouble to home cities. There had been such a build up to the outbreak of war, much speculation had probably taken place, particularly for Iris's father with his work colleagues, as he worked at a factory which had already constructed a 'shadow' factory and was operational in the production of Stirling Bombers.

After Iris had left school at 14, she had gone to work as a seamstress for a lady in Northfield. By the time war broke out she must have been quite experienced having worked there for three years. Her manageress sounds like quite the enterprising sort because she was very good at identifying the next niche in the market. Initially, the population were prepared for the feared gas attacks, through the issue of a standard gas mask, which came in a gas mask box. A cumbersome and awkward thing to have to carry around. As Iris recalls:

"We all had boxes... with our gas masks in... well, course there was a problem because it was a box, so we made a bag with straps so you could carry them on your shoulder... so, for quite a few months it was non-stop making the little bag... (she chuckles)."

There must have been a high demand for these little bags, for Iris agrees that there must have been thousands produced in their little firm. Then Churchill was observed wearing a new item of clothing, he would now don a 'siren suit' whenever the air raid siren went. This was meant to be a suit which would, to some extent, seal a person from the gas. How effective they actually were is debatable, however, once Mr Churchill was seen wearing one they became an instant 'must have' to the populace at large, and another niche market to exploit.

As a worker in textiles, Iris was to some extent protected from compulsory work orders, because she could be making uniforms which were seen as vital to the war effort. Between, the gas mask bags, the siren suits and various uniform contracts, Iris was kept in gainful employment for the first half of the war. Particularly through the period of the terrible blitz on Birmingham, Iris writes in her own words:

"The bombing of Birmingham was shocking. I trembled from head to foot when I heard the sirens, the German planes had quite a different sound to our planes, so you knew when they were overhead. As the raids worsened people came out of the town to spend the night on the Lickeys, My mother took pity on a family of four and gave them shelter. They used to spend the nights with us and go back home in the mornings, that went on for weeks. The fact that Longbridge was never bombed I think, was the clever way they camouflaged the factory."

Iris was fortunate (compared to those living in the heart of the city) to live out towards the Lickeys, beyond where the 'Austin', Longbridge factory was situated. A point not lost on those who were seeking places to situate the 'shadow' factories, as the more rural they were the less likely they were to suffer from raids. Although there was some enemy action her way it was no way nearly as concentrated or intensive as it was over the central part of the city, which emphasises how centralised and targeted the German operations were. However, that is not to say that raids did not bring the same fear and dread that it brought to all, Iris writes:

"Once the sirens had gone, and the enemy planes were overhead, this was a very fearful time, as you never knew where the bombs were coming down. Our defensive ack ack guns were going off and the searchlights were on, it was a very traumatic time for everyone. On the night that the city was on fire, we saw the incendiary bombs dropping and because we were high up, we could see right the way across the city. You never knew where the bombs were going to fall, people were out with buckets of sand and shovels to put out the fires. We got no sleep, on nights like this and had to go to work the next day, and carry on working. I remember saying, if it wasn't so wicked the light display was like a fireworks display, with the lights coming down. But we knew what danger we were in and the reality of it all."

Like the others in this book, Iris describes the shelters as being 'cold and damp' and not very nice places to go to, as a consequence, seldom frequented by Iris, as she writes she took the 'risk of being bombed instead'.

The blitz did touch Iris's personal life, very deeply in November 1940. She had been put onto a contract to make and fit uniforms for nurses in a local hospital. There were two ladies in particular, that Iris had got to know and had got friendly with who were killed when a bomb struck The Woodlands Hospital in Northfield:

"...one was from Scotland and one was from Ireland... they were older than me... one was called Sister Galloway and the other was called Sister Daniels..."

According to Carl Chinn in an item of research from the Birmingham Post Supplement 8th May 1945:

"Two nursing sisters were killed at the Woodlands Hospital in Northfield, when three bombs hit the building as they were eating their supper..."

Iris was deeply distressed by this, especially as she had been working on their uniforms at the time they were killed.

The effects of rationing, began to have a detrimental effect on Iris's occupation:

"Well the sewing trade was getting very slack because of the rationing... it was cheaper and better to buy, than to have them made... because by the yard you spent more on coupons you see, so that was why it was coming to a very slow end..."

She says that she knew she had to do something, something more important to help the war effort:

"...they were telling you that you had to go, in the papers, those that were not in essential jobs, had to go into the Army, or the Land Army..."

She has qualified this since in her writings, in that she had no desire to leave home, and she decided to follow her sister into the factory at the age of 19. It must have helped already having two close family members working there, her sister and her father, although he was in the factory that had been producing cars. Iris decided to report for work at the 'Austin Aero' and went to see the Personnel Office there. She was the only woman to report for work that day, though according to Iris, the factory itself was employing hundreds, she describes the place as 'massive'.

According to Iris, at the Austin Aero, they recruited women to work as labourers to the men, generally one woman to one man. They also had a 'leading hand' as an overseer. At that stage in the war the efforts at Austin Aero were concentrated on the production of the Stirling bomber. As we have read in other chapters, the Austin had experienced particular problems in fulfilling their previous government contracts, and the Air Ministry did not have full confidence in them. However, there was always a shortage of aircraft, so any that were produced were desperately needed, the Austin plodded on.

Iris was set to work helping to assemble the wingtips, as she recalls:

"...there were six of us putting on the wing, and my partner, was putting on the wingtip."

This was not a speedy process, and they could only assemble two a week. The women were given difficult and awkward jobs to do:

"We didn't have half of what the men... we had the dirty work to do... we all worked with a man... you just went in and you did what you were told... there was no training (she laughs)."

She added to this later when she wrote:

"But the men had full responsibility. Work had to be very accurate. Every stage of the operation had to be inspected as the safety of our airmen was paramount."

It was a particularly obscure section to work on, and a great deal of the task required the women to use mirrors inside the sections of the wing they were responsible for, Iris explains:

"Well, there was the riveting... we'd got concertina rivets... and then we'd got the guns... they'd drill the holes, well if you could imagine, I don't know whether I can explain it to you, I could draw you a drawing, inside the wing was like trellis work... there was a square there at the bottom, where you used to have to go up... with mirrors... we used to have a dolly... a chappie used to be on top of the wing, and we was inside... well you could just about get part of you inside... you used to have to get the dolly, and wait for the rivet to come down, and then you had to hold the dolly, while they gunned it down."

She further explained this in her written additions:

"The men were putting the rivets in and we signalled from inside to let them know you were ready to receive the gun, from the inside. Vibration was taking place and you had to be very precise in sealing the panel."

Iris started there in 1941, and she had gone from non-shift work to shift work which must have been a shock to her system:

"...I worked a fortnight about... I did from 8 o'clock to 5.30... and then for a fortnight, and then... for the next fortnight we went on nights... and that was from 7 o'clock till 6.30 in the morning."

She was pleasantly surprised by the amount she was getting paid, as a seamstress she had been taking home about £2 per week, at the Austin Aero that rose to the considerable sum for a woman of £5 per week, but no doubt still substantially less than the men were getting paid. Of her partner there she recalls:

"Well I was fortunate, I had a nice one that I worked with... he was a very kind and very nice chappie... I was very fortunate... but some of them they were really dreadful to the girls..."

She wrote, that she never got used to the bad language and the way they spoke to the girls. And the place itself was cavernous, having to hold numbers of fully constructed bombers, Iris remembers the bleakness of nightshift work:

"...the night work used to get me down... I used to feel the cold so much... it was a big barn of a place..."

She recalls in her writing that 'shift work at the Austin took up substantial amounts of her time' and that with the hazards of the blackout and having to carry torches, made the few dances that did happen, difficult to attend, especially with everything finishing by 10 o'clock:

"You didn't get a lot of social life... there were cinemas to go to... I can remember going one afternoon, I was on nights and I went to the pictures... in the afternoon, and the sirens went... and I just stayed put (laughing)... it went off one afternoon when I was at the cinema..."

And in the same raid:

"...my sister, who worked at 'The Austin' as well... she was actually machine gunned going to the shelter... by a German, and he was brought down... I think it was in the Tewkesbury area..."

She recalls a particularly sad story:

"...I lost a friend at Arnhem... he was in the parachute... he was a friend from home... it was rather sad... he met a girl in London and they married, and she came to Birmingham and she got two rooms, one up and one down, and they went out and bought the furniture but he never saw it... in their home"

And of the hardships of war such as the rationing, Iris recollects:

"Well we never really went hungry you know... because people helped each other and shared what they had... the most difficult thing that my mother had problems with, was tea... but a neighbour would always come, when we were nearly at the end of it..."

She does not feel particularly hard done by, to her everyone was in the same boat. Things teenage girls take for granted now were either in very limited supply or simply not available, but as Iris says:

"We just got on with it... there wasn't the clothes about that there is today... (she chuckles)... we only had small wardrobes, so you can tell how many clothes we had..."

By far the best thing about the Austin Aero and the opportunities given by wartime for Iris, was meeting her husband Eric, like for others in this book, had she not been thrust into this artificial work environment, heavily masculine-centred, she would not have had the chance to meet him. A meeting that in a place that employed hundreds and was the size of multiple aircraft hangers, was chance anyway, as she recalls, with glee:

"I met him going to the loo (she laughs)... we used to have to wear dungarees... the loos were down this passageway... my husband was working on this section you see, where no women worked… well two of us were walking down and met two girls who were walking back, and of course we were all talking together, and all of the men were (she wolf whistles)… the day after I went on nights and I thought nothing more about it… well on the Monday morning I came back onto days… and I went to the loo to put on my dungarees on you see, and there was this man with a big grin on his face… and I turned round to see who he was grinning at… and it was me…"

The Austin Aero came to an end as a manufacturer of Stirling bombers, as the plane was considered too cumbersome and it was succeeded by other more efficient planes. Iris had got together with Eric, and they were married in 1944, at St Lawrence church in Northfield.

They managed the wedding by saving their coupons to buy her wedding dress, whereas Iris being an excellent seamstress could have made her own, but the material in coupons would have cost more. They had a chocolate cake through her cousin who was in in the Catering Corps. All her family and friends got together to provide a 'tin of this and a tin of that' to help the festivities go with a swing. They were lucky enough to have a reception for about twenty people, in the hall over the Co-op on Bristol Road. She was fortunate enough to have a bouquet of beautiful red tulips, which stand out from her white wedding dress, on the colourised photograph she keeps.

The couple shared two rooms in West Heath in Birmingham with a friend of Eric's. She continued to work at the Austin until the end of the production of the Stirling, and then she had a son, who was born in 1946.

Eric was called up towards the end of 1944 into the Royal Signals, eight months after they were married. He had been protected from call up due to his age and finishing his apprenticeship. It must have been quite a change joining the army, from having been a sheet metal worker at Longbridge. He was posted to India and then to Singapore. When he was eventually demobbed in 1946, he applied to, and was accepted for the Warwickshire Constabulary.

She remembers, the first Police house that her and Eric were given to use: "Yes we got a police house in Sutton and it was like going back in time… because the house was a rented house it wasn't a police house… and it was all gas… with an old black grate, and a boiler in the kitchen and no running hot water… and I went back to a zinc bath! And a loo up the garden… I had to put up with that for four and a half years…"

She managed to bring up her toddler in those conditions as well. However Eric was not for the city, he wanted 'a country beat' and he got it in Curdworth. That changed their outlook on life totally, and they were happy there for nineteen and a half years. Eric as the country beat policeman, would have made many friends and been well respected, and as the policeman's wife, Iris, in her own right earned the same respect and friendships, which are still there for her to this day. Her daughter was born in Curdworth in 1955. Sadly, Eric died in 1999, three months after they romantically celebrated their 55th wedding anniversary in Paris.

So the war and the 'Austin Aero' brought Iris many significant opportunities and experiences that peacetime probably would never have had, as she says:

"...I have a lot to thank 'The Austin' for."

FOR IRIS

Stitch, stitch, we win the war,
Stitch, stitch, another stitch more.
Stitch, stitch, with nice neat ends,
Stitch, stitch, for my dear friends.

Bomb, bomb, down they came,
Bomb, bomb, more the same,
Bomb, bomb, fall down on our head,
Bomb, bomb, my dear friends are dead.

Drill, drill, hang onto the dolly,
Drill, drill, here comes the rivet, golly!
Drill, drill, we smack it back,
Drill, drill, now that is that.

Chapter 12

WIN'S WAR

Win Hinton is the elder lady of her family, a part of a close community, which was accentuated by her daughter Pat, joining in on the day I interviewed her, which helped to add detail to her story. Win is 87 years old, but you don't call her Winifred, just Win. Like other ladies that I have interviewed, she hasn't moved far from where it all began. She is a very composed person, I don't think that Win is one to panic, or worry unduly, she just gets on with things.

Her parents came from Solihull originally, and during the war her aunt still lived over that way, not far from Grove Road, as Win reflects at that time Solihull was considered to be very rural. Her father had been a prisoner of war in the Great War, as had her uncle (her mother's brother). Win's family name was Patrick, and before the war the family lived in Bournbrook, an area associated to Cadbury's, being situated so close. Her parents were called Ellen and George, and Win had three brothers; Maurice, Sid and Phil. The whole family, including grandparents (Annie and Harry), and in-laws, lived in Bournbrook, in fact they all lived in the same road, George Road.

She left school when she was 14 in 1934 and started work for Boxfoldia making cartons, in her words:

"I left school on the Friday and started work on the Monday."

She met her husband before the war they worked together for a while and then he worked for 'The Austin', prior to his call up. The day that war broke out she was living in Kings Norton, her daughter was 6 months old, the day was nothing special to her, as she says:

"I didn't really take any notice, it was just an ordinary day to me."

As her daughter says, things didn't really effect some people immediately, they just sort of 'erupted' much later on. Win says that her next door neighbour reminded her:

"Don't get panicking and running, she said, remember you're a soldier's daughter!"

At that time she was looking after her daughter in Kings Norton, then in 1940 she moved to a cottage on Bristol Road and H. C. Ward had started recruiting in 1941, so she went to work for them, leaving her baby in the care of her grandmother:

"She was the best carer in the business" Win reflects.

And at Ward's, Win did a bit of everything, she continues:

"Well they make everything, they make the machines from scratch. Even to the screw... I shaped the gears out of a piece of steel... they had every department you could think of where they made different things... the drill shop... another section where they made the screws... the grinders..."

Her daughter can remember at 5 or 6 years of age, watching the big capstans tied down with big 'hawser', leaving the factory gates in the large lorries, which emphasises the important role that Ward's had in the war effort. It 'made the machines that made the munitions', and the level of skill of any person working there had to be high. Win states:

"All over the world they went, they used to say if you can get a job at Ward's you can get a job anywhere!"

When the men were called up, women were called up for Ward's to fill in. She worked through till the birth of her second child in 1947. There weren't that many women working there, although some conscripted women were brought from Scotland to supplement the workforce. According to Win, a few thousand men worked there with possibly a hundred women, and they worked for a flat rate of just over a £1 a week, with a bonus once a month, depending on what they had turned out in that month.

"Sometimes we used to get two or three quid extra, we used to go barmy then."

She says.

"I went on this capstan to learn from scratch, a lathe, I learnt to do the gears and that's what I stopped on, that and something else, a rod. I used to have to use a micrometre. I used to have to be spot on, to a thousandth."

She reflects on the good times that they used to have there, although she never stayed in the canteen for lunch because she only lived around the corner, she can remember the concerts that the workers had. She says laughingly:

"Me and our mum, used to get our dinner and whatever, and a cup of tea and go back and listen to what was on... It was only what they had got on between themselves, people in the factory. I mean Stan James, oooh he'd got a wonderful voice, he was a singer. And then there was Arthur the capstan man, used to play the trumpet, oooh he could play the trumpet, course he was in a band, and there was different ones that could do different things."

She reminisces that the raids were interesting, Ward's had their own shelters which were situated up on the canal bank, and rather than go to them, they used to stand on the canal bank and watch the dog fights.

"When the bombing was really bad, and I would be there most nights, I come back (one night) and I'd got no windows, there wasn't a window in the house... Just inside Hubert Road, all the houses were flattened, and nobody got hurt!"

She says amazed:

"We used to watch the dog fights over 'The Austin's'".

They remember the 27th August, 1940, the night the Germans got the Market Hall in Birmingham, according to Win's daughter they had been trying to get the railway line near Heeley Road and they missed and that's how they got Hubert Road as well. As for repairs, it seems she was lucky and her windows were covered temporarily and then replaced very quickly.

Her husband George was called up as a fitter to the RAF, he used to load the bombs onto the aircraft. He was stationed in the last 'post' in India before the 'Japs' took it, and quite literally as he left, it fell, later he was in Ceylon (Trincomalee) and he was very lucky not to have been taken prisoner. By all accounts the fleeing British troops took some flack, her husband got wounded and was sent to the military hospital at Mae Khalung (better known as the hospital in the film 'The Bridge Over The River Kwai').

"He got blowed into a ditch, his head was bad."

She remembers her daughter used to walk him up and down the garden, they used to joke about him being bald, he used to laugh and say it was the sun. But they later found out, his treatment had involved UV light and he had fallen asleep in front of it, on one or more occasion. When he had left to fight, he had a full head of wavy hair, and when he was demobbed in 1946, he just had hair round the sides.

The house that she lived in at the time she owed to her tight-knit family. Her Aunt Floss (Win's mother's sister) had a family who had been called up and she wanted a smaller house and thought of Win needing somewhere bigger to live, with her growing family. Win describes living in a little cottage, with a pokey kitchen and a big room, with two rooms upstairs, they lived there till Pat was 11. It almost backed on to Win's grandparents' garden, which meant that it was easy to let her little girl climb over the wall and walk the eighty yards to her great-grandparents house. She was very lucky to have a close and supportive family who as she says "all pulled together" she continues:

"to tell you the truth, we never really went without anything. My husband being in Ceylon, used to send me a box of tea... and then he'd send my mother a box of tea and that's how we'd go on."

When clothing was required, she used to turn to the black-market, like many others, she says in hushed tones;

"Where it come from?... you never asked".

They tried to keep Christmas as they had before, and very lucky for them they had turkey, which her daughter remembers fondly helping to pluck, over a big tin oval bath. The lack of refrigeration meant that everything was fresh. Win's grandmother, still made the Christmas pudding and the mincemeat. Paper chains made out of gummed, coloured papers strips, were lovingly assembled by available willing hands. One memorable Christmas was when the 'yanks' had arrived, Win's cousin George, turned up with 'a couple of coloured girls'. Win's grandfather was slightly 'taken aback', all had a really nice Christmas and enjoyed each others company immensely. Win reflects:

"During the war, were some of the best Christmases we ever had."

This spirit of pulling together, translated into every area of life, Win recalls how special events called for some special skills, when there was a wedding everybody would do something or supply something, wedding dresses were loaned, food found. One of Win's talents was bottling fruit, which could be used on such occasions. Birthdays were not such an event, they were not considered so important until the American influences, came and went.

Win never really used to venture out in the blackout, though her daughter reminds her towards the latter part of the war, that Pat as a little girl used to go to the shelter under Burtons with her grandad and more often than not, the one in the park, probably whilst Win was on nights.

When she had been working at Ward's for a short while, her foreman said to her that he thought she ought to see Mr Ward and ask for a rise, she continues:

"...I went down and I got half a crown... there were four of us that got the rise..."

Her daughter remembers waiting outside for her mother and grandmother to finish, and the surge of thousands of men coming out the factory. Win's says that sometimes:

"Our mum used to have Pat (her daughter) of a night, and we used to go out a group of us... that was nice... we was treated like they was."

So, Win used to find the men easy to work with and she never had any problems. In her words she had some 'lovely times there', especially the times when presentations were made. Her own mother was presented with a gold watch for long service, made by the queen's jewellers. Her mother had been in her 70's when she had finally retired, in Win's words:

"My mother had worked at Ward's... my mother and my grandmother."

They had been employed in the same way in the Great War, as Win was in the Second World War. As her daughter emphasises, women like Win and her mother, and her grandmother had kept production going and received no recognition for the service they had given, and more so, women who had filled shells and suffered from poisoning and explosion. They were not recognised at the time, so as not as to give information to the enemy and they have not been recognised since.

It was a time as Win says:

"When you all helped one another. You never shut your doors to anyone."

With the same spirit all those in the neighbourhood pulled together, and Win's mother had a simple philosophy:

"Always pay your bills, keep a roof over your head and a good pair of boots... and a bed to lie on, you can make do with the rest."

In her opinion (and Pat's), young people these days rely too much on credit, instead of making do, and building things up slowly by not borrowing, they expect all things 'yesterday'. At the time of this interview, the looming 'credit crunch' was a glimmer on the horizon, how wise they are. Win even decorated her house, and put up curtain rails and shelves, because she had to, and her mother did the same, a very practical woman. Once George had returned, things were different, and he liked to do it all.

The saddest story that Win recounted to me during our interview was the story of her brother Maurice's death and the subsequent effect that it had on another member of her family. Her brother Maurice had been serving in the Navy and had been killed in February 1943 while at sea, she says:

"He was 20 years old in the December, and he was killed in the February."

But Maurice had a big fan in the family, their cousin Len, who looked on Maurice as an older brother, there was 7 months between them. They had been inseparable and had always gone everywhere together, except to war because Len had been too young to enlist at that time. Eventually, Len did enlist in the Navy. Len was devastated by his cousin's death, she says that:

"He joined... they'd be called the commandos today, but it was a special unit... when he joined up he said 'I will kill every German I lay me hands on' and he did."

She continues:

"You couldn't write to him, you had to write to the War Office, he'd got no rank or number... they used to go in the midget submarines... they was on Anzio beaches, the actual landings, they was already there. And then they put him to the Japs and that's what done him in."

She reflects carefully:

"They were putting them big mines on Jap ships... and he was bringing his pal up... his air pipe... he come up too quick... and he hit his back on the ship... and they never heard... my aunt Floss, where he was or what he was doing for nine months... he was in Australia in a hospital... and when he come home he was as white as the driven snow... and they sent him for a cruise when he come back to the West Indies... the doctor on board the ship was his own doctor at home."

He won the Military Cross, though the feeling was he should have won the Victoria Cross for what he'd done.

Win's husband George was demobbed in 1946 and when he came back it was a really bad winter, so he helped clearing the roads, and then on the many construction sites around the city. Win carried on at Ward's till 1947 just before her second child, she did try to go back for a short while after, but she couldn't settle and felt that George didn't like her working there with all those men. Her brothers Sid and Phil went off to work for 'The Austin' and Land Rover respectively.

And what became of the air raid shelters? They became stage sets and dancing studios for the likes of Pat and her friends, who put on many a show in their purpose built little theatres. As Win says:

"There are a lot of people worse off than me."

She has her family, who all look out for her. The sense of community is very evident, and the sense of family that builds that community is what comes through strongly, Win is certainly very fortunate to have so much support, and in such close proximity, so many have not.

FOR WIN

Any day now, they say,
The bombs will come.
Any day now, this
War will be on.
Any day now, we will be
Fighting through.
Any day now, I will be
With you.

Any day now, there's a
War to win.
Any day now, our
Lives will begin.
Any day now, all dreams
Will come true.
Any day now, I will be
With you.

Any day now, there will
Be an end.
Any day now, my love
I will send.
Any day now, you know
It's true,
Any day now, I will be
With you.

Chapter 13

SUDS AND SINGING – REFLECTIONS ON EVERYDAY LIFE

"LOUDSPEAKER. DOWN TOOLS. SEVENTEEN HOURS. DOWN TOOLS. THE PIECE-WORK WAY MEANS BETTER PAY"

(The Shadow Factory – A Play – Anne Ridler, 1945)

There is no doubt that the war changed the pattern and rhythm of life for everyone, probably no more profoundly than for the many women that found themselves thrust into factory life. Whereas their lives would have been shaped by a short period of work, probably not in a factory, followed by courting, marriage and motherhood, the war forced extreme differences to that pattern. Those working before the war that had married and had the marriage bar applied on them, like Win and Evelyn, found themselves back at work through the Essential Work Order. Those that had started in factories pre-war and were unmarried, as were Daisy, Eileen, Iris (flag) and Kathleen, found their production changed over to munitions. The others Iris and May had been in occupations previously protected were compelled by government edict into factory working, as did Jenny with the added trauma of transferring many miles from her own home.

Marriage became either delayed by the effects of being parted from a boyfriend, or not having the opportunity to meet anyone. All normal social opportunities had changed, in some cases horizons were broadened, Iris met her husband at the Austin, Jenny met hers at the BSA, May and Kathleen did not meet their future husbands till after the end of the war. Some marriages became an urgent necessity from fear and emotion, and then these relationships had to endure a forced separation, followed by housing and employment problems after the war.

Families were fractured by the mobilisation of the majority of the male population, many young children were evacuated for their safety. Women found themselves with immense responsibilities that they had not had to deal with pre-war. Food and clothing were in short supply and rationed as a consequence. Entertainment may have been considered too frivolous or inappropriate and as such was muted. During the bad period of raiding, entertainment was very limited, or curtailed when the sirens went off, and the necessary public transport ceased operation making any journey, potentially, a very dangerous undertaking. Life had always been centred around the home and hearth, and if anything during the war years it became more so.

Throughout the entire duration of the war the home-front life emerged, evolved, and changed, it was severely disrupted by the panic and devastation of the raids, and then settled into new rhythms, that surrounded the factory shifts, the need to shop for food, look after the family and the home, 'to keep the home fires burning'.

Before the war, for those that worked in factories life had been relatively simple. The lived near where they worked, the women in this book were at this point in time, generally unmarried women living at home with their parents. They had left school and had the expectation on them to earn a living not only to pay their way, but also contribute substantially to the household income. They worked in private factories where conditions varied dramatically, some were fortunate to have a canteen of sorts, but most would take sandwiches. They were normal girls in their late teens, sharing cosmetics, dressing their hair into the latest fashions, making the best of what they had (Todd, 2005). With the advent of the war the emphasis shifted, they became the majority workforce within the first few months.

They found themselves, on new machines possibly making new things, with little training or explanation. Rates were set, and they were set to work to achieve their targets, the more they made, the more they were paid. This rise in income brought the opportunities to buy small things, unless of course most was going in 'keep' to their parents, but shortages were now a problem. With the whole of the country being turned over to war production, of one form or another, things were not so easy to come by, they had either been stockpiled, or were no longer being manufactured. Money could be spent on a night out, a trip to the cinema, or the Hippodrome on a Saturday afternoon (if it did not conflict with their shifts), or go to a dance hall, like Amy's or the Palais de Danse (if their parents permitted). After all, these were a new generation of younger women with greater social freedoms, many of their mothers had worked during the Great War and had led the way of emancipation for their daughters.

Most would have gone home after work, to help their mothers with the younger children. The mothers had shopped for food, and once rationing had been instigated collected the rations for the families, and stood in long queues for goods that were more difficult to buy. Food had to be cooked for the family, a house needed cleaning, younger children needed entertaining. In their own time, those that could, turned their hands to a bit of needlework, while material could still be obtained, making something for themselves. Throughout the war, the Ministry of Information and the Ministry of Food, published various small booklets as guides, such as; 'Wise Eating in Wartime', 'Make Do and Mend', 'How to Keep Well in Wartime', and 'The ABC of Cookery'. These information books were used to help the housewife make the best of rationing and recycling.

The wireless which had become such a focus in a home pre-war, took on an even more important role in wartime. Whereas, it had been the entertainment for the women, while they washed, ironed and sewed (Beddoe, 1989). It became the link to their male relations and friends progress abroad, it became a communication channel from the government of what was to be done, it gave the escapism in drama and laughter, and subliminally reinforced the 'must do your bit' message. Even the comedy which became so popular to lift wartime morale, pushed the war effort by poking fun at bureaucracy (Gardiner, 2004). ITMA (It's That Man Again), featuring the Ministry of Aggravation and Mysteries, with the Officer of Twerps made light of the ever prevailing officialdom.

In April 1940, life changed and became a chaotic and unstable time. All the rhythms that had been adjusted to, were fractured on an almost daily basis, it was more important to get from day to day through each raid, than to plan for anything. Getting to and from work, posed a problem for these girls. After a raid, there was the smashed remains of what had happened the night before, sometimes prohibiting buses from running, hose pipes and rubble making walking hazardous. At the end of their day, they could be caught running for service shelters, unable to reach the safety of home, finding the bus that they should have been travelling on with the lights out and the bus stopped. Evenings were a critical time, many of these spent in the make-shift shelters at home, cold and damp, meals curtailed and spent in blackness, fear prevailed constantly. Sleep was disrupted for days, making each successive day even more difficult to cope with, and the long arduous, monotony of working on a production line on piece-work rates dangerous due to sleep deprivation.

Life became urgent and to be lived for the 'here and now', those that could get out and enjoy themselves, would take the opportunity to do so, anything to change the pattern of fear. In some ways, it was better to be caught in a cinema in a film during a raid, at least the escapism into a fantasy world, in the 'pictures' was better than the alternatives. "Gone With The Wind" went on general release in the early part of the war, and provided the colour and romance that many found missing from their lives. It was also a very long film, and as such an excellent evening's entertainment. Many films were released to promote wartime patriotism, such as; "In Which We Serve" (1942), "Millions Like Us" (1943) and "The Way To The Stars", which were to keep the support for the war at the forefront of people's minds.

Then there were the dance halls, as Kathleen recounted being in the YMCA at a dance during such a time, they carried on dancing. These little breaks in the unfolding dramas, and the relieving of the tensions of daily living were vital to everyone, but particularly to young people. And if the journey home, meant a long and dangerous walk as in the case of Iris (flag) or Daisy, it was better to be in the familiar surroundings of their home territory, than to be forced to spend the night in a packed, inhospitable, city-centre shelter, the risk was worth taking whatever.

For a year, they endured the almost nightly torment and everyone must have breathed a collective sigh of relief by the time of May 1941, when the blitz subsided, even if there was some persistent anxiety that it may return. By this time, the Essential Work Order was coming into being, the whole of the country was being turned over to the Total War Economy (Appendix 1). The vast majority of those that could work in Britain, were being compelled to work in one form of war production or another. This is no more true than in Birmingham, which was the industrial beating-heart of the nation, and by logistical circumstances had ended up with the most strategic production concentration of aircraft and arms as compared to any other industrial centre. Everyone was needed, and many more from other places besides. By 1942, when all of these ladies were employed in their wartime work what was life like in and out of the factories? What did an average day in their lives consist of?

Jenny's day started with two-pieces of toast and a bus ride to the BSA in Hall Green, May had a very long bus ride from Balsall Heath to Solihull. When the girls arrived at their respective establishments, clocking-in the punching of the time card ensued. Win used to enter the enormous gates at H. C. Wards, through a foyer, clock-in and then into the cavernous workshop that seemed to stretch for miles, filled with many machine tools, constructing more machine tools to fill the unremitting constant need, which then went to build all those things so desperately required for the war effort.

Iris used to have to change into her dungarees before she could start work, probably wearing a turban on her head. Many refused to do so, for fear of flattening their carefully coiffured hairstyle, rolled around a stocking as was the fashion of the time, for there was no hairspray to anchor unruly locks. Some factories had purpose built facilities for the girls to change in, but many were built without thought to those needs, leaving girls to change in toilets.

Then to the machines, a machine that they may have already spent three years on, in a production line. Machines that were built before the days of the Health and Safety Executive, poorly guarded and constantly in production, so very dirty. The work was set by themselves generally and required suds to cool the cutting or milling operations, suds that ran down their aprons into their shoes, that damaged hands and nails through constant use, without barrier creams. Their shifts were long, and piece-work rates were driven by volume to earn the money, only the works entertainment could break the monotony many had 'music while you work', which brought the much needed cheer and distraction. In some cases the government made provision for both canteens and speakers for the 'music while you work'. Jenny talks of singing along, though the noise of her machine drowned her voice and innate shyness. Iris (flag), she used to sing along to them all, and cry when she sang the sad songs.

Under the Provision of Canteens and amenities in Factories Engaged on War Work, a factory employing 250 persons or more should install a canteen, but employers were not obliged to do so. Only the government factories, such as the Royal Ordnance factories and Agency factories had these facilities built and supplied by the government, the others if they were considered stable were offered government loans.

As a consequence, many factories only had what was already in existence pre-war, and may have taken some assistance to install speakers but not necessarily. The new 'shadow factories' had been built with all of the facilities, and proper changing and rest rooms, but most of girls experiences are of poor facilities, which did not offer the same comforts. The war brought the revolution for the sales of Tampax for women, as the pre-war alternatives were not practical for those standing on the production line for 12 hour shifts, with no adequate toilet facilities (Gardiner, 2004).

The camaraderie of the production line, was as true for the women as it had been for the men that preceded them, but probably more so. These were difficult and sad times. Girls made friends with their neighbouring girls, they shared intimacies and laughter and sadness. When a husband was injured or killed, when a bomb fell on a neighbouring street, all was shared and comforts given by these others who lived with the same constant fears everyday. Those that worked on the vast production lines, share common stories of old men that were very nice and supportive.

These were the men who were too old to fight, left behind to work, the younger ones who were reserved set and maintained machines, made machine tools, they were the skilled workers. Working often as not, in separate areas, the women worked in one vast section they worked in another, there was very little fraternisation. As a result, only limited contact and a 'them and us' mentality, which only seemed to reinforce the 'otherness'. The women were still 'outsiders' doing a job that would not last, and they would eventually be gone. Only Iris at the Austin, had a very different story of negative behaviours and language towards the women, probably because of the very different working practices. The women there had to partner with the men, and work in a small team with a leading hand, this meant there was much more daily contact and possibilities for derisory comments, regarding substandard working by the women.

The arduous shift was only broken by a lunch break, for most it was a chance to step outside, breathe clean air and eat the sandwiches that they had brought from home, rather than eat in an unappealing canteen. Others, loved their canteens, a chance for a hot meal, in Jenny's case it was a decent hot meal, she had survived on two slices of toast since breakfast. There was not much in terms of variety, meat was in short supply, it was mainly vegetables, but it often had the accompaniment of a 'turn'. A talented employee, singing a song or playing a musical instrument. At the Rover, May was fortunate enough to have a restroom to go to after her lunch before the start of the second half of her shift.

Every now and then a special event would happen, it may be a show put on in the works canteen by the workers, 'Me and My Girl' at The Hercules with the loan of Iris (flag) and her wedding dress. Or the night, that Daisy got the surprise of her life, to find Joe Loss and his band in their canteen. It must have been such a thrill and what a change from the long endlessly, cold nights working, to be dancing to such an amazing act in their factory.

Many other factories, especially the government owned Royal Ordinance Factories, were fortunate enough to have more professional shows courteously of ENSA and CEMA. ENSA (Entertainment National Service Association) was set up primarily for the entertainment of the troops, but did tour various lucky munitions factories. CEMA (Council for the Encouragement of Music and Arts) was seen to be the more cultural alternative, offering a classical entertainment, and viewed by some as less accessible for the masses, particularly Ernest Bevin (Gardiner, 2004). There are some records from the Ministry of Labour, of both organisations making the odd trip to Birmingham. In 1943, ENSA proposed a tour of 10 cities (Birmingham was one), although none of the women in this book can recall any such show coming to their places of work. However, it is more likely that CEMA, which tended to use less well known classical artists did appear at some factories, as they toured with much greater frequency and tended to be used by ENSA to fill in where the larger ENSA troop could not appear. The CEMA organiser in Birmingham, Mr H. G. Vincent, reported that the CEMA tour that took place between 7th and the 24th of July, 1941, had been 'a great success'

Pilots and other air force personnel were sent on morale visits to factories, to provide inspiration to those who were employed in the making of the aircraft. Just occasionally, politicians and royalty would make surprise visits to cities and factories, again to boost morale. Very little evidence remains of these visits, for security reasons they were kept very quiet. Both Iris and Eileen talk of General de Gaulle's visit to the Austin and the BSA, however actual recorded documentation is probably not in existence. Although Queen Elizabeth, the Queen Mother, is known to have visited the BSA and there is some evidence at the National Archive of other royal visits, none of that particular visit remains. Which leads me to believe that there were possibly a number of such visits particularly by Churchill and other royals for which we have no recorded information.

King George VI is recorded to have visited the Austin on the 11th March, 1938, when the push to re-arm was becoming a priority and the Austin factory being one of the first 'shadow aircraft factories' was commencing the work. He had originally, planned to make the visit to two or three of the shadow factories (Austin, Rover, Daimler, Humber and Standard) in the previous year, but the palace had been advised by Thomas Inskip, that none of the factories were in full operation and that it would be a very long day to see very little. Sir Thomas wrote at that time that he considered that:

> "...I believe any visits that the king can pay will not only be tremendously appreciated by the workers, but will be of real value in giving prominence to the wide range of new activities in our re-armament programme."

At that time, because of the practicalities of arranging a trip to the Midlands and concerns regarding the King's health, he was restricted to London and Bristol. Early in 1938, the palace enquired if it would be possible to arrange a visit to the Midlands.

Inskip felt that it would be possible, but that it would be more advantageous if the King could visit all five (which were located closely together with three in Coventry and two in Birmingham). The plan that Inskip suggested was that:

"He might take the train which would run into the Austin siding at Birmingham where He would see the construction of both air-frame and aero-engines. From there He would pass to the Rover Aero-Engine Factory and a short ride would take Him to Coventry where the Daimler, Humber and Standard aero-engine shadow factories are all situated."

Further he added:

"...I should suggest His going to the Austin and Rover factories at Birmingham, partly because Lord Austin is Chairman of the Shadow factory Committee and partly because He will see both sides of the shadow factory work, i.e. both air-frames and aero-engines."

The visit was duly arranged, and the King travelled up by train the night before to undertake the visit the next day. The report in The Times, recorded the following:

"Birmingham, March 10.

The King has visited to-day five of the shadow factories engaged in aircraft production for the Government. To the inexpert mind there would seem to be little shadow about it and much substance – endless miles, that is, of machines unceasingly at work turning rough steel into highly finished parts... It has been throughout a day of interest, mainly in seeing a great variety of mechanical processes and occasionally of learning of some skilled operator having come into this active branch of industry from the depression of the special areas."

Of the day itself, The Times records the following:

"The royal visit has been a private occasion in that it has been free from civic and other formal ceremonies. The King arrived at Birmingham last night and the Royal train remained at a siding of the Austin factory Longbridge, and the King was received by Lord Austin, chairman of the Austin Motor Company, Limited, and others connected with the firm."

The Times records in some detail the two Birmingham visits:

"AIRFRAMES AND ENGINES

The Austin factory, for the manufacture of airframes and aero-engines, covers 15 acres of ground. Production is in hand on about 75 per cent. of various components of "battle" aircraft, and in the aero-engines section crankshafts, reduction gears, oil supply and controls for V.P. airscrews are being manufactured for the Bristol "Mercury VIII" engine.

The first process which the King watched was the blanking of main plane ribs in a 350-ton hydraulic press. From that he went onto see the assembly of the fuselage and the welding of fuel tanks. The assembly of wing ribs was watched with special interest by the King, who spoke to some of the men about their work. In the engine section of the factory propeller tests were in progress, and those who looked on were provided with cotton wool to deaden the terrific noise in their ears. As he left the factory the King was cheered with great enthusiasm by the vast crowd of workers who had gathered at the main entrance.

The royal party travelled by road to Rover factory at Acocks Green on the other side of Birmingham, and at many places along the route there were dense crowds of people who cheered as the King's car passed on its way. Occasionally the children of a school on the route were lined up and joined with great vigour in the cheering.

At the Rover factory the King was received by Mr. E. Ransom-Harrison, chairman of the Rover Motor Company, Limited. The factory is engaged in the manufacture of connecting-rods, pistons, valves, and gears for the Bristol "Mercury VIII" engine. Among the many operations which the King watched with close interest was the sodium filling of valves. This has still to done by hand, and the young man inserting a sodium "worm" into a very small bore of a valve managed his task bravely in the circumstances of the day."

The King realised the importance of such visits in boosting morale (and production) in the factories. In 1939, it was suggested that he make a special message to be addressed to munitions workers to help with the production drive at the same time he asked to make more tours of factories. Included in his extensive itinerary was a visit to ICI Metals Limited (formerly Kynoch Limited), which he made on 26th October, 1939, there is also some reference to visiting the BSA in Redditch though no detail remains. He expressly stated at that time that he felt it was inappropriate for any member of the government to accompany him, as it was considered that this would attract publicity which he did not want. This may explain why no more of his visits were recorded in detail, combined with the added press censorship.

He received an information booklet from I.C.I. Metals Limited explaining its connections to Kynoch Limited, and the processes that were undertaken there. According to the information given, the factory was by then covering an area of 300 acres, and employing 6,000 personnel. In his visit the King toured most of the departments there, and was introduced to the many processes and operations that were being undertaken to produce shells and small munitions.

Churchill's visits were particularly welcome as excellent motivators to the workforce across the country, he is known to have made many visits in and around the Midlands, again limited evidence at the National Archive remains. One visit is recorded, a two day trip that he made to Coventry, Birmingham and Liverpool, on the 26th and 27th September 1941. It seems he had planned to visit the previous October, but the blitz was in progress and it was probably considered too dangerous.

He spent the first morning in Coventry visiting Armstrong Siddeley and Armstrong Whitworth, before proceeding to Birmingham by train, where he transferred to a car. He inspected the Civil Defence Authorities and the War Room, before driving around the extensive bomb-damaged areas of the city, this may have been the time when Eileen saw him outside the BSA in Golden Hillock Road. He visited a tank manufacturer in the city, Mechanisation and Aero, before ending the visit by touring the (Nuffield) Castle Bromwich factory and watching a demonstration of the flying Spitfires.

Interestingly, he travelled by train that evening to Liverpool, where the next day he undertook a visit to HMS Indomitable, while it was in docks. From the details of the visit available the crew was on board, so it is more than possible that Evelyn's husband, Chris Cookson, was probably party to that particular visit.

The maintenance of morale was treated as an essential part of the war effort, and every possible means were employed to keep morale high, whether it was the management of news in the papers, or programmes on the wireless to focus minds on the home and the need to drive the war economy forward. The short propaganda films played in the cinema before the main feature, or the many poster campaigns around the city that reminded everyone how vital it was to take their part, it constantly prevailed in all areas of life, including the factory walls and the canteen.

Day shift workers gave way to their night shift colleagues, and ventured out into the daylight (in summer) to make their way home. Most times because shifts ended in the early evening they would find the blackout, when they left work, and the hindrances this caused to any movement. In autumn, the smog could add further hazards to the blackness making it almost impossible to see a few feet in front, even with the aid of a carefully masked torch pointing downwards.

The blackout was one of the most gruelling aspects of the war that the population had to endure and had been enforced since the outbreak. It infringed many social freedoms that people had taken for granted, and caused a whole new regime of investing in material to mask windows, and a constant checking (and re-checking) to make sure the blackout was not being broken. Car headlights had to be masked, and white painted stripes applied to the edges, despite this in the first year of the war there was a dramatic rise in road deaths which was directly attributed to these measures. As Gardiner, 2004, notes:

"...in Birmingham they rose by 81 per cent in December 1939, which saw the highest number of road deaths – 1,155 – since records had been kept, while a further 30,000 people had been injured."

Further, according to the surgeon to the King reporting in the British Medical Journal, again quoting from Gardiner, 2004:

"...that by frightening the nation into blackout regulations, the Luftwaffe was able to kill 600 citizens a month without ever taking to the air..."

The blackout in factories had been enforced since the outbreak of war. An effort was made by the Secretary of State (Air Chief of the Air Staff), to have this repealed in July 1943, as it was considered to be hampering aircraft production. It was met with a very firm 'no' from Churchill, who on the advice he had been given, still considered it to be too dangerous in guiding the odd stray bomber to sensitive sites of production, and too costly, as many of the new factories had been built without windows.

The night shift workers, entered poorly lit cavernous hangars, which were very badly heated. Iris remembers the coldness of the Austin at night. Very often the facilities available to dayshift workers were at a minimum at night. Those who were fortunate enough to be working in the larger factories, probably still had an adequate hot meal, many of the smaller private factories did not, making the night shift a particularly gruelling experience, and in the blitz a very frightening one.

When shifts ended, day or night, normal living had to be resumed. For many of the women in this book, that posed problems but not so great for those ten years or so older, who had families to maintain, but no others to support them in doing so. These women are long since gone now and unable to recount their difficulties but evidence still remains of their particular problems. The government had been very careful to handle conscription, so as not create a bigger problem with employment once the war came to an end. Although, there were those who considered that there should be no exemptions made for any women between certain ages, there was a realisation by some that to insist on those with domestic responsibilities taking on a working role would create a situation of custom and practice, that had the potential to destabilise the society. Married women with children,

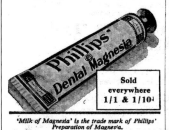

Advertisements from the ATC Gazette – 1944.

Here's a grand way to

SALUTE THE SOLDIER

It may be some time before you are on "combined operations," giving air cover to our soldiers as they go into battle. But you can give your support to the soldier now — by backing him up with your Savings to the fullest possible extent. Support this great Savings drive—the biggest ever made. Buy as many National Savings Stamps as you can, and turn them into National Savings Certificates as quickly as possible.

BUY NATIONAL SAVINGS STAMPS

6d. - 2/6 - 5/-

Learn to Ankle your BSA Bicycle

"Ankling" will make your B.S.A. run even more easily.

"Ankling" is the experts' way of pedalling that gives you more "pedal power" for the same amount of energy.

Flex your ankle to drive the pedal round its full circle.

Study the illustration and you'll see that the old stiff ankle method was "up and down" driving through 180° only—the new method is "round and round" driving through the full 360°.

It's worth learning to "ankle" your B.S.A. Bicycle — you'll find long journeys shorter — short journeys quicker —all journeys easier.

Your dealer will help you to get your B.S.A. Bicycle.

War-time standard models, with pump and tools (but without toolbag), from the B.S.A. Dealer in your district

£8.19.5
Including Purchase Tax.

BSA

BICYCLES AND MOTOR CYCLES
Every part a little better than it need be!
B.S.A. Cycles Ltd.. Birmingham, 11.

Advertisements from the ATC Gazette – 1944.

BOMBER COMMAND

Air Chief Marshal Sir Arthur T. Harris, K.C.B., O.B.E., A.F.C., Air-Officer-Commanding in Chief, Bomber Command (left), Air Marshal Sir Robert H. M. S. Saundby, K.B.E., C.B., M.C., A.F.C., Deputy-Chief, Bomber Command. The aircraft depicted illustrate the progress of Bomber Command's equipment during the war. At the bottom there are Battles, above them a pair of Whitleys, then a Wellington and a Halifax.

Bomber Command – ATC Gazette – 1944.

Advertisements from the ATC Gazette – 1944.

Advertisements from the ATC Gazette – 1944.

An early Austin car.

The first Austin car.

An advertisement for Austin.

Handbook of Austin Ten - Four.

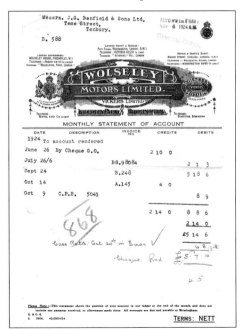

Invoice from Wolseley Motors Ltd 1924.

Lord Nuffield – William Morris.

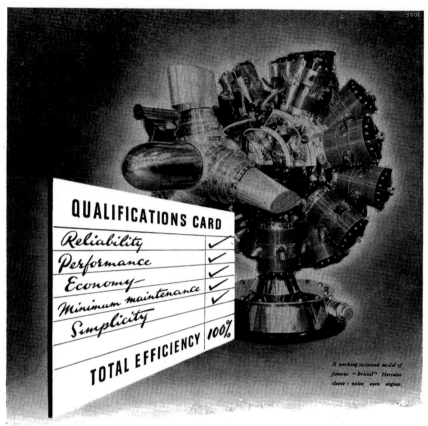

A working sectioned model of famous "Bristol" Hercules sleeve - valve aero engine.

. . . five features contributing to sleeve-valve supremacy

Of all the qualifications that can be " ticked " to the credit of any aero-engine design, those counting most in the future will undoubtedly be . . . all-round economy and minimum maintenance. The " Bristol " sleeve-valve engine—based upon a principle of exceptional simplicity—has a high efficiency relative to these factors. With a " Bristol " sleeve-valve engine there is no grinding-in of valves ; no spring inspections or replacements ; no tedious tappet adjustments ; the only maintenance necessary is the usual servicing of ignition and carburettor ; and occasional filter checks. Coupled with this is economy in fuel and oil . . . inevitable result of simplified design, and logical support for the assertion that the SLEEVE-VALVE WILL BE THE PRINCIPLE BEHIND THE POWER OF THE FUTURE.

 *pioneered and developed the single sleeve valve engine*

THE BRISTOL AEROPLANE COMPANY LTD. ENGLAND

An advertisement for Bristol Engines 1945.

Advertisement for BSA cycles 1920.

Joseph Chamberlain (1836-1914), Mayor 1873-76,
MP for Birmingham 1876-1914.

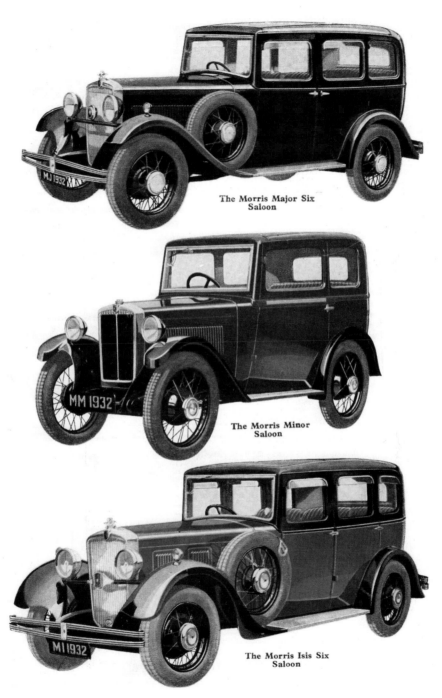

The Morris Major Six
Saloon

The Morris Minor
Saloon

The Morris Isis Six
Saloon

A selection of Morris cars.

MORRIS MOTORS LTD.

SIR WILLIAM R. MORRIS, BT.
` ` ` CHAIRMAN ` ` `

` ` E. H. BLAKE ` `
` ` MANAGING DIRECTOR ` `

MORRIS
(Reg⁰ Trade Mark)

COWLEY, OXFORD

WHEN REPLYING PLEASE
QUOTE OUR REFERENCE

SALES DEPARTMENT

2. WMT /NS

YOUR REF _____

March, 1932.

GREATER VALUE THAN EVER

Dear Sir,

You will have gathered from the National Press the wonderful stride forward to still greater value in Morris cars for 1932. Morris production always has been based on a bigger interpretation of car values and the 1932 models carry the tradition a long step forward and bring old standards to a still higher level.

Important improvements for this season include:-

- An elegant entirely new radiator, chromium finished and, on six-cylinder models, with automatic shutters.
- New "Eddyfree" front to all Saloon and Coupe models.
- Petrol tank at the rear - an extra safety feature.
- Twin-top four-speed gearbox on all six-cylinder models.
- Lockheed hydraulic brakes (on all cars except the Morris Minor), providing extra powerful brake action.
- Wide doors - more generous seating - softer upholstery - Pytchley sliding roof - added convenience and comfort.

That a high degree of economical running is always being maintained by Morris cars is clearly demonstrated by the report of the R.A.C. trial reprinted on page four.

We extend to you a cordial invitation to visit the showrooms of your nearest Morris Dealer. This will not imply any obligation on your part and our Dealer will welcome the opportunity to demonstrate to you the wonderful British craftsmanship embodied in Morris cars and the "after-sales service" and the payment-out-of-income facilities which are offered under the Morris plan.

Yours faithfully,

Morris cars are
guaranteed for
2 years.

Wm. W. Thomas.

Director and General Sales Manager.

Public Relations letter from Morris Motors Ltd.

An advertisement for Lucas Research 1945.

THE PRIME MINISTER
THE RT. HON. NEVILLE CHAMBERLAIN, M.P.

THE PILGRIM OF PEACE
BRAVO! MR. CHAMBERLAIN

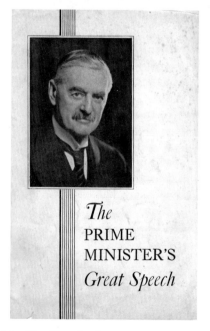

The
PRIME
MINISTER'S
Great Speech

PEACE THROUGH STRENGTH

Mr. Chamberlain's Great Speech delivered at the mass meeting of women Conservatives at the Royal Albert Hall, London, on Thursday, May 11th, 1939.

IT is almost exactly a year since last I addressed you in this hall, and what a year it has been! Whatever may be the ultimate verdict on the events through which we passed in those 12 months, and which have left their mark on some of us—whatever may be the verdict on the part which has been played by the British Government, we can be sure that the year 1938 will stand out as one that is memorable in the history of the British people.

I feel I have a great opportunity this afternoon in speaking to you who have come here from all parts of the country, and I want first of all to give you my thanks for the consistent and loyal support that you have given throughout the year to the National Government. I seem in these days to be the target for a lot of rotten eggs, but I can assure you that does not keep me awake, because I believe that I have the support of the women of the country and that they have a clearer vision than some of those whose sight is obscured by party or personal prejudice.

Neville Chamberlain (1869-1940), Lord Mayor 1915-16, MP for Birmingham (Ladywood) 1918-24, MP for Birmingham (Edgbaston) 1924-40, Prime Minister 1937-40.

"Mars are marvellous"

They certainly are! Just chunks of sheer delicious goodness made with chocolate to sustain, glucose to energise, milk to nourish.

Mars

ZONED TO THE SOUTH

Refreshments in PARTY frills

It's a pleasure to break away from the serious side of cooking sometimes; what better excuse than a children's party? Without too great a strain on the rations, and with a little ingenuity you can give your refreshments those colourful and festive touches that will delight your little guests. Here are some ideas:

ICING WITHOUT ICING SUGAR

When you ice your cake you can save on sugar in the cake recipe, which can be quite plain in itself, so the idea is not so extravagant after all.

FUDGE ICING
½ lb. sugar, ½ pint milk (fresh milk, or household milk in which you have melted a small knob of margarine, or richest of all, unsweetened evaporated milk), flavouring and colouring. Put all ingredients into a saucepan and boil, stirring occasionally, until a little dropped into cold water will form a soft ball. Remove from stove, cool a little, and then stir briskly until mixture is thick and opaque. Spread while warm on to the cake with a knife dipped in hot water.
Flavouring: 1. Dessertspoonful of undiluted coffee essence. 2. Two level tablespoons cocoa. 3. Yellow cookery colouring and lemon or orange flavouring to taste. 4. A few drops red colouring, and vanilla to taste (vanilla should be stirred into the mixture just before taking off stove). Fudge icing is more quickly made in a frying-pan than a saucepan.

CAKE OR SANDWICH FILLINGS

DATE FILLING: 4 oz. chopped dates, 6 tablespoons water, 1 level tablespoon soya flour, few drops lemon essence, pinch mixed spice. Cook the dates in the water until soft. Mix in the other ingredients and leave to cool.

CHOCOLATE FILLING: 1½ tablespoons sweetened condensed milk, 2 level tablespoons cocoa, 1 level tablespoon soya flour, 1 teaspoon vanilla essence, 1 tablespoon hot water. Mix all the ingredients very thoroughly together.

JELLY WHIP FILLING: 2 level tablespoons flour, 1 pint water or fruit juice, 3 level tablespoons gelatine, 1 level tablespoon sugar, flavouring essence, colouring.
Gradually add the liquid to the flour, stirring well to prevent lumps, boil gently for 5 minutes, pour on to the gelatine and sugar and stir till dissolved. Set aside until cool and just beginning to set. Add flavouring and colouring and whisk until thick and foamy.

(S.136)   **ISSUED BY THE MINISTRY OF FOOD**

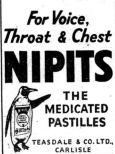

Advertisements in Titbits – 1945.

In an age that thinks too often in terms of quantity and pays too little attention to quality, the craftsmanship and technical excellence of the Rover Car assert themselves with a quiet insistence that compels attention more surely than could any amount of high-pressure salesmanship. Truly, it is its own advertisement.

ROVER

One of Britain's Fine Cars

THE ROVER CO. LTD., SOLIHULL, BIRMINGHAM & DEVONSHIRE HOUSE, LONDON

CV3-68

Advertisement for Rover Co. Ltd – 1945.

were housewives, married men worked to support their families (Holloway 2005). The status quo had to be maintained in order to keep economic life stable, so only those married women without children were forced to take work, however many volunteered, such as Win and Evelyn. They were able to manage their dual roles due to the support of their female relatives minding children. In Evelyn's case it was her mother, in Win's case her grandmother, as Win's mother was working alongside her at Ward's.

Rationing posed particular problems for working women who found themselves on long (sometimes cold) shifts, on very low calorific-value meals. In 1939, all households had to register with local shopkeepers, this was to offset the lag between the issue of ration books and to ensure that each shop got the correct entitlement for its customers. By 1940, the pinch was beginning to be felt by many, meat was rationed to just over a pound per person, tea was restricted to two ounces per week, all cooking fats (including margarine and butter) two ounces a week. These rations varied further according to the season. You could be restricted to half an egg (rather than two), or half a pint of milk (rather than two), some rations such as; sugar and meat could rise in quantity (Minns, 2006). The housewife had to become very creative (and adaptable to what was available) in how to give her family a wholesome meal every night, and the factory worker was often grateful for the canteen. Soups and stews (that mainly used vegetables) became a staple of wartime fare, and nothing was wasted!

In particular, for most shopping caused great difficulties, especially in the early days of the war (Holloway, 2005). No time was given to allow women to shop, which led to women being late or even absent from work, in order to collect rations or stand in the ever longer queues. A point that had not been lost on the Germans who were experiencing the same difficulties, a document from "Das Schwarze Korps" 10th July, 1941, had been intercepted and translated that described such queues in these terms:

"Wherever there is a crowd it becomes bigger! Where there is a queue people imagine there is a scarcity; where scarcity is presumed, irrational appetite arises. Scarcity causes more queues, queues increase the urge to get "just one more". The queue sets its teeth in its own tail and becomes endless… There has, in fact, developed a professional queuer, a malignant odious breed looking on the expectant and prolific mother or the war worker as an unfair competitor;"

The government looked at introducing measures to ease difficulties, but they soon realised to impose any sort of mandatory regulation on employers to release women with particular difficulties to allow them to shop could create insurmountable problems with production and the management of other workers. They decided to seek regional solutions, through negotiation at a local level with employers and shopkeepers.

The government surveyed regional offices of The Ministry of Labour and National Service in August 1941, for their opinions of the progress of these negotiations. Birmingham's response mirrors that of many centres of production across the country:

"Our problem is not only one of easing the difficulties of married women already in the industry, but also of being able to make some public gesture to convince women not yet working that, if they come forward to play their part, reasonable shopping facilities will be available to them. As we want to get as many women working a full shift as possible, the time is probably not opportune for us to press too hard for a large extension of short shift and part time working, which would give the best single answer to shopping difficulties."

They had arranged a meeting with the Chamber of Commerce and the Retailers Association, and had been met with a negative response:

"The meeting was, from our point of view, very disappointing as, despite our stressing the importance of retailers making special efforts to meet the needs of the munition worker shoppers, their attitude was completely negative, and, whilst they did not refuse to give further consideration to the matter, a recital of their wartime difficulties left no doubt in our minds that considerable pressure must be put on them before any comprehensive co-operation can be expected."

The regional office concludes their letter by offering suggestions as to how these problems may be alleviated:

"Among the new standard suggestions for assisting the shopping workers, the retailers suggested that pay days should be brought forward to Thursday, mentioning that at points where factories had adopted this procedure, the Friday and Saturday morning rush was eased. They also suggested that the day off should be staggered over the week. The suggestion of opening shops during the lunch hour, either generally or for munition workers only, was countered with the complaint of staff shortage, which answer was also given when the ordering system was mentioned. Being a retailers' conference, we did not stress adjustments which could be made by the factories, though in Birmingham every factory which has been approached is giving some official or unofficial time off to married women for shopping. In some areas local shop keepers are co-operating, but in others the reverse is the situation."

It seems these problems were insurmountable, and possibly it was not in the government's future interests to solve them. For if it was made easier for married women to work, then this situation may continue and become irreversible after wartime. Little was done other than to leave these difficulties to local arbitration, and family helping family to cope with their own particular difficulties.

The women in this book bar two, were either married by this time or engaged, which precluded them from gadding about. They now had to wait at home for their loved one's return. Reducing social opportunities, to those that happened when their boyfriends and husbands were on leave, or when there was a family gathering or special event. The home and hearth became the centre of their lives, assisting their mothers, sleeping and returning to their machines the following day or night. In Jenny's case it was her landlady's table, and a shared bed, all for her £2 per week. Iris (flag) did live in a flat away from her mother for a time, and did have to shop, with her friend Margaret, when they could between shifts, but at least they only had to care for themselves.

Christmas was the highlight of the year. Not the over-commercialised Christmas of today, where presents and television dominate most households, these were the simple family celebrations of yesteryear. It was the coming together of extended family, where a chicken was a feast and a turkey or goose was particularly rare. Win's daughter remembers having to help her grandmother pluck the turkey into a large tin bath. Christmas pudding was made, paper chains were painstakingly gummed together, and strung about the house, and Christmas stockings were simple offerings of basics, nuts and fruit and small toys for the children.

Those that married during the war years, such as Daisy, Iris and Eileen, talk of everybody providing something for their special day. A borrowed wedding dress, or in Iris's case one that she could have made but it was more expensive on coupons to buy the material than it was to buy the dress. People brought bottled fruit and cakes. Music was played by local friends. Flowers were what could be got at the time, Iris had red tulips.

The other guests dressed in their best clothes. The hat was still a mandatory item of social etiquette for women, even just day-to-day wear. I remember my own mother's collection of beautiful hats that she had kept after the war; felt berets, pillbox hats with veils, and the Robin Hood style felt trilbies complete with the beautiful hat pins. Each of the ladies had the same hats, and loved to wear them, it added the touch of glamour to otherwise austere time. Clothes were in short supply, Win mentions the black market as the only way that they could keep acquiring clothes, Jenny bought a beautiful dress and had it cleaned and never saw it again, a sign of the times.

When trying to build their homes, and save for their bottom drawer, new things tended to be a luxury, although utility furniture became a feature of the post-war period, most of the women in this book were totally dependant on the help of their families. What things could be given, or borrowed, things were passed through the family, which gave each of them a start.

Life was hard, but they managed as best they could, each and everyday. After the first few frantic years, it must have seemed at times that the war would never end, and there would be no such thing as 'normal' again, but eventually it did.

THE SHADOW FACTORY

Act 1 – Scene 1 – page 12

Director:
"...I tell you, it's certain this world is Coming,
Whatever we do. Then be a realist,
Accept our age for what it is;
And then accept your function in it.
Here is a factory still in the making,
Malleable still as a molten bar:
Won't you help us bring it to birth?
Or, to use a more modern metaphor,
Won't you be the catalyst?
We're building a new canteen; I plan
To make it the hub of factory life.
The central arch is design for murals:
These are to set the tone of the whole,
And while they refresh the eye, to strike
A note of optimism. What do you say?
Will *you* undertake them? You've heard my ideas,
Put them into paint?

A Ridler – 1945

Chapter 14

MAY MAKES HER WAY

Of all the ladies that I have interviewed, May Allen is the one who has moved the least distance since the war. In fact, she lives opposite to her mother's old house in Runcorn Road in Birmingham, at number 84 as her mother lived at number 87. May's mother managed to buy her house for £350 pre-war, they are worth considerably more now. May lives in a terrace of linked town houses built in 1905, they were built on the old artillery fields, and railway bridges cross the streets. The houses are close to the road with short front gardens and arched open porches, they have no cellars, just nooks under the stairs, which were going to be their main sanctuary during the bombing. May's own family were going to be profoundly affected by the war.

May's father was John Charles James, son of John James of Redditch, needle manufacturers. John Charles had a weak chest, a common complaint in the family and one from which his sister had died, so this must have been a cause for concern for his father. He had been born in August 1883 (May's mother was born in June 1883) and he must have met up with his future wife by the turn of the century, for his father insisted on him going to South Africa around 1902 to 1904 to Johannesburg. Medical advice had been sought and the warm climate was considered most beneficial to him. May recalls, the large yellow trunk that her father used to have with all his keepsakes in that he had collected on his trip. However, May's mother was not at all happy about him going and refused to answer his letters in the two years that he was away.

May's mother, Susan, middle name Mary, was probably born in Sparkbrook, and must have met John Charles in Redditch. She kept her silence for two long years until he returned, he must have missed her, for on his return he married her. After a few years, they set about the business of producing their family. There was; John Charles, Alfred John (who died in infancy of cot death), Florence Beatrice, Frank Albert, William Henry, Walter Fredrick. With the last three May says:

"Mum got tired when she had the last three so we had the one name..."

So with the last three Suie, May and Edie, that was eight living, even for those days this was a large family. A family of children were an investment opportunity for parents, being the old fashioned equivalent to an 'old age pension', as their children they would provide for their parents.

During this time, they lived firstly in Redditch, where pregnant already, May's mother had to scrub the workshop floors with cold water, she had two children quickly, suffering associated painful maladies. She was very grateful to move back to Birmingham even to a small two up, two down, back-to-back, in Alfred Street. It had two rooms upstairs, where all the boys slept in one room and all the girls slept in the other. Downstairs, the parents used the front room as their bedroom, and the back room was the living room and main eating area. There was a small back kitchen, and the toilet was in the yard. There was no bathroom. And as May says, her mother lived to the age of 91 without ever having a bathroom, or owning a washing machine.

Meanwhile, John James must have died for all his business interests were sold and a pot of money put aside for his son, which was going to become vital in the ensuing years. May's father served his time in the Great War, bridge building in the Suez. Unfortunately, he fell ill and contracted enteric fever, which hospitalised him in Alexandria for quite some time. It was a private hospital, and without money you did not get treated. Every week Susan would draw out £8 from his inheritance, she would keep £1 to live on while sending him £7 for his treatment, which was a considerable sum of money. Meanwhile, Susan would sew for the army, having all these small children and a sick husband. Eventually he was made well and came home to produce the rest of his brood.

Life carried on, Susan got sick of the cramped conditions and moved her family into 87, by this time all eight were established. John Charles junior, went off to the army to become a professional soldier, and Florence Beatrice married George and moved out.

May was born in 1922, and she attended the Council School on Stratford Road, in the last year before she was due to matriculate, the city reorganised schooling so that different age groups, were schooled separately. Her school would now only take children to the age of 11, it meant for the last two months of her education she was moved to Conway Road School.

She had told the Labour Exchange that she wanted to work in accounts, May explains that the:

"Nearest I could get to learning accounts, was sitting at a cash desk in a butchers shop at the Bullring... I stood up all day, it was so tiny, a little circle with a trap door… for the butchers to bring the money up and you give them the change…"

As she says she learnt nothing and she looked for something else.

Her sister Suie, was working in the laundry on Ladypool Road, this laundry was part of a chain around the city, mainly dealing in industrial contracts for works towels and overalls, similar to 'Initial'. May got a job there, she had to sort and mark the dirty laundry, and then sort the clean and pack, she got paid £1 10shs for that, this was around 1938.

May still had higher ambitions and tried for the GPO as a telephonist, usually a job reserved for grammar school girls. As May says it was a mentally very demanding job because:

"…we had books to learn all the codes… on Post Office telephones we had to know when somebody wanted to make a call… Coventry to Leamington was CV/LG…"

She was not over enamoured with the work expectations, she did not like the idea of shift work, or indeed having to work Christmas Day 2 till 10. The final straw for her, was that if any mistakes were made, i.e. 'giving calls for free', it was deducted from your wages. They were constantly monitored by supervisors who would listen in. Once May had such a call:

"…It was Christmas I think… one girl… I think it was a nurse phoned me and said she'd got no money and it was desperate… and I put her through… they are listening, you see they have a plug to plug in… if they catch you out, you cop out, and you have to pay for that call…"

So in 1942, May changed her job again to work for Dare's the Brewery on Belgrave Road, she was employed on the switchboard. Working for them she became classified under the Ministry of Food, and was protected for the first few years of the war. She worked there for 10 years until she was nearly 30, apart from her break for 'war work'.

Meanwhile, with a professional soldier in the family there must have been considerable talk of the impending war. Suie's husband George was already a member of the Territorial Army, and as a consequence one of the first to go, he went into the Royal Engineers. One of her other brothers bought an Alba wireless for the house, a luxury they had never had before, and like many families on that grey Sunday in September they sat around listening to Chamberlain. She was young and as she says, 'it didn't really mean much' at that particular time, but when 'our planes' started to practise their low flying over the houses then it began to sink in.

Immediately, Bill (William) and Wal (Walter) got their 'call up'. Bill into Warwickshire Infantry, and Wal into the Coldstream Guards (tank regiment).

Frank was in a protected occupation he worked at the BSA in Golden Hillock Road. John Charles had already been serving as a professional soldier in the Royal Engineers for 22 years. Their father had been an unofficial fire warden, and carried on standing outside watching for incendiaries, all the fire buckets carefully placed in each archway along the street. May enlisted into the voluntary fire service, and she had to report for duty one night a week to a fire station and wear a uniform.

Then came Dunkirk in June 1940, her brother-in-law George, had to be evacuated and obviously suffered from the shock. Soon, the bombs began to fall all along the neighbouring railway line, and the surrounding streets, this was August 1940. She can remember George's outbursts as the planes rumbled overhead:

> "...when he came home for a few days after Dunkirk... the bombs were dropping on the night... (she laughs) he could know when the bombs were near... cause he shouted 'duck'... and we all ducked!... I've never forgot it... (she laughs)... under the table!"

There was a mobile Ack Ack gun on the railway line above the street which according to May:

> "We had a gun along the railway that moved along and back... that's probably why we got a lot of bombs... coz they'd see that gun and it used to move backwards and forwards..."

There 'dropped a whole pack of bombs' along the street and to this day May still has a crack in the front wall of the house. The houses above the railway line were totally destroyed and replaced in 1947 with quickly built (Gerry built) houses, which were later pulled down to make way for factory units.

There were brick built services shelters along the avenue, which were round in construction, May recalls that they were:

> "...just bricks, no lights you had to take a torch... we went in once and tried it... but after that time... no, no, never again... but they had them on the Moseley Road... under the shops, the cellars you could go down, but we never went down those..."

They just trusted to their cubby under the stairs.

During the bad November bombing, May remembers one particular bomb which was responsible for laying waste to their old street, and reducing Alfred Road to rubble, the bomb was known locally as, 'the golden ball for the BSA', it was meant for the BSA but was off target. November 19th, 1940 the night the BSA got hit, Frank her brother was not working, because fortunately he never worked nights.

She can recall the local doctor, (Doctor Cronin) having to perform an emergency amputation of a leg on a man who had become pinned down in a raid on Moseley Road. The same doctor, lost his own son who was in the RAF, not because of enemy action, but unfortunately due to a lightning strike. With the raids, she recalls that it got to the stage that:

"You didn't take no notice, because it was there all the time."

May got her call up for essential work, in 1943. She applied to join the Land Army, which by that stage was full, and she was posted to the 'shadow' Rover factory in Solihull instead. Whereas, she had walked to Dare's each day, suddenly she had to face a very long coach journey back and forth to Rover, with twelve hour shifts.

The first day they gave her some meaningless task to perform so in May's words she 'took a day off' when they asked her why, she said:

"aww the paraffin made me feel sick... well I came here to do a job, ok so I will do a job... and they thought 'oh she's a big head we'll show her'..."

So they gave her 'a man's job to do', she explains:

"...they put me on a man's job, polishing artic rod pins... I will never forget it, but it was hard work... it was a lathe that you had to place this piece of metal in... you got to have a long strip of emery paper, you put Vaseline on it... and you got what we used to call mutton cloths, what the butchers used to wrap the sheep up in... because you had that as a duster, to hold it with, cause you wore you finger out... and you put it round, and then you moved it up and down to polish it... and then you had to have it tested to see if it was right."

They paid her £6 per week for her work, whereas a man doing the same job would get £24, and this was for 12 hour shifts. A month of days, then a month of nights. The canteen was a very good one, offering a good range of food, May feels that people were healthier then than now, and of course, there was 'music while you work'.

May and an Irish women called Edith, were the first to go onto the 'automatic' (numerical controlled) machines. They would set the work, and set the tool to the piece, and press the buttons, but as she explains with a wry smile, when it went wrong 'the setter didn't know how to set it' you had to call for the foreman:

"...Ooooh hoo you just had to watch... and all of a sudden the foreman had gone... with a mutton cloth round his hand... that's what you got to learn not to do... put you hand on the wheel..."

Before she started at Rover in Solihull, she used to have time for a social life. She and a girlfriend, used to 'go up town' sometimes to the Hippodrome or the Casino Dance Hall, or even the Moseley Swimming Baths, which used to be boarded over as a make-shift dance floor. Her friend would sometimes try and palm her off on a 'yank' that she had 'picked up', no fear! May was not a woman like that, 'they were here just for one thing'. However, once she was on essential work, with the long shifts at the Rover, and the long journeys, she was too exhausted to even consider a social life. Poor May was suffering more than ever each month for which the men never made allowances. Still she would push herself to the limits, even though she had stopped as an ARP, Dare's were so short staffed they asked her to help out. While doing nights at Rover, she would come and work days on the switchboard at Dare's, she was burning the candle at both ends, as she says:

"…you're young and you do it… but I wouldn't do it again… my legs felt like they were bursting."

Thanks to Dare's though, May was able to have something that many of the women missed, a very good twenty first birthday party. As she was in under the Ministry of Food and protected until she was twenty one for the Essential Work Order, she was able to save a bottle of complimentary drink each month (not spirits) and eventually the day came, and her family used the Clifton Road School which can still be seen from her backroom window. She can remember carrying the alcohol and food through the 'gully' with her sister, and a train carrying American soldiers passed, a bit of banter took place between the men on the train and the girls down below. To which, the 'yanks' helped with the impending festivities by throwing Camel cigarettes out of the train windows to the girls.

Her brothers Wal and Bill, were being made ready for D-Day and the Normandy landings, operation Overlord was struck by bad weather initially and they weren't ready to go. Bill and Wal probably landed with the area designated 'Sword'. Bill travelled all the way through France and Belgium, ending up heading for Arnhem across Holland, they became 'pinned down at the Nijmegen bridge' in May's words:

"…they called 'em ducks, they dropped down as they went over the water, he was one of the first Bill was… he went right through to that bridge… that's where he got hurt… because on the film you saw them, how many were just sat there singing 'Abide with me'… he got hurt and eh… they asked the Germans to stop the war for a few hours… to get those there into hospital in Brussels…"

Wal made good progress initially, he was in charge of a tank and his regiment made it as far as Falaise Pocket outside Caen. There disaster struck, they came under shell fire and he was looking out of the tank. His head and face 'got all smashed up', while still under sniper fire, he had to get himself down below and get his fellow soldiers to bind his head together. Then he got out of the tank, dodging bullets to get medical attention. He was brought back to Basingstoke, the Park Prewitt Hospital, where a doctor of facial reconstruction whom May describes as 'an artist' called Mr Gillies, put him back together again.

It was a long and painful process. They had to cement his teeth together to make his jaw immobile, they took a painful bone graft from his hip and kept it alive on his chest until they were ready to finish the procedure. Bill was never the same person afterwards, suffering severe shell shock and stammering. He went back to being a butcher after the war, and although he had been told to take things easier he never would. After suffering several heart attacks he died at 46. Bill just 'changed' as May says, he was one of the silent ones never talking. Only once or twice mentioning how green (and how quickly) the corpses of the German S.S. troops used to go, because (in his opinion) of all the drugs they were given.

May split her time, working and visiting Wal, at Park Prewitt Hospital in Basingstoke, witnessing the 'nuts and bolts' and severe head injuries.

She does recount some very amusing stories. Once, while working at the Rover, when she had just had lunch she decided to go down to the restroom for a break, where as she recalls:

"…there was a Scots girl who was a bit of a case… and she stood up this once and she said 'stand up all ye who are virgins?'… and nobody stood up (laughing)…"

And then there was Bunty and Marie, her two friends from Banff. They seemed to be very close but May was very naïve, and Marie was always mentioning her boyfriend which no one ever saw. As May remembers:

"…these two girls one was like a boy and one was like a girl. I hadn't got a clue, you know… they were always going in the toilet together…"

The war was coming to an end and Rover was winding up the munitions contract, work was slack and boring, May recalls she was immensely glad when it did finally end and she was able to return to Dare's and the accounting machine she was learning to operate. Dare's asked her to do some relief work in a hotel they owned in Earlswood called The Reservoir at weekends. While she was there she invited one of her old factory colleagues up from London to help her celebrate New Years Eve at a dance they had organised.

That evening a group of young chaps were sat by the bar, and one cheekily asked her for a 'kiss for Christmas', she duly obliged. The following day she got a call from an eager young man, in her words:

"...is this Derrick? (laughing) and he said 'No... it's Dennis' (she laughs)... that was the start... 'Dennis the menace'..."

Den had not had an easy war. He had been in the Carlton Cinema, on 25th October 1940, the night the bomb fell on it, they were all told to shelter under the circle. Nineteen people were killed, with no obvious injuries, it had been the blast that had caused their deaths. He was one of the lucky ones, he had lived, but with severe hearing loss, which was only rectified slightly in much later years with an operation. May started seeing Den, who got his call up for National Service in the Royal Engineers. They married in January 1953, eventually they had two sons. Den died in December, 2000. May still lives in her house opposite where she lived as a girl. She says to me she is glad she is old, because she would not be able to put up with sub-standard workmanship and materials like young people have to do today. She has always been a generous and kind lady, like her mother, and like her mother has given most away, which has consequences. As I leave her and look towards the railway bridge, just down from her house, I imagine, low flying planes, Ack Ack guns, fire bells and hanging buckets, so much has changed.

FOR MAY

They rumbled deep overhead,
The fireworks are going to start he said,
They dropped the pretty lights to light the ground,
And then them big boys followed all around.

One hundred fell, and one hundred more,
Bang, bang, whoa, whiz, roar!
The world shook, and heaved with fright,
On that bloody awful Guy Fawkes night.

Remember, remember the 19th of November…

I will tell you what I remember well,
That evening was utter hell,
When all the world seemed to explode,
An' all was on fire down our road.

Oh God, the heavens opened on us hard,
The landscape, battered and scarred,
The walls, they came a tumbling down,
And every place was laid waste around.

And now the silence in the dark surrounds,
On the bloodied nose of this hurting town,
We breathe a sigh and intake our breath,
Another night, survived, our meeting with death.

Chapter 15

IRIS – 'THE FLAG'

"I started writing a book... it was for my step sister... we got the same mum like... when I was 8 my dad died... my mum was still a young woman and she started courting again... so my sister Maureen, whom me mum had when she got married again... said you saw our dad more than we did, will you write about him?... I mean I was only 8, but I can remember this man come courting me mum, so that's what I wrote about."

This is Iris Lodge, she is 84 years of age and she has not had the easiest of lives, but she retains an enormous optimism about all things, and like many of her generation does not dwell on the past, or problems, she just 'gets on'. She explains to me that her family lived in Nechells, that is her father and mother, her brothers Harry and Ron. Her father had sustained a leg injury in the Great War and never really recovered:

"When I was a little girl he went in hospital, me mum said it was his legs... one day she said, don't go to school, keep the fire going, I'm fetching your dad home. And then when she come home on the night, I said 'where is he?' and he had collapsed when they got him out of bed and I never seen him again."

Her mum eventually remarried, her step-dad, (who Iris refers to as her dad) couldn't get work at first in Nechells and used to cycle all the way to Wolverhampton, before he managed to get a job in the local tar factory. With mother and father out at work all day, their kind next door neighbour, used to mind the 'kiddies' during the day, the culture of Birmingham (and of the time) where neighbour helped neighbour. Two sisters were born, Maureen and Beryl, and a younger brother Clifford.

Iris attended Elliot Street School, where she got the nickname 'Flag' after the Iris Pseudacorus or yellow flag iris, because there were two girls with the name Iris in the school, and to limit confusion the teachers gave her a pet name because she was considered to be tall and stately, as her mother used to say. She enjoyed school, but unfortunately Iris contracted scarlet fever at 13, in her words:

"I had the day at school and I can remember we were cutting some worm and I felt really sick doing it. And when I come home, I told my mum I felt ill and I must of looked ill 'coz she fetched the doctor, and I was in the fever hospital for about six weeks. And it was ever so frightening, because I remember it was pitch black when I went in, and they had these gas heaters and they were throwing these shadows out."

Her poor hard working mother, who had 5 of her 6 children at that time, was having to cope with her very poorly teenage daughter, whilst, holding down her job working on the large grinding machines at British Timkins. Mind you, when Iris's sister, Maureen was a baby, Iris can remember her mother coming home of a lunchtime to breastfeed her. She died at 58, and Iris says that she was a 'lovely looking woman'.

It was an interruption to her final year at school, for she would have left at 14, but after her 6 weeks in the fever hospital, she was not allowed to return to school because she was still 'skinning', her legs and hands peeled for a long time. This is because the bacteria that causes the illness can still be highly infectious in those whose skin is peeling after the main infection and fever has abated. Her mother took her to 'The Hercules' then a manufacturer of bicycles, where she started in the chroming shop, school life ended, and her working life began.

In the meantime, her social life consisted of going to the Mission Hall in Nechells, in Cuckoo Road. Her brother Harry was in the Boys Brigade run by Captain Scott, all the boys used to go and some girls too, so Iris joined. While in the Mission Hall on one occasion, she felt a young man called Sam, giving her the eye and again later as they all walked up Nechells Park Road, boys in the front, girls at the back. As they got to the corner, the young man concerned stopped and offered to walk Iris home:

"That was the start of our courting, and I was with him ever since."

She was 14, he was 17.

After a short time, she left Hercules and went to work at Lucas, this mobility between jobs being common. She started work there as a 'viewer' a quality controller of the time. She was noticed by the commissioner there, who obviously felt that Iris had a bit more about her, and asked her if she wanted to work in the time office. She was very happy with the move, and she started work on the following Monday, no overall! She was taught typing, and her main undertaking was to check on the time keeping, adding up the time roll each week. With that and her young man, Sam, things were going very well. And then the war broke out...

That Sunday, Sam wasn't allowed around her house, in fact he was never allowed around until the day he left to fight. She remembers feeling very upset that day, as everyone in the house was, listening to the wireless. She was coming up to 16, her young man who her mother wouldn't countenance till the day he came to say goodbye was elsewhere and faced going off to fight for his country. Sam joined up under age and lied to get in, as many men patriotically did.

Iris remembers the fear that she was struck by the following June when she heard about Dunkirk on the radio, she knew that Sam was there. The announcer said that all those soldiers that could be evacuated had been, and that if you had not heard anything that all hope was gone. For a few days she lived with the fear of having lost Sam forever, but soon enough he made contact, he had been evacuated to Weymouth and it had taken him longer than most to be repatriated, Iris breathed a sigh of relief.

At that time, Nechells had been coming under fierce attack, and the bombs had fallen heavily. Iris's mother had had enough, she had relatives in Wolverhampton and decided the whole family should go and stay there. Iris was devastated, she loved her job at Lucas and protested to her mother that she didn't want to go. Her mother insisted but Iris was reluctant and even though her family were leaving at the weekend Iris still hadn't asked for her cards from Lucas. She had to stay with Sam's mother for that weekend before leaving Lucas on the Monday and joining her family in Wednesfield:

"My mum took me to the Eveready factory, me cousins worked there, ooh and they got ever so black from the stuff they put in the batteries... I thought oh my god... they put me on this line... oh I hated it... I wanted to go back to Birmingham and live with Sam's mum."

But Iris fell on her feet, she was noticed by the foreman, and very soon she started as his booking clerk, working in the office.

Things changed again. Her mother didn't really like living there, sharing a relatives house is not like having your own home, and she made the decision to move back to Birmingham. She found a big house in Hunton Hill in Erdington, and ever a one to help those who had helped her, she asked Mrs Fletcher, the kind neighbour who had minded her children for her, to come and live with them too.

Iris started at The Hercules again, but this time, 'Manor Mills' in Cuckoo Road, they had been making bicycles and then they moved over to munitions. By this time in the war, there were no choices, because you couldn't leave or change jobs, labour was in very short supply and this was the government's way of ensuring a consistent workforce, of course it did mean there were 'no sackings' either. She was put to work making igniter shells, Iris reflects:

"Oooh you should have seen this capstan I was on, it was ever so big! And the steel we used to cut... oh God! it was hard!... and when you had a night off you go back on, and your hands would swell... because you would have to drill, and drill, till you got through."

Her mother was working there too, and advised Iris to wee on her hands, so that the ammonia would harden them off.

Iris remembers that the men 'were absolutely fantastic' to work with and particularly the foreman Mr Beresford. One Christmas she had to go somewhere and a man tried to kiss her, and Mr Beresford appeared like a knight in shining armour and said he had come to meet her, for he 'had guessed what might of happened'.

It was not all joy though, one night Iris was going into the works and had entered the works yard to clock in. Whereupon a 'Lister truck' loaded with sheet metal shifted its load while passing her after it got caught in a pothole. The load cascaded out onto Iris's feet and legs, injuring her quite badly, and ruining a pair of new shoes. She was taken into the infirmary, where she lay all night in agony and where she should have had stitches. That night they brought her mother in too, who unbeknown to Iris was suffering from a thrombosis in her leg, and was having a bout of phlebitis. Both mother and daughter were on nights and both, spent that night in the works infirmary in neighbouring beds. This was a time where there was little or no concern for works health and safety, and no compensation claims for works accidents.

"I did 7 till 7 every night, half hour for dinner... 12 hours a night... I did that for over four years. I was like a strip of wind" she reflects.

For her troubles, Iris was on piecework, but she could turn out 300 shells a day, which would amount to a princely sum of £6 per week, far more than any of the others in this book could earn. The shells were made at Hercules and then filled at IMI in Witton.

Iris made friends with another young lady called Margaret. They had much in common, Margaret had lost her mother and looked after her father. Her young man was away fighting as a submariner, sadly she lost him. Iris and Margaret became 'best pals'. They bought a tent together and every weekend, it was their treat along with a third friend called Tilly (Matilda), to pitch their tent at the Stratford Lido. They would rent a punt on the river, and take a wind-up gramophone along. It sounds like an idyllic heaven, what a break from the blitz-ridden Birmingham. Both Tilly and Margaret were catholic girls, and would leave Iris to a quiet Sunday morning reflection, whilst they went off to church together. It was a good time for Iris, for working nights meant that she didn't get any opportunity for a social life.

Life always changes, and in 1942 when she was 18 years old, she and Sam got married at St Clements Church in Nechells, they chose this church because of its connection to the Boys Brigade, which of course is how they met and very romantic. She managed to get a flat for 10 shillings a week in Nechells, a little one roomed place, with the sink on the top of the cellar steps. She remembers her two sisters Maureen and Beryl coming over to keep her company:

> "...they used to come and sleep with me, because I was scared... they used to come and sleep with me... and we used to put the wireless on, 'The Man in Black', Valentine Dyall, then we was too frightened to go to bed... I used to think if I lock the door they can't get into me, but if I lock the door we can't get out."

Sam's, Uncle Ted, used to take her out for tea in Needless Alley on a Monday and to the Odeon, because she had Mondays off. He had been fulltime in the army in Egypt, and he came back to England just before the war.

There were things that she didn't like and she honestly recounts:

> "Do you know what I used to hate?... When we'd had an air raid and you used to go out the next morning, and find all the streets all blown up and all the houses gone."

During the raids sometimes she used to go and stay with Sam's parents, his dad was an ARP warden:

> "If we'd had an air raid we used to go in the air raid shelter... Sam's dad used to do the fire watching like... this one night there was nothing but incendiaries come on the garden, it was terrible... frightening."

And working when the raids were on:

> "Sometimes we'd just get in from work, when I was on days, we'd just get in from work, and the sirens would go, perhaps we'd had no tea, and we'd have to go straight down..."

Being war work, they were not allowed to take nights off:

> "It was like being in the army it was."

One night during a raid all her electricity went, and she wasn't feeling too well, so she took a night off. The next evening she was made to explain her absence, and when she told them what had happened, they sent an electrician around, perhaps being helpful, or perhaps to check her story.

Shopping for food was extremely difficult, trying to fit this in around shifts, time-off for shopping was not allowed. Often, when they got to the shops they found them empty, so apart from the rationed food, extras were often difficult to come by. Although, having the amount of money that they had never experienced before, made it possible to buy things that would have been considered luxury. Once her and Margaret were so cold they took a bus into town to buy a blanket.

Working in the factory had some benefits. A hot meal, which could on occasions be edible, although Iris had a preference to go to the other canteens which were around the city. Her first experience of venison was in one such canteen. When 'music while you worked' played on the speakers, she was able to sing along to all the tunes of the day, her voice drowned out by the noise of the machines to protect her natural shyness. She used to sing all the songs and as she says:

"...the sad ones... I was nearly in tears by the time they finished".

At one time when they were getting raids every night, they had to walk all the way back from town because the buses had stopped, and as Iris says:

"...we walked all the way through it, and we got home and he said 'go down the shelter'... and I said 'I just walked all from town!"

She continues:

"You'd get up of a morning, or you'd go out of a morning to go to work and you'd gotta' walk coz the buses couldn't get through, or there'd be flat ground where the houses once was."

For Iris there were a few small pleasures besides her weekends with the girlfriends at Stratford, at the Hercules there was a canteen where they used to put on shows:

"The one show we done... I don't know if you remember the song 'Me and my girl'?... well two of the fellas and me and my friend Margaret, the four of us done it, and I took my brides dress and I wore that."

But, they never got paid for any time off and being a very male factory, nobody cared for women with 'monthly problems' or the associated aches and pains.

When the war had ended, they put her on days, but changed what she was making without giving her any instructions about what she should do. They set brass in the lathe which was totally different to cut than the steel she had been used to, as a consequence, the first time she tried the brass being so soft she 'cut her fingers to ribbons'. After that experience, she couldn't settle and decided to make a go of something else.

Sam had a war he didn't want to talk about. He had spent over two years in the tank regiment in Italy from 1939 to 1942, during which time she never even heard from him. When he was demobbed his lips remained tightly sealed, although years later, Iris met one of his friends, who earnestly said to her that Sam had saved his life.

Iris had found a shop, a general grocery shop, two doors down from her mother's in Aston Church Road. The old man who owned it was selling up, and Iris had saved one hundred pounds. It was the time of rationing, and he could only sell her some of the stock. She tried to make a go of that after leaving Hercules, and because they were short on stock, she had to make ends meet by taking a job as an usherette at the picture house on Alum Rock Road. She got by, but Sam being shy never took to being a shopkeeper, and the need to start a family was becoming a pressing concern, after all they had been married for four years, so they traded their shop and started their family. When the baby did arrive, the birth cost £6 at Dudley Road Hospital, and she was ordered (by an officious midwife) to 'cut her nails'. Sam settled down to being a polisher in the Jewellery Quarter.

Many years have passed now, as has Sam. Iris is not the strongest of ladies physically, but mentally she is astute as ever. She never thought about what she was making as something that could kill, it was far too abstract for that. She was another who had a job to do, to get the 'boys' home, and she just got up and did it.

FOR IRIS

The clawing darkness bites at my throat,
And eats at my battle-scarred spirit,
It scratches at every inch of my soul,
To find my absolute limits.

It seeps into my veins, and brings chill,
As it takes my very last reserves,
The wind that blows through, bring all ill,
As I walk in the night of shattered nerves.

Its coldness heralds, only troubles ahead,
As its exploring fingers find their mark,
It finds the separation between the living and the dead,
And conceals all our fates within the dark.

The black death of poison that it brings,
Will take away our city's pride,
The evil destroyer to all things,
The grim reaper of human lives.

Chapter 16

SHADOWS OF THE PAST
– THE LAST 'ALL CLEAR'

In comparison, there is not in existence the wealth of data at the National Archive, for the latter period regarding factory working, that exists for the earlier period of the war. This is in part due to the desperate recruitment problem that the government was faced with for arms production and the subsequent need to recruit personnel quickly, which generated a considerable amount of documentation. The government did not display quite as frantic a need to terminate employment, although, exactly how that enforced-exit from factory working for the 4,500,000 munitioneers was to be managed did raise one or two serious questions, before aiming at solutions.

Added to this, what few records do remain, can give a very confused impression to the reader. That there was an expectation by the allies that hostilities would cease much sooner, than they did, in fact the allies believed this to be the case. So the dating of these documents during 1944 and 1945 (and some in 1943), appears to be based on these premature assumptions of the end of World War Two. As a consequence, the information available has to be first considered in the context of the progress of the war, both for the position of the German aggressors and the allied advance into enemy territory, and then re-examined with a view to the actual chain of events in order to make sense of the eventual outcomes.

As far back as 1942, according to Boston (1980) the Women's Advisory Committee to the Ministry of Labour had been set to address the problem of letting the women go, once the war ended, she reports that the initial suggestions were:

"Women who had worked before the war should be given priority either in re-instatement in their pre-war jobs or in new employment. Those women who had entered work for the first time during the war should either be given a lump sum (if they wished to leave employment) or be allowed to have their claim for a job considered by a tribunal. The committee also recommended that the school leaving age should be raised to fifteen to avoid flooding the labour market with school leavers."

These suggestions had been based on a very different pre-war economy. Most of the UK industrial manufacturing sector had been turned over to war production, the remnants of what remained lacked skill, investment, materials and most importantly, a market which the goods could be sold. It would take a while to re-establish a manufacturing economy. In the meantime, nearly 5,000,000 armed service personnel would be returning to try and find work. It would be almost impossible to hold pre-war jobs for the women, never mind trying to find lump sum payments in a war shattered economy in order to buy them off. It was better to reinforce the discourse of the 'temporary' nature of their role and their expected return to caring for their families. This was done through constant advertising and reinforcement as Williams (2002) notes:

"Married women and working mothers had also been subjected to a constant barrage of wartime propaganda which reminded them that their services at the war factories were temporary and would not be required once the wartime emergency was over."

In fact with the nurseries that had been founded for the war effort closing, some women would be left with little or no choice (Holloway, 2005).

The first significant impact that began to turn the tide of the war in Europe was the eruption of the Japanese war. The American naval base at Pearl Harbour was attacked in December 1941, causing the allies and the Americans to declare war against Japan. In a counter measure, Germany, Italy and the Soviet Union declared war on the USA, which pulled the somewhat reluctant American government into supporting active military service of US personnel in Europe. Added to this, the RAF had increased the strength of the air force substantially despite the intervening 'Battle of Britain' in 1940 and 1941.

In 1942 alone, 17,731 operational aircraft were built and delivered to the existing force, this with production rising rapidly, with over 1,500,00 million already employed building them (combined with the USSAF force strength one quarter the size) the RAF had gone on a counter offensive in retaliation for the bombings in UK. In spring and summer of 1942, the allied blitzkrieg caused substantial and overwhelming devastation to the cities of Cologne and Essen.

Essen that April experienced the first super bombs of 8,000lb, in May the first 1,000 bomber raid by the RAF attacked Cologne. On July 27th and 28th the allies bombed Hamburg with incendiary bombs creating a firestorm, causing the loss of 40,000 lives. These attacks were carried out in waves of 'carpet or blanket' bombing with hundreds of planes dropping thousands of bombs. This was combined with the concept designed by Barnes Wallis who had developed the technology of the bouncing bomb famously employed by 617 Squadron to blow the dams in Ruhr in May 1943, in an effort to hinder factory production, – 'The Dambusters'. The industrial heartland of Germany had been hit substantially, causing a huge loss of production of steel, and the manufacture of arms and equipment at a critical time for Germany.

By 1943 and into 1944 Hitler had stretched his military capacities to their limits, he was fighting wars on several fronts, and it can be argued that his forces were now militarily over-extended. He had continued occupations in most of Western Europe and Scandinavia, and those that were not subjugated were facing almost daily attack and were using all means of resistance against the German forces. There was a major ongoing campaign in the deserts of Africa. Hitler had gone one stage further and broken his pact with the Soviet Union and had opened up the Russian front, in the first instance allied to Mussolini, whose own position as Italian leader was becoming untenable. The ensuing extended Russian campaign would drain the German resources and morale to breaking point.

The allies made comprehensive plans, to advance into enemy occupied territory, and regain a foothold in mainland Europe, a move not considered since the evacuation of Dunkirk in 1940. Americans, Canadians and British strategists proposed Operation Overlord, the Normandy Landings. The plan first developed in 1943, committed to simultaneously landing both 150,000 men, airborne and seaborne. Confidence was high, maybe a little too high, there was a general feeling that if these advances could be made that 'war would be over by Christmas'.

With these thoughts in mind, there were decisions taken to downsize the munitions production capacity and rationalise production significantly with the impending cessations of hostilities in Europe. It was taken as read that the demobilisation of troops would follow, bringing home those who went first. As men, it was accepted that they would desire to return to a normal working life as soon as possible (Holloway, 2005). Throughout 1943 the Ministry of Supply records show that munitions and arms production was constantly reviewed to reduce output especially with the smaller firms that had been employed to plug the gaps. As far as Birmingham was concerned, a few smaller firms were released and at Cadbury's Bournville, the filling programme was stopped (it was the same for many other filling factories around the country), however, the larger factories such as Lucas and Austin although reviewed were kept in full production, due to changes in contracts.

In 1944 the more difficult problem of dismissing women when the time came, had to be addressed. During the period of recruitment of female factory workers (through the Essential Work Order) the government had always been conscious of the effects that women working could have on home and family stability. Pre-war society had been soundly based on these underlying principles and the depression of the twenties had either forced those still in factories back to domestic service, or home and family. Following their initial suggestion, the Women's Consultative Committee wrestled with the problem, but as Boston (1980) suggests, their deliberations were based on unfounded assumptions:

"The Women's Advisory Committee assumed that after the war, many women would have to return to domestic service and drew up a memorandum offering suggestions as to how women could be persuaded to do so... The assumption that many women would be redeployed in domestic service was one which they shared with the government. In 1944 a pamphlet issued by the Ministry of Labour claimed that 'domestic work is a priority job'."

This was the considered the natural order of things, and the way the government had always proposed that after the war life would return.

Operation Overlord (D-Day) took place on the 8th June 1944, although the British, US, Canadian, and other allied troops lost in excess of 10,000 men.

Hitler still had one card up his sleeve in order to try and break the UK. In the summer of 1944, the first of the fully automated V1 rockets launched from the Pas de Calais and fell to earth over the UK. These rockets (or Doodlebugs as they were commonly called) were soon being launched in mass raids, against London and the South East of the country. These rockets were sinister devices, having no pilot or conscience, just a pre-programmed direction and bombing range. A killing automaton. They had a range of 150 to 200 miles, so as a consequence all the Germans efforts were concentrated on the London area, causing as much destruction and catastrophe as possible.

The V1, had been first developed back in 1942, but the need for them was not considered essential at that time, as the war appeared to be going Germany's way. The V1, carried just over 1,800lbs of explosive and had a range of 150 miles. They were the first jet propelled engines, a form of cruise missile and the potential of these weapons to develop quickly was there. The V1 could be heard and seen, as its cruising speed was 360 mph, between June 1944 to March 1945, over 8,000 were launched against London, over 2,500 of those were on target. In September 1944, the first V2 rockets caused real fear and panic to be instilled into Londoners. Although these rockets carried a slightly smaller payload of explosive at 1,600lbs (although some sources quote larger amounts up to 2,000lbs), they flew at a much higher altitude 50 miles above the earth, travelling at a speed in excess of 3,000mph.

Whereas, the V1 was a daunting prospect, especially as you would hear the distinctive engine noise above your head, followed by the stalled silence and had ten seconds to take cover, the V2 was silent and fast and undetectable, it could not be shot down by the hard working Ack Ack gunners on the coast. 16,184 people were killed and nearly 18,000 were injured by the V1 rockets, 1,400 V2 rockets were launched against London between September 1944 and March 1945, causing in excess of 9,000 deaths.

No one will argue that this second blitz was not the absolute end of Londoners' morale and stamina. As a nation, we had already been engaged in five years of war, the country was tired. Short rations, less protein, 12 hour shifts for most, the second shift on returning home for women. The family fractured by disunity, young children evacuated, a rise in juvenile crime, as male role models continued to be absent and non-influential in young people's behaviour (Minns, 2006). Enough had been borne by everyone. One can only begin to imagine how tired people were having suffered five winters in the blackout, and blacked-out factories depriving factory workers of sun even in the summertime. The V1 and V2 rockets were the final straw for most, and were said to have completely destroyed morale in London, Gardiner (2004) argues that this can been borne out in the figures of migration out of the city:

> "By September over a million in the 'priority classes' (mothers with infants under five, school age children, expectant mothers and the old and infirm) had taken part in the evacuation scheme which the LCC had announced on the 1st July…"

It is not hard to imagine the consequences, had the range of these rockets extended to 250 miles or even 300 miles. There is no doubt that the rockets technology was increasing daily and had the war been further prolonged, and more importantly had the Germans not been moved from their French launch sites, the targets could have easily become the Midlands. Then aircraft and munitions production would have ceased in Birmingham, completely changing the final outcome of the war.

The allied forces were hindered in their plans to liberate Europe, and the war was not going to end by Christmas as first thought. It was not quite cut and dry for the allies, progress across France had been painfully slow, unsurprisingly with hindsight, there was significant resistance by the German troops. Operation Market Garden (the attempted advance across Belgium and Holland into Germany) proved a complete disaster. The Germans were not going to give in as easily as predicted and made a counter-offensive on the Ardennes in December 1944 which lasted a month. During 'The Battle of the Bulge', the Americans lost 19,000 men, whereas the British lost 1,400 men.

At the end of 1944, the Women's Consultative Committee responded to the government White Paper on the re-allocation of manpower between civilian employments after the European Cease Fire by offering the following proposals to retire women in class K, such as; married women with domestic responsibilities (either with a child under 14 or elderly relatives) who had been the last to have been conscripted; and those women who wished to rejoin their husbands once they were released from active service, and any women over 60 (although it had already been decided that those who wished to leave who were aged 50 or over would be allowed to retire). This was intentional, it was giving a clear message to women and society in general, that their place was in the home, and that there was no intention of promoting a culture of working women. When plans to reduce production were first muted it was these women who were firmly placed at the top of the list to be returned to civilian life as soon as possible.

The common understanding was that women would want to join their husbands returning, and would need time to prepare for their return. Many households were in complete disarray because women were unable to keep up with the demands of home life and working fulltime. The Ministry of Labour decided that a period of two months should be given to allow married women to resume normal domestic life and make adequate preparations for the imminent return of their husbands. In fact as Holloway (2005) points out:

"The lay-offs in munitions factories began quite a while before the end of the war and, even then, women were re-directed into other work, such as aircraft construction where production was still increasing. However, again, the general expectation was that married women would want to return to the domestic sphere and that young single women would return to 'women's work' in the interlude before marriage and starting a family. Many women expected only to be employed in the particular work they were undertaking for the duration of the war."

The decline in production, combined with the feelings of the imminent ending and the associated change, brought an undercurrent of instability and boredom, to those who worked in the factories. As women found themselves with less and less to do, and colleagues leaving, the greater monotony of repetitive work, now seemingly with limited purpose, became a drag. They knew that their worlds were about to change again, and lived with the excitement of a post-war prospect, to leave the blackout and shortages behind, and most importantly see families and communities reunited again.

By the end of 1944, Birmingham had begun to feel the real effects of the lessening of production. According to Ministry of Supply minutes of November, the BSA, Shirley (where Jenny worked) had the production of the rifles limited to 1,000 per month. By December the minutes record that it was being considered to 'transfer in whole or part' production at the BSA, Small Heath (where Eileen worked) to 'Service cycles and motor-cycle repairs'.

It was at this time the fate of the Shadow factories came up for consideration and discussion. These factories were government factories, whose capacity for aircraft (engines and airframes) and munitions production was lessening significantly. There had already been moves by the Ministry of Air Production to dispose of redundant and obsolete jigs, tools and gauges back in May 1944. By the end of 1944, the agreement was already being considered as to how and when production might cease in the numerous shadow factories dotted around the British Isles. The intention was that these factories would either be turned over to civilian use, or retained to provide reserves for the Ministry of Supply for the duration and beyond. The decisions to be made were which factories could be sold onto private industry and which would prove useful to hold onto in the short term.

Eventually in the early months of 1945, the allies began to push German forces back and it was not more than a matter of months and the war in Europe had collapsed. First at the end of April, Mussolini was captured by partisans, and executed, and then Hitler committed suicide as the Soviet army fought their way into Berlin. Meanwhile the allies were advancing into Germany. Finally, on May 8th 1945 the allies accepted the German unconditional surrender which had been offered on the previous day.

It was over, in Europe at least, it would be a few more months before the Japanese would succumb to the bombings of Hiroshima and Nagasaki and offer their surrender. For those on the home front VE Day (Victory in

Europe), was the end of years of fear and deprivation, it marked the end of hostilities, the boys would be home again soon. For most it was the beginning of the end, either they still had loved ones fighting out in the Far East, or they were faced with the enormous task of reconstruction. For a city as damaged as Birmingham had been, the prospect of re-building was daunting to say the least.

It was the end too for the coalition government that had kept the country together. Labour pulled out of the coalition two weeks after VE Day, and in so doing forced a General Election on July 5th. Churchill had been just the charisma that the country had needed to lead the effort during the war, but he was now viewed as too old, and too much of a maverick, people were demanding a change. The Socialists ideals of the welfare state, with 'cradle to the grave care' were being formulated and for a war torn country this was more than just a little appealing. Labour won the election by an absolute landslide with a 146 seat majority (393 Labour, 213 Conservative, 12 Liberal).

Women found themselves released from work to return to normal family life. However, life was far from normal, there was an acute housing shortage in Birmingham, many remained living with parents until they could find somewhere to live in the coming years. Women, who had been used to financial independence, now found themselves reliant on the returned breadwinner. Their independence was also built on real terror, that they had endured; the horrors of the blitz; they had to 'make do and mend'; they reared children as single mothers, they were changed as people. These women probably worked harder, probably suffering bomb shock, as much as their men folk were altered by the atrocities of a long war suffered at an impressionable age.

Many men found it hard to adjust to civilian life (Minns, 2006). To return to jobs previously held, which in many cases were no longer in existence due to the war shattered economy. They had to learn to live with their families again, to share homes with their wives, many war marriages had never had that uninterrupted experience. These men who may have greater authority with women before the war, found themselves up against war-hardened, feisty women, less demure, less deferential. This caused many challenges, and there was an increase in domestic violence, because the rules of moral behaviour had been unbalanced by war. Women had sought comfort with others, as had men, this may have led to marriage break-up and divorce, illegitimate children and venereal disease. There were many cases of wives suffering serious physical injury (even death) at the hands of their husbands, who due to war, had forgotten how to control the innate violence that had been drilled into them.

For most although adjustments were difficult and took time, the experience of coming back together was a joy not a burden. Houses were found, built, rented and moved into, children were born, the shortages became less. However, the initial plans that had been brought to fruition to retire women from essential work backfired on the government. Many of the 5,000,000 returning were not able to replace the gaps that suddenly appeared in engineering and manufacturing (Holloway, 2005). Many men were employed on the heavy work of re-construction. Birmingham had a history of employing more women than men in the metal and allied trades (A Vision of Britain). Nationally there was a shortage of skilled labour, within a year of the end of the war, women were having to be recalled to fill the vacancies in these fields, Holloway, (2005):

"This was particularly acute in the engineering sector where, between 1943 and January 1947, the female engineering workforce was nearly halved but had not been replaced by sufficient numbers of men because the school leaving age had been raised to 15 and conscription of men into the forces was still continuing."

As for the sixty 'Shadow Factories' that remained in the UK at the beginning of 1945, most had ceased production and had been sold off to private production. Of the sixteen left at the beginning of 1946, only the Austin employing 407 people was still under Ministry of Air Production, all others in the Birmingham and Coventry area were now private.

By the end of the 1940's the problem of a labour shortage had to be addressed with some urgency, the government was forced to act, Holloway (2005):

"The shortfall was so large that during 1946-7 the government was obliged to restore employment controls so that they could direct workers into essential work. This was seen as a campaign to persuade women to return to work in key industries again."

However, as is clear from the women's stories, the tasks that they now found themselves carrying out, were more simplistic and less challenging, as a consequence, of many more skilled men having returned. Jenny never found her new role in industry as interesting as she had been used to, Kathleen had gone back to cigarette cases and compacts, Eileen was drilling brake drums at the BSA, and eventually was too pregnant to continue. The BSA by then had been turned back to motorcycle production, and sadly despite a remarkable war effort (with the immense tragedy) and tradition, the BSA in Small Heath would never make arms and munitions again.

The statistics for war production and in particular Birmingham's contribution to that war effort are astounding. At the peak of the war (and by that fact production) in 1943, the population of the UK was approximately 44,000,000. The Statistical Digest of the War gives the total working population at approximately half that figure, 22,285,000, if one assumes that that figure is divided equally between the sexes (as it was the case in Birmingham at that time), then there were approximately 11,000,000 women available to work across the UK, with 1,000,000 serving in the armed services. The total number of personnel (mainly men) on active service were 4,906,400, reducing the available working population to 17,000,000. There were nearly 265,000 killed while on active service and nearly 107,000 civilian deaths.

There was still a necessity to run the country and keep essential services active. The employed civil defence personnel (including fire and police) was 323,000. National and local government employed 1,786,000 and Agriculture and Fishing employed 1,047,000. Government figures give a peak production total of over 4,500,000 in munitions and aircraft production, over 1,500,000 were women. In other words across the whole of the UK nearly a quarter of the available population worked in these fields.

Birmingham according to the Vision of Britain website, had a population of just 1,000,000 at that time, again equally divided between the sexes. If the national statistics are extrapolated, then it would follow that only 500,000 would be the working population of the city. According to Black (1957), 100,000 were enlisted on active service, and a remarkable 400,000 were employed in munitions work. Through this astonishing statistic it is safe to say that the whole of the working population was dedicated to this very serious war effort. No other city can take the honour of having been so totally focussed towards the war production.

The city still had to function; local government, schools, shops, medical services, it is not hard to understand why the civil defence for Birmingham was made up of part time volunteers and veterans. Equally, why there was such a pressing need to draft women in from other parts of the country to fill the gaps in production. It is hard to imagine now in what circumstances that one quarter of a million women (at least) could be so driven and dedicated to such an immense effort, in one very concentrated urban area.

Birmingham responded to call to arms quite literally, to every man and woman. It made Birmingham a very vulnerable and strategically very sensitive area, and although much of the production was eventually expanded nationwide in the highly successful Shadow Factory scheme, there can be no doubt that when it counted, at the time of most fear, the blitz, the city received the brunt of Nazi aggression, and did indeed come through victorious.

CONCLUSION

There is no doubt whatsoever, that Birmingham played a significant role in the war effort, but what has become apparent to me throughout the research for this book, is how great a part that Birmingham actually contributed. It was a curious hand of fate, both nationally and internationally that caused the confluence of both industry and politics to come together in the heart of the country at that time, which has made the story even more intriguing. One of the most interesting questions emerging from this is, had Neville Chamberlain not been Prime Minister during this period, would the incumbent in that high office have had quite the same empathy or understanding of the need for such an industrial capacity, or the local knowledge? Indeed, would Birmingham have proved so critical to the war effort, or would it have been Manchester, or Liverpool, or even London?

I am of the opinion, that our Prime Minister having come from Birmingham was a significant factor, but there were many other reasons why no matter what the political machinations had been, because of Birmingham's central role in industrial and entrepreneurial enterprise, it would have emerged as pivotal to war production come what may. A major factor, I firmly believe, that influenced that drive is the character of the people. Although it had a relatively short pedigree as a city (probably that was significant also) it brought together people who were second and third generation with the determination and enthusiasm to get on. The women were shown to be as equally enterprising and hardworking as their men folk, with a tradition (again short) of working in non-traditional female occupations, metal and allied trades, a feature not common in the rest of the United Kingdom.

The majority of women in this book never saw what they were doing as particularly abnormal, it was common practice for women to work in industry, being second or third generation they may have aspired to other things had it been a time of peace, but when it was imperative for them to support their country and they did not back away from or shirk that grave responsibility, they embraced the challenge and did more then they had to. The ladies of that time were very much emblematic of the 'Dunkirk Spirit', soldiering on whatever the hardships and deprivation, facing up to bombings and blackouts, the tiredness and fear.

This book was primarily about saving their voices for posterity. A generation that because they were so close to a previous devastating conflict, and set great store about commemorating their act of remembrances for the previous generation, to some extent have been forgotten by subsequent generations. The feeling of having more time to share with them, to gather what they have to say, to reveal their histories, is a false one. The reason why so few women are represented in this book, is simply the fact that these few are some of the youngest of the women that would have been involved in this mammoth effort. Their ages at the outbreak of war range between 17 and 22, when we consider that by 1943 women were being conscripted up to the age of 60, and would now be some 30 years older than this sample it becomes clear. The ladies represented here are now in their late eighties or early nineties, the vast majority of their forebears would be into their hundreds. They have gone and we have lost them.

History is a recounting of and preservation of the past, it is a subjective view of what went before. As I emphasised in the introduction, it is far better that the view is based on first (primary) sources, than stories retold by others, further and further removed. That is why it is so important to preserve these precious narratives, for the future generations, who have no connections with this dreadful time. This is not to simplify the task, because it is a complex one, utterances made now are affected and influenced by many things, which can affect their re-telling and understanding.

First, there is hindsight, to tell a story after it has occurred, re-shapes it in the telling, because reflections of what may have been (and what actually occurred) affect one another and change the sense and feeling of the narrator. Secondly, these stories have been re-counted from seventy years ago, they are not as clear as they were, and may have shifted their meaning in time, what words and understandings meant to people seventy years ago, are very different to values that are commonly held today of language and society in general. Thirdly, they are not single narratives (I do not believe any narrative is) because they have been told and re-told, and have evolved in that process; the women have shared with others (family and friends) and their evaluations through shared discussion can change the narrative (thus it becomes multiple): and my influence, I have a profound part to play, I have influenced the further re-telling and then made my evaluative decisions over what to include and what to discount. My impact upon the re-telling of a narrative, can change the whole emphasis of that narrative completely, or can reshape it in part. I can lose the nuance of the language, because of the primitive translation of speech into written text. Intonation can not be relayed effectively to the reader to enable a feeling of being there and listening to the storyteller. In my own clumsy, subjective, way all I can hope to do is give an impression, a sketch, a snapshot view, and hope that is enough to create understanding.

So it is with the history, I have never claimed to be a historian, I just have a passion for a place I used to call home, and often as a researcher a passion is a good place to start. My knowledge of that place has increased beyond belief, yet I thought from familiar experience and understanding, I knew so much already. I was always aware that Birmingham was an industrial giant in the UK economy in times gone by, but the identified causes of that success and exactly how important the city has been, became considerably clearer during my investigations.

As I have already alluded to, it was this fatefully timed convergence of; resources, inventive creativity, entrepreneurial vision and political influence, that converged at the same time. There were significant players in that process such as; Herbert Austin, William Morris, Joseph Lucas, and of course previously Joseph Chamberlain. However, it was as much about the many people drawn to work for these enterprising men, as it was about them, themselves. Birmingham emerged as the cutting-edge place to be, where everything was made to a high quality. The munitions industry was already in existence, when the early car industry started, but without that car industry the facilities to produce aero engines and airframes, and the manufacture of these vital components would have been difficult to find anywhere else.

The Chamberlain family knew business, they understood the city and how to get the best out of it. There is no doubt that Joseph Chamberlain is still viewed as the most influential of men. It is hard to live in the shadow of someone so great and (constantly be compared to them), and judged on their merits and skills. That is how it must have been for Neville Chamberlain the whole of his life. He was not as outgoing as his father (probably very shy) and was continually observed as being uncaring and unfeeling, from his apparent aloofness.

It cannot be argued that he had made an excellent Chancellor of the Exchequer (one of several cabinet posts that he held) and had seen the country through probably the worst financial crisis to date, that the world had ever seen, the effects of which had been monumental on Great Britain as history records. It had meant that defence had been cut back severely, when you have the choice between feeding your people and defending your nation to make, there is only one way to go. Chamberlain understood that we were woefully under-resourced for defence. He knew that Germany was on an opposite course. He was a 'peacemaker', he had been through the Great War, he had witnessed the carnage and the returning many invalided men, old before their time, he did not want to see another war.

He took the risk that Hitler would bankrupt Germany before any great catastrophe occurred, he was wrong, but a man should not be condemned for trying to secure a peace at a time he knows that his own country cannot possibly wage a war. Had it not been for the 'phoney war' we would never have been able to defend ourselves the way we did in 1940 and that was despite of having been actively rearming for some two years. He tried through international diplomacy to head off the challenge posed, hindsight is a wonderful thing, and as we know from later parts of the war Hitler was excellent at agreeing to do one thing with his so called 'allies' and then doing something else. Diplomacy has to be built on a degree of trust, that what is actually negotiated and agreed between parties, will be validated, in this case it was not. Churchill once made a scathing remark about Chamberlain saying that he was an:

"...old town clerk looking at European affairs through the wrong end of the municipal drainpipe."

An unfair observation of a man, whose only crime was to try and keep his country free from trouble.

What is accepted is that at the time, the country was very grateful for Neville Chamberlain's attempts to keep peace, and had there not been subsequent acts of aggression by Germany, he would have remained as a national hero. It is the fickle nature of the voting population that has judged him harshly latterly, but in my opinion he was the safe pair of hands that was needed at that time.

Churchill, on the other hand, was the iron fist. He was exactly what was required by the country at a time of war and led from the front as was his way to do. He had always been judged a maverick and was a self-confessed egoist. He had walked across the floor of the house with ease, when it was within his interest to do so, and as such could work as an effective coalition leader, which is what the prime ministerial role required at that time.

Churchill knew how important it was to manage morale and he understood that war was a challenge of managing the morale of the population to keep the efforts of every man and woman dedicated to achieving victory. That required a propaganda campaign both at home and abroad that was extremely finely tuned with no negative messages that could create disenchantment, or disunity, and a degree of firm censorship that filtered all information in whatever form.

It can be argued that propaganda and censorship are for defence purposes, but the question that remains is how that is employed for defence? Was it just to keep the enemies from having access to sensitive information that could be detrimental to the outcome of the war, or was there another far more controllable objective of this campaign? I have argued that from the evidence of the time, it was clear that many of the reasons given for keeping the country unaware of Birmingham's plight was not because of feared subsequent enemy aggression, it was to keep the general morale of the country high. As the editor of the Trade and Technical Press (Mr Percival Marshall) had made abundantly clear in his correspondence, Hitler was only too aware where all the sensitive sites of production were (at that time). He would have sight of comprehensive journals and other documents in British Consulates (in pre-war Germany), which would have initially enabled the Luftwaffe to make maps and landmark guidance for their bombers.

Without the continued confidence of the people the war would have been lost through fear, it was necessary to limit and colour all information that may be now reported to general population to enable a continued effort. This is as much true for the people of Birmingham who endured during these dark times. The less they actually knew about the wider problems that the city was facing the more they were likely to keep going in adversity, and they did.

A second piece of evidence from which the same conclusions might be drawn, is from the words of one lady in this book, Jenny. She was conscripted under the Essential Work Order, and as she is at great pains to draw our attention to, she had no idea about the bombing of the BSA factory in Small Heath (she was assigned to the BSA in Hall Green). For had she had one inkling that it had happened she would not have come, I am sure that would have been true for many of the other conscripts that were brought in from far flung places to fill the same factory.

Indeed the effects on Birmingham had been so severe, that when the government was drawing up specific plans for a propaganda campaign for the German people, it was research data gained from their own Home Security survey (amassed after the year of the Birmingham blitz), that they used on which to base their campaign. Further, the effects of mass-incendiary bombing on the city were reported and analysed by the RAF, and then used in their counter attacks with devastating results over the industrial heart of Germany.

At the outset of the war, because of the wealth of skills, and available technologies, Birmingham became the most concentrated area of production in the country. Later in the war, when the Shadow Factory scheme was effectively deployed and operating to the further reaches of the country this over-concentration on Birmingham was lessened. However, at the time of the aerial bombardment upon the United Kingdom it was extremely vulnerable, something that the government had realised and voiced amongst themselves immediately after Churchill assumed high office. There was a key understanding that if France fell, and if Britain were subjected to air attack, that the knock-out blow could come through raids on Birmingham and Coventry.

It is said that Hitler actually lost the war the day that the expeditionary forces evacuated from Dunkirk, for that was the UK's time of peak vulnerability. We still had insufficient arms, munitions and aeroplanes at that time to defend ourselves effectively, and we left what little we did have on the beaches of Dunkirk. If Hitler's panzer divisions had followed us across the channel, it would have been the end, the first bit of good fortune for Britain was that they did not. The second, was the night of the 23rd of November, when Birmingham had been smashed to pieces, and had 700 fires raging around the city. Had there been one more night of enemy action, Birmingham would have been finished, and the production of aircraft with it. This was the predicted fear of the government, without our concentrated aircraft production we were lost as a nation.

If the bombing had continued for one more night, we could not have withstood anymore. Birmingham had no water. Canals were being drained to put fires out. There is no doubt production could not have continued under those circumstances, and the astonishing numbers of weapons and planes pouring out of the city at that time would have ceased, so soon after Dunkirk. Finally, Birmingham's third bit of good fortune (but not for the devastated London), was that the V1 and V2 rockets did not have the range in 1944 to reach the city, but what is clear is that the technology was advancing at such a pace that it is impossible to say for certain if there would have been some serious repercussions for the whole war effort had the war continued another six months. After all London felt the brunt, and it destroyed the morale of the Londoners, these same cataclysmic effects would have been felt in Birmingham.

My only regret is that there were not more personal reminiscences to share from other women, but time and fate have intervened to make that population shrink dramatically. All the stories that were shared, are as individual and different as would be expected from such a diverse population, and they all bring a different perspective. In common, they all share the fear and the anguish that they suffered through very troubled times, they talk of friends made through their work, and how each leant on the other for support. As it was, in order to give each narrative deeper analysis, having so few meant that I was able to concentrate on the quality of the accounts rather than amassing quantity, which has enabled me to re-tell their stories with depth.

They had much to say about their lives pre-war and post war, which I believe was essential to include in order to contextualise each of the women and give added texture to their memories. Each woman in this book gave of her up-most during their trials and tribulations, as all were expected to do at that time. Their lives were changed forever by their experiences, as were their families lives following the war.

Figures and statistics, have substantiated the fact the city of Birmingham can hold its head high when held to account, that to every last woman and man, each and everyone did their bit. No other place can boast such absolute and total commitment. Nationally ten percent of women were involved in the manufacture of aircraft and munitions. It is safe to say that almost one hundred percent of the working population of the women of Birmingham were committed towards the same, hence the need to bring so many more in from other places.

Bevin had been one of those who envisioned a Total War Economy (Appendix 1), where all aspects of life were dedicated towards the necessary war production. There is no doubt in my mind that Birmingham became the absolute epitome of that belief and discourse. Primarily, because of the efforts of all those women who gave selflessly, above and beyond the call of duty, and until this day remain unrecognised. They have never been publicly thanked (or honoured) for their stalwart efforts, without the contribution of 1,500,000 women around the entire British Isles, the country would not have endured World War Two and emerged as a free nation.

To you all – Thank You.

Appendix

THE DISCOURSE OF TOTAL WAR

To proliferate a war is a very costly business, not just from a financial perspective, but from the costs of time and labour; normal peacetime stability within an economy becomes unbalanced by the absolute focus towards wartime production, as Broadberry & Howlett (2002) notes;

> "An economy that produces guns but no butter will quickly collapse. The armed forces and the munitions workers need to be fed, clothed, housed, transported from home to work, industry needs to be provided with energy, etc."

Meanwhile, less essential activities and occupations are suspended. Normal day-to-day activity has to be curtailed in order to expend as much time towards the war effort as possible, all those who work in sectors that do not actually contribute towards the effort must be identified, and encouraged to become part of that war machine.

This is where the discourse of the 'Total War Economy' is born. Chamberlain had focussed the country's efforts and attentions on rearmament pre-war. As Broadberry & Howlett (2002) notes:

> "Britain was a relatively large and rich country in 1938 devoting more than half the national expenditure to the war resulted in a formidable effort."

It had stimulated the post depression British economy, giving those who had experienced severe unemployment a sense of purpose again. Chamberlain had concentrated on the expensive and radical expansion of the air programme, which had to be paid for. When his leadership came to an end and Churchill and his new cabinet assumed power, a rapid reassessment of the economy was needed in order to increase the war production. Prior to Dunkirk, the government had established that their true vulnerability was through the predicted economic isolation that would ensue once France fell. The only way of remaining able to fight the Germans and inhibit an invasion, was to maintain superiority in the skies, and keep the essential centres of air production (Birmingham and Coventry) secure. This is evident from the Cabinet paper of May, 1940 'British Strategy in the Near future'. Neither, of these challenges would be easy to meet, the

Germans had a military strength four times greater, they had the information of where our sensitive sites of production were located, and these sites were centralised, rather than spread widely like the German factories in the Ruhr.

Ernest Bevin was Minister of Labour during this time, and is credited with the promotion of the Total War Economy, which is the absolute mobilisation of all; labour, materials, power and leadership towards war. Although, there are no extant papers that point to this system being adopted, all text; cabinet papers, speeches, propaganda, ministerial documentation is threaded with the discourse.

Discourse is the underlying story or message, that gives rise to collective opinion, it is not necessarily hidden, but sometimes it is never made explicit, it is assumed by all who hear, or read it, to be there, and the more that it is repeated the more evidential it becomes. As Foucault (2002) argues discourses are 'practices that systematically form the objects of which they speak'. By analysing a discourse it is possible to understand; how it evolved and is perpetuated; how it became a collective understanding and what attitudes, characteristics and themes it is composed from. Not all texts will display all the composite parts, but by studying a range of narratives, it is possible to reveal the range of composing themes of that discourse. In this appendix I have examined three such sources of literature in order to analyse what themes composed this discourse, that was so influential in achieving the aims of mobilisation.

I have taken three documents, that were initiated in May, 1940, though not necessarily immediately published. The first source are five extracts taken from a narrative script produced for a Ministry of Information film that was made available in July 1940, entitled 'Behind the Guns'. The second are two extracts taken from The Man-Power Survey commissioned by Ernest Bevin and the Ministry of Labour in May, and produced by William Beveridge in November, 1940. The third source is one extract from the very famous speech made by Churchill to the House of Commons, on 4th June, 1940, 'We Shall Fight on the Beaches'.

To put these three pieces of text in context, our soldiers had come back from Dunkirk defeated, leaving much of their arms and ammunition behind them. Britain was militarily alone and isolated, we had no allies at that point and we were facing attack from the Luftwaffe. There was now a munitions shortage where there had been at one point an over production, accompanied by a drastic labour shortage. These problems of production were exacerbated by the fear of nightshift work that was beginning to establish itself, due to the April blitz. The government realised that a real push was needed in order to meet all needs.

Behind the Guns

Extract 1
Every time our fighting forces go into action they depend upon the skill of the workers of Britain. To equip our fighting men on land, on sea and in the air, the labour and the skill of many different trades are enlisted – an army without uniform. In Britain now by day and by night in all the workshops of war that huge army without uniform is on active service. They win their victories by making machines to beat those of the enemy in output and efficiency.

Extract 2
The Bren is a comparatively new invention but the men who make it have years of engineering experience behind them. Their eyes, as the eyes of the soldiers who will later look along the sights. Here are the men whose hands have been trained in peacetime in assembling of complicated parts which might belong to an inoffensive sewing machine, but the final result is the most formidable of all small arms, the Bren Gun. These men, whose grandfathers made rifles combine the old craftsmanship with the new science; they hold victory in their hands and when each gun is tried as every gun is before going into service it finds the mark with all the accuracy of a piece of British precision engineering.

Extract 3
These are the men who, father and son, have tested the big guns for generations. They fire a charge through the guns six times more powerful than that for which it was built. But while some workers fashion the gun to a fine degree of precision, other men must match it with the precision of the missile that it must fire – the shell must be perfect. British light engineering resources, speedily adapted on the outbreak of war, are feeding the guns with constant supplies of shells and bullets. Although vast quantities of shells are being turned out everyday, the munitions factories must always hold themselves ready to switch over from one type of shell to another, should the need arise. The resources of skilled men and up-to-date machines must be ready to meet any demand that war may suddenly hurl at them.

Extract 4
Women, too, take their place in the ranks of this army without uniform. There are places in the ranks where their special ability for certain work gives them the right to serve. The quick and accurate fingers of these girls are as important to the fight as the vital supplies they are maintaining.

Extract 5
Land, sea and air supremacy is won not only in battle but months before during trials; for these hazardous jobs the army without uniform has no shortage of picked men. Our aerial victories are won not only with bombs and bullets but also with set squares, slide rules and all weapons of the mathematician. In the aircraft factories of Britain our workmen are trained to build to the most severe standards of accuracy in the world. When we read that 'all our aircraft returned safely', we can sometimes hardly imagine how they managed to withstand the hail of bullets and the strain of manoeuvring to which they have been subjected. Here is the answer: in air braces strengthened over and over again by cross braces; in work carefully carried out by none but the most competent craftsmen; in assembling that is content with no superficial result but insists of the best possible job. Our speed-up in production is a big achievement which has not been obtained by skimping the work, nor is there any stinting of quality where the lives of our airmen are at stake. This is the attack of the craftsman rather than the machine. This is the front where skilled hands assemble part by part the machines which are to give us superiority in the air. So when each aeroplane is assembled, wing and fuselage joined, engine rigged, petrol tanks fitted, tail assembled, air screw lifted into place, every part has been tested and re-tested until human ingenuity can do no more; and even then, before the aeroplane is passed out, it is submitted by experts to every conceivable test, both on the ground and in the air.

Man-power Survey

Extract 6
This conclusion applies to all total war. It applies with special force in the circumstances of the present war, when in a small island, subject to aerial attack and threatened by invasion, the fighting men

and the members of the civil defence services stand under discipline cheek by jowl with the industrial army. Success in this war depends upon three indispensable partners in the war remaining continuously at work under constant risk. There is reason for hoping that actual damage to our factories and industrial equipment by successful bombing can be kept within limits not seriously affecting total output. The main problem – one of the critical issues of the war – is that of maintaining continuity of work and output by night as well as day, in factories which are threatened but not hit.

Extract 7
The safety of the country requires that workpeople engaged on vital war production should act as if they were in the front line, should take its necessary risks, should not retreat from the line except under order to avoid excessive risks. They will be more ready to act in this way if they regard themselves as servants of the State than as employees at a bargained wage. The industrial workers of this country are of the same metal as those enrolled in the fighting forces and in civilian defence; they would be as ready under trusted leaders for service and sacrifice; there is no need to lure them to tasks by hope of personal gain.

We Shall Fight on the Beaches

Extract 8
They had the first-fruits of all that our industry had to give, and that is gone. And now here is this further delay? How long it will be, how long it will last, depends on the exertions we make in this Island. An effort the like of which has never been seen in our records is now being made. Work is proceeding everywhere, night and day, Sundays and weekdays. Capital and Labour have cast aside their interests, rights, and customs and put them into the common stock. Already the flow of munitions has leaped forward. There is no reason why we should not in a few months overtake the sudden and serious loss that has come upon us, without retarding the development of our general program.

Within these eight extracts I have identified ten themes which reoccur to generate the discourse. I believe these themes combine with equal weight, and it is their combination that gives the force to argument, it is this discourse that is repeated in every corner of society becoming an established mantra.

The first obvious theme is that of 'patriotism':

"...when in a small island, subject to aerial attack and threatened by invasion."

The narratives perpetuate British sovereignty, of possessing a nationhood and spirit. There are references to Britain and British in extracts 1 – 5, and then in both Beveridge's and Churchill's narrative to 'island'. In extract 7 there is a reference to 'country' and 'State'. Most importantly, it is the people's relationship to their country, as; 'workers' and 'servants of the State', that their 'duty' has to be done, which emphasises the patriotic undercurrent of the discourse.

Although there are no direct references to god or religion, there is underlying spirituality to the texts, a feeling of a crusade, a military undertaking for god. It becomes particularly apparent in The Man-Power Survey in both extracts. The statement referring to the conjoined efforts of the army, civil defence and the workforce that;

"Success in this war depends upon three indispensable partners in the war remaining continuously at work under constant risk."

This evokes triumvirate imagery, a trinity of the vital exponents of war. The triangle is the strongest structural frame, three together are the ultimate strength. Further, in extract seven this religious dimension is accentuated with the reference to sacrifice.

The theme of skill is most apparent; 'skilled men', 'skilled hand', 'old seamanship' is one that particularly appeals to the male worker, they were skilled, or semi-skilled, as the women were not considered to be. There are many references to skill and craftsmanship throughout extracts 1 – 5. Other references such as; 'fashion', 'precision' and 'tested' are linked in sentences to the words; 'men', 'father and son' and 'grandfathers' as to qualify the male domination of skill. In fact, in extract 4 which refers to women, only their 'special ability' is mentioned not skill, they are expressly divorced from that claim.

There is the theme of engineering threaded, once again throughout extracts 1 – 5. Engineering is different to skill, it is technically specific and new, words such as; 'up-to-date machines', 'invention', 'science', 'precision', 'mathematician' evoke this message. It becomes particularly apparent in such statements as; 'severe standards of accuracy in the world' and 'submitted by experts to every conceivable test'. With these statements, the common worker has been elevated above the status of shop-floor blue-collar, to a white-collar engineer, and of course because of dilution and the need to promote skilled men on, and move women in to fill the gaps, this is how these men were advanced through the discourse. Again in extract 4 which is the only direct reference to women, no mention of engineering is made, the connections are kept to purely a supporting role;

"Women too, take their place in this army without uniform."
Interestingly, in extracts 6 – 8, which are generated by the government, a higher social class of men, no acknowledgment of the working man's professional level is mentioned, they are referred to as 'industrial workers'.

As would be expected there is a strong militaristic theme running throughout all the narratives. From the outset the workers are referred to as 'the army without uniform', that is on 'active service' and this is emphasised by the statement:

"They win their victories by making machines to beat those of the enemy in output and efficiency."

Also, references to what went before war in 'peacetime', further articulate the state of war. Women are given 'the right to serve' in 'this army without uniform', but they are merely 'maintaining' the 'vital supplies' 'important to the fight', they are not using levels of precision to fashion them.

Even the engineer is mobilised within this army as is clear from this statement:

"Our aerial victories are won not only with bombs and bullets but also with set squares, slide rules and all weapons of the mathematicians."

According to Beveridge in Extract 7 he says that those:

"...engaged on vital war production should act as if they were in the front line..."

And further to this he stresses that they:

"...should not retreat from the line except under order to avoid excessive risk."

The underlying thread of industry is apparent throughout all the narratives. It is explicit in terms such as; 'trades', 'workshops', 'industrial workers/army/equipment', 'labour'. The feeling of urgency, that rapid intensive production is vital, and everything is needed in larger amounts, 'vast quantity of shells', 'a constant supplies of shells and bullets', 'speed-up in production', 'the flow of munitions has leaped forward'. It is perpetuating the need to do more faster, but with care to protect our fighting men; 'each gun is tried as every gun is', 'the shell must be perfect', 'the quick and accurate fingers of these girls' and most apparently:

"Our speed-up in production… has not been obtained by skimping the work, nor is there any stinting on quality where the lives of our airmen are at stake."

There is a theme of patriarchy particularly apparent in Extracts 1 – 5. There is much emphasis on the male input into the war effort, the men who have many years of 'engineering experience', their 'hands' 'trained', they have a pedigree of other men with the same skills behind them, their sons too, take the same paths in skills and craftsmanship. 'Skilled men' use 'up-to-date machines', they build to the most 'severe standards', they 'are of the same metal as those already enrolled in the fighting forces and in civilian defence'. The women are merely supporting actors to the men, in fact they are patronised as being 'girls' with 'quick and accurate fingers' that only have 'special ability for certain work', it is the men who are the main protagonists of the triad of war. The 'State', the 'trusted leaders' they are men too, protecting the interests of the 'working men' proliferating the fight.

An interesting theme to emerge is that of anti-capitalism, almost verging on borderline Marxism, but is this in support of unionism or a challenge to it? In both Extracts 7 and 8 are references to a Marxist mantra. In Beveridge's report he says that the 'workpeople' should:

"…regard themselves as servants of the State than as employees at a bargained wage."

Of course the unions would have been the protagonists in any pay bargaining, but this statement has associations to Marxism, as does statement that in his opinion:

"…they would be as ready under trusted leaders for service and sacrifice."

We are all part of a collective team, it is not about individualism or a free-market economy, it is pulling together, which he qualifies furthers by stating:

"…there is no need to lure them to the tasks by hope of personal gain."

Churchill refers to 'Capital and labour' the owners and the workers, having:

"…cast aside their interests, rights and customs…"

Traditional practices of working are no longer applicable, the rights of the worker through the unions, custom and practice – Sunday a day of rest – no longer applies. It all has gone into the 'common stock' the soup of industry, or the stockroom for the factory.

There is a theme of competitive challenge, that the more we can push ourselves the more that will be achieved. The workers 'make machines to beat the enemy', while workers make fine guns they are matched with ammunition. Workers must be prepared to be responsive to changing productive methods if the 'need arises' and they:

"…must be ready to meet any demand that war may suddenly hurl at them."

A challenge from Beveridge that:

"The safety of the country requires that workpeople engaged on vital war production should act as if they were in the front line, should take its necessary risks, should not retreat from the line except under order to avoid excessive risks."

He is calling for a total effort from all the workers, to stay at their posts night and day, in whatever dangers as Churchill does in his narrative, he states:

"How long will it be, how long it will last depends on the exertions we make in this island. An effort the like of which has never been seen in our records is now being made. Work is proceeding everywhere, night and day, Sundays and weekdays."

And as if that challenge is not quite enough, we will find a little more, as he says:

"There is no reason why we should not in a few months overtake the sudden and serious loss that has come upon us, without retarding the development of our general program."

Finally there is a theme of heading toward victory, the positive thinking of winning, of being better, stronger and fitter than the enemy. 'They win their victories by making machines' and making weapons which then allows them to 'hold victory in their hands', and through their skill in aircraft production they 'give us superiority in the air'. As Beveridge points out 'success in the war' depends on the triad of the army, the civil defences and the 'army without uniform'.

The combination of these themes is what created the discourse of the 'Total War Economy', the discourse was then repeated endlessly through every section of society, bringing the thoughts and feelings into practical actions. As Broadberry and Howlett (2002) notes the term of 'total war economy' must be justifiable according to the figures in the index of munitions, production in 'the first quarter of 1944' was 'six-and-half times the level of the last quarter of 1939'.

A mobilisation of all the forces had been achieved, not just the armed forces or civilian defence, but the economic forces of; man-power, wages, raw materials, energy, and collective co-operation of a people determined to win. This is due in a large part to a discourse which emanated in the war cabinet in 1940, and became common currency nationally within a very short time, the final result justified the hardship encountered in 1940, as Broadberry and Howlett (2002) concludes:

"The British war economy was a success, at least in terms of the overriding objective of achieving victory. Britain overcame early strategic setbacks to mobilise economically without causing internal unrest, managing to raise, equip and maintain armed forces that would fight on three major fronts: in Asia, in Africa (and later Southern Europe), and finally Western Europe."

BIBLIOGRAPHY

Books

BEDDOE, D. (1989) *Back To Home And Duty: Women Between The Wars*. 1st Ed. London: Pandora.

BOSTON, S. (1980) *Women Workers And The Trade Unions*. 1st Ed. London: Davis-Pointer.

BUNCE, G. (2003) *Lucas In Birmingham*. 1st ed. Stroud: Sutton.

BUNCE, G. (2004) *Lucas Birmingham & Beyond*. 1st Ed. Stroud: Sutton.

BUTLER, J. (1999) *Gender Trouble*.

CADBURY, E. (1907) *Sweating*. 1st Ed. London: Headley Brothers.

CADBURY, E. (1909) *Women's Work And Wages*. 4th Ed. T. Fisher London: Unwin.

CHINN, C. (2007) *Brum Undaunted: Birmingham During The Blitz*. 2nd Ed. Warwickshire: Brewin.

DRAKE, B. (1917) *Women In The Engineering Trades*. 1st Ed. Allen and Unwin: London.

DOUGLAS, A. (2006) *Birmingham In The Forties*. 3rd Ed. Warwickshire: Brewin.

FOUCAULT, M. (1998) *The Will To Knowledge: The History Of Sexuality: 1*. 1st Ed., Penguin: London.

GARDINER, J. (2004) *Wartime Britain 1939 – 1945*. 2nd Ed. London: Headline.

HOLLOWAY, G. (2005) *Women In Work In Britain Since 1840*. 1st Ed. Oxon: Routledge.

MILLS, S. (2004) *Discourse: The New Cultural Idiom*. 2nd Ed. Routledge: London.

MINNS, R. (2006) *Bombers And Mash*. 4th Ed. London: Virago.

RIDLER, A. (1945) *The Shadow Factory*. 1st Ed. London: Faber & Faber.

TODD, S. (2005) *Young Women, Work And Family In England 1918 – 1950*. 1st Ed. Oxford: Oxford University Press.

WARD, R. (2005) *City – State And Nation: Birmingham's Political History 1830 – 1940* 1st Ed. Wiltshire: Cromwell Press.

WIGHTMAN, C. (1999) *More Than Munitions: Women Work And The Engineering Industries 1900 – 1950*. 1st Ed. London: Longman.

WILLIAMS, M. G. (2002) *A Forgotten Army: Female Munitions Workers Of South Wales 1939 – 1945.* 1st Ed. Cardiff: University Of Wales Press.
WOOLLACOTT. A. (1994) *On Her Their Lives Depend: Munition Workers In The Great War.* 1st Ed. London: University of California Press.

Cabinet and Ministerial Papers

Air 20/209: Birmingham Small Arms Co. March 1940
Air 23/2379: Aircraft Factory Visits 1939/40
Avia 10/229: Correspondence Joseph Lucas
Avia 10/34: Birmingham Small Arms Co. 1939/40
Avia 15/3766: Factories, Manufacture and Production. 1938/39
Avia 15/3825: Shadow factories closing. 1944/45
Avia 22/501: List of firms, reduction in munitions production 1943/45
Avia 22/663: The Provision of Canteens in Factories. 1941/44
Avia 22/668: The Provision of Music in Factories. 1942
Avia 22/1119: The King. Visits to Munitions Factories.
Cab 6/7/49: Supply and Man-power – Note by the Chancellor of the Exchequer. January 1940
Cab 23/83: Cabinet Conclusions. 25.2.36
Cab 23/90a: Cabinet Conclusions. 22.12.37
Cab 24/239: The Position of the Private Armaments Industry in Imperial Defence. 7.4.33
Cab 24/264: The Report of the Royal Commission on the Private Manufacture of and Trading in Arms. 10.10.36
Cab 24/265: Note by the Secretary of State for Air on the policy of His Majesty's Government in Relation to the production of Aero-Engines. 27.10.36
Cab 24/267: Cabinet – Report of the Royal Commission on the Private Manufacture of, and Trading in, Arms. 1.2.37
Cab 24/269: Cabinet – The Organization, Armament and Equipment of the Army. 3.2.37.
Cab 24/273: Cabinet – Defence Expenditure in Future Years. 15.12.37
Cab 24/275: Cabinet – Statement Relating to Defence. 1.3.38
Cab 24/276: Cabinet – Officials Secret Act. 29.4.38
Cab 24/278: Committee on Overseas Broadcasting. Broadcasting in War – Report. 22.7.38
Cab 65/5/7: War Cabinet Conclusions. 18.1.40
Cab 65/7/61: War Cabinet Conclusions. 14.6.40

Cab 65/8/19: War Cabinet Conclusions. 18.7.40

Cab 65/10/15: War Cabinet Conclusions. 25.11.40

Cab 65/10/18: War Cabinet Conclusions. 28.11.40

Cab 65/10/30: War Cabinet Conclusions. 27.12.40

Cab 65/21/1: Conclusions. Confidential Annex. 13.1.41

Cab 65/17/5: War Cabinet Conclusions. 13.1.41

Cab 65/18/41: War Cabinet Conclusions. 23.6.41

Cab 65/19/8: War Cabinet Conclusions. 21.7.41

Cab 66/7/49: British Strategy in the Near Future. 26.5.40

Cab 66/11/19: The Munitions Situation. 29.8.40

Cab 66/14/12: The "Daily Worker". 23.12.40

Cab 66/14/30: The "Daily Worker". 11.1.41

Cab 66/28/23: Munitions Production – January – June 1942. 3.9.40

Cab 67/1/36: "Stop the War" Propaganda. Memorandum. 14.10.39

Cab 67/6/45: Compulsory Censorship. Memorandum. 11.6.40

Cab 67/8/84: Man-Power survey. 6.11.40

Cab 67/8/54: Air Raid Damage. Censorship. 7.10.40

Cab 67/8/114: Air Raid Damage. Censorship. 25.11.40

Cab 68/2/38: Supply and Production. Third report by the Air Ministry. 31.10.39

Cab 68/4/23: Supply and Production. Fifth monthly report by the Minister of Supply. 5.1.40

Cab 68/5/55: Publicity in Enemy countries. 29.3.40

Cab 68/6/23: War Cabinet – Propaganda. 11.5.40

Cab 104/109: Munitions Factory: Inspection by His Majesty The King. March 1938

Ho 192/1210: Birmingham Economic and Social Survey – Morale. March 1942

Ho 192/1234: Birmingham Small Arms Co. 1940/41

Ho 192/1240: Effects of Morale on Industrial Capacity

Ho 192/1245: Joseph Lucas Ltd. Effects of raids.

Inf 1/254: Reports of the Home Emergency Morale Committee. 1940

Inf 1/522: Defence Notices. 1939

Inf 1/523: Defence Notices. 1939

Inf 6/422: Ministry of Information Film. "Behind the Guns". 1940

Lab 8/378: Questions of rates of pay and recruitment of women in the engineering branch of the munitions industry and their retention in these industries. 4.3.41

Lab 8/492: Drift of Female Labour from Industries of National Importance. 1941

Lab 8/611: Munitions Labour Shortage Committee. 1943

Lab 8/920: Release of women with household responsibilities from essential work. 1944

Lab 26/35: Provision of Entertainment CEMA. 1941

Lab 26/40: ENSA Entertainments to Munition Workers. 1940

Lab 26/61: Shopping Difficulties. 1941/43

Pre 3/93/6: Blackout in Factories. 16.5.43

Prem 4/38/2: Mr Churchill's visit to Birmingham. September 1941

Prem 1/439: Press Censorship: Functions of the Ministry of Information. October 1939

Prem 4/40/4: Alleged Slacking in Factories. June 1941

Prem 4/40/5: Article in Daily Mirror Alleging Mismanagement in Munitions Factories. August 1941

Websites

Arnhem: *www.d-daytovictory.com/battles/battle-arnhem.htm*

Arnhem: *www.bbc.co.uk/history/worldwars/wwtwo/battle_arnhem_01.shtml*

Austin: *www.austinmotor.co.uk*

Austin: *www.austinmemories.com*

Battle of the Bulge: *www.bbc.co.uk/history/worldwars/wwtwo/battle_bulge_01.shtml*

Battle of the Bulge: *www.battlefieldexperience.com/html/ardennes_offensive.html*

Birmingham population statistics: *www.visionofbritain.org.uk*

BSA: *www.bsaguns.co.uk*

BSA: *www.bsaowner.co.uk*

Neville Chamberlain: *www.jgames.co.uk/title/Neville_Chamberlain*

Neville Chamberlain: *www.jgames.co.uk/title/National_Liberal_Party_UK*

Neville Chamberlain: *www.oxforddnb.co.uk*

Kynoch: *www.staffshomeguard.co.uk*

Joseph Lucas Ltd: *www.madeinbirmingham.org/lucas.htm*

Joseph Lucas Ltd: *www.lucasmemories.co.uk*

Lord Nuffield: *www.spectator.co.uk*

Lord Nuffield: *www.nuffield-place.com*

Operation Overlord: *www.thehistorychannel.co.uk/site/features/d-day.php*

Operation Overlord: *www.d-daymuseum.co.uk/overlord.htm*

Rover: *www.rover.org.nz*

Spitfire Manufacture: *www.sciencemuseum.org.uk/on-line/spitfire/321.asp*

Quotes Statistical Digest of War: *www.dasa.mod.uk/nat.stats/ukds/2000/ukds.2000pdf*

V1 and V2 rockets: *www.battlefield-site.co.uk/v_weapons.htm*
V1 and V2 rockets: *www.theotherside.co.uk/tm-heritage/background/v1v2.htm*
V1 and V2 rockets: *www.flyingbombsandrockets.com/v1_into.html*
Wolseley: *www.gbclassiccars.co.uk/wolseley.html*
Wolseley: *www.wolseley.co.uk*

Miscellaneous Papers and Theses

BROADBERRY, S. & HOWLETT, P. (2002) Blood, sweat and tears: British mobilisation for world war II. *draft chapter for* CHICKERING, R. and FORSTER, S. (eds.), *A World at Total War: Global Conflict and the Politics of Destruction, 1939 – 1945*. Cambridge: Cambridge University Press.
DEBNEY, J. (2006) Engineered Careers? A study of women engineers in the Offshore Oil and Gas Industry. (unpublished thesis) UEA.

BY THE SAME AUTHOR

If Only

Sal and Issie would never have met had it not been for WWII; their lives were completely different, Sal living a leafy-suburban existence in Birmingham, working in a dress shop, Issie coming from the poorer part of the city.

Sal longed to work at 'the aero' with all the sophisticated girls making munitions and earning good money. As the war approaches she gets her wish and meets the vivacious Issie. There starts their longest most enduring friendship, that would eventually bring them together as family; sharing many moments of joy and sadness, fear and sacrifice along the way.

ISBN: 978-1-85858-460-7

£6.95